POLICING SAME-SEX RELATIONS IN EIGHTEENTH-CENTURY PARIS

POLICING SAME-SEX RELATIONS IN EIGHTEENTH-CENTURY PARIS

Archival Voices from 1785

EDITED BY JEFFREY MERRICK

THE PENNSYLVANIA STATE UNIVERSITY PRESS | UNIVERSITY PARK, PENNSYLVANIA

Library of Congress Cataloging-in-Publication Data

Names: Merrick, Jeffrey, editor.
Title: Policing same-sex relations in eighteenth-century Paris : archival voices from 1785 / edited by Jeffrey Merrick.
Description: University Park, Pennsylvania : The Pennsylvania State University Press, [2024] | Includes bibliographical references and index.
Summary: "An English translation of recorded depositions by men arrested for sodomy or pederasty in eighteenth-century Paris, exploring complex questions about sources, patterns, and meanings in the history of sexuality"—Provided by publisher.
Identifiers: LCCN 2023055341 | ISBN 9780271097114 (hardback) | ISBN 9780271097121 (paper) | DOI https://doi.org/10.5325/b.20249489
Subjects: LCSH: Male homosexuality—France—Paris—History—18th century—Sources. | Sodomy—France—Paris—History—18th century—Sources. | LCGFT: Primary sources.
Classification: LCC HQ76.2.F82 P655 2024 | DDC 364.15/36—dc23/eng/20231222
LC record available at https://lccn.loc.gov/2023055341

An open access digital edition of this book is available with the generous support of The Pennsylvania State University Libraries under the Creative Commons Attribution-NonCommercial-NoDerivatives 4.0 International License. To view a copy of the license, visit https://creativecommons.org/licenses/by-nc-nd/4.0/.

CC BY-NC-ND

Except for the uses authorized by this license as well as brief quotations for reviews and critical articles, no part of this book may be reproduced, in whole or in part, in any form, without written permission from the publisher.

Copyright © 2024 Jeffrey Merrick
All rights reserved
Printed in the United States of America
Published by The Pennsylvania State University Press,
University Park, PA 16802–1003

The Pennsylvania State University Press is a member of the Association of University Presses.

It is the policy of The Pennsylvania State University Press to use acid-free paper. Publications on uncoated stock satisfy the minimum requirements of American National Standard for Information Sciences—Permanence of Paper for Printed Library Material, ANSI Z39.48–1992.

*In memory of my maternal grandparents,
George Arthur and Edith Willson Small,
and their son Robert Newton Small
and for my aunt Virginia Grace Small*

CONTENTS

Preface (ix)

List of Abbreviations and Note on the Texts (xi)

INTRODUCTION (1)

DOCUMENTS (18)

Appendix (213)

Notes (217)

Works Cited (233)

Annotated Index of Men (235)

General Index (247)

PREFACE

When I entered graduate school in 1973, there was no such field of study as the history of sexuality, let alone homosexuality. If there had been, I would have avoided it because I intended, at that stage, to immerse myself in the European and American Enlightenments. During the next decade or so, sex migrated from the margins to the mainstream in history and related disciplines, and I migrated from Diderot in the stacks to deviance in the streets: suicide, sodomy, and spousal conflict. In the course of the 1980s, I finally acknowledged my identity as a gay man and recognized my vocation as a social historian.

After publishing more than a few articles and books about this subject, I never expected to produce the present volume—not until I read these police reports, located and photographed by Bryant Ragan and Eric Albrand, during the COVID-19 pandemic. These impressive and instructive texts deserve more readers than the few academic historians who have examined the manuscripts on site in the Archives Nationales. *Sodomites, Pederasts, and Tribades in Eighteenth-Century France: A Documentary History*, published by Penn State University Press in 2019, illustrates the variety of published and unpublished sources for the study of same-sex relations. This volume presents all the relevant archival documents from one year, a splendid sample of records that invite more detailed quantitative and qualitative analysis.

My objective is not only to make more French material available to Anglophone scholars and students but also to encourage them to study it with smaller as well as larger issues in mind. We know that humans have imagined, experienced, conceptualized, and regulated sex in different ways in different times and places. How did the police and the men they arrested understand sex between men in Paris in 1785?

To answer that question methodically rather than anecdotally, we must analyze what they said (and did not say), how they said it, and the context in which they said it. As a humanist who does research about ordinary Parisians in the archives, I write not about systems and structures but about patterns and exceptions, with more emphasis on language than figures. For that reason the index includes many words and phrases used in the documents. At the same time, readers more inclined toward numbers will find lots to count in the following pages.

With any luck, I am not only older but also wiser than I was when I published my first article on this subject in 1998. The more I ponder the extant sources, the more informative and complicated they seem to me. My scrutiny has become more aggressive and my conclusions have become more tentative. I fully expect others to challenge my version of the subculture, as I have challenged the work of historians who explored it before me.

This volume represents my last word on this subject, or so I think at this time. In any event, I should thank a long list of scholars who have assisted and supported me over the years, but I will simply express my gratitude to Eric Albrand, who deciphered more than a few strange names and difficult passages, and to Bryant Ragan and the two anonymous readers, whose comments improved the introduction significantly. My thanks as well to everyone at Penn State University Press involved in the production of this book. It has been a pleasure to work with Ellie Goodman and her colleagues again.

ABBREVIATIONS AND NOTE ON THE TEXTS

arr. Parisian *arrondissement*
C   commissaire's verdict
I   inspector's account
OP other places frequented by pederasts
P   imprisoned
PP pederasty patrol
R   released
S   signed promise to avoid suspect places at suspect hours
U   unable to sign
W warned to avoid suspect places at suspect hours
X   unwilling to sign

The records from 1785 begin with formulaic language (reproduced only in #1 and #18, the first pederasty patrol) and include three parts: the inspector's account of the arrest (I), the prisoner's statement, and the commissaire's verdict (C). I have summarized the inspector's account in my words, including quotations within quotation marks and additional information within parentheses. I have translated the prisoner's statement verbatim, indented it to distinguish it from the preceding and following parts, and enclosed additional information within brackets. Most prisoners signed their statements, and I have reproduced their signatures as written, within slashes and without correction. Some would not sign (X), and more could not sign (U). I have abbreviated the commissaire's verdict and included any comments of significance within quotation marks. The commissaire released some prisoners without further ado (R) and others after he gave them a warning (W) or after they promised not to frequent suspect places at suspect times (S). He consigned many to prison (P) but rarely indicated which one.

    Text within {curly brackets} is crossed out in the document, while text within +crosses+ is added in the margin.

More than a few reports mention coins in circulation in 1785. One gold louis was worth twenty-four livres, and one écu was worth three livres. One livre (or franc) was the equivalent of twenty sols or sous. One sol or sou was worth twelve deniers, and one liard was worth three deniers.

I have added the province or country in parentheses after the names of cities and towns, but I have not annotated Parisian streets that have changed names or vanished. For these details, see Hillairet, *Dictionnaire historique*.

I have retained a few French words, without italics, in the translations. The noun "commissaire" refers to one of the forty-eight officials responsible for public order in the twenty districts of Paris, as opposed to the commissioner of police in modern cities. The preposition "chez" means at the residence or business of, in just one word.

Introduction

The police records in this volume include evidence about several central topics in the history of same-sex relations across cultures and centuries: patterns in age and role, urban subcultures, and sexual activities versus identities. The traditional model of younger passive males and older active males, of course, dates back to Antiquity.[1] Adolescents played the receptive role in anal (or intercrural) intercourse but switched roles as they aged and later married and produced children. Greeks and Romans stigmatized passive adults and oral contacts. No one has synthesized recent research on medieval or early modern Europe, but we can see both continuity and change between 1400 and 1800.[2] We know more about same-sex relations in this period because we have more sources to work with, especially series of criminal records that document the lives of more people over more decades. In late fifteenth-century Florence, for example, the majority of adult men had been incriminated for sodomy at least once.[3] After playing the receptive role in their teens and the penetrative role in their twenties, most, though not all, married in their thirties. Florentines did not consider oral sex in the active role degrading for adults.

Sodomite subcultures emerged in the late seventeenth and early eighteenth centuries in Amsterdam, London, Paris, and other cities.[4] Records of surveillance and judicial proceedings show that men who desired men, mostly workingmen, knew where to go and what to do to locate others like themselves, with or without exchanging money for sexual services. Extant sources reveal more variety in Enlightenment Paris than in Renaissance Florence: some active adolescents and passive adults, some pairs of males of more or less the same age, no stigma about passivity and less stigma about orality, more masturbation than penetration, more male prostitution, more unmarried men. The French sources document the persistence of as well as divergence from the classical model of sexuality and masculinity. At the same time, they do not, on the whole, exhibit the behavioral and conceptual connections between sodomy and effeminacy that Randolph Trumbach has discerned on the other side of the English Channel.[5]

Early modernists have refuted Michel Foucault's notable and quotable but simplistic distinction between sodomitical acts before and homosexual identities after 1800.[6] The fact that eighteenth-century men did not have the modern medicalized and psychologized notion of homosexuality available to them does not mean that they—not to mention the police—could not understand sexual difference in other ways. By the same token, the fact that jurists collected all types of nonprocreative sex acts, from anal or oral intercourse within marriage to bestiality, under the umbrella of sodomy, does not mean that the category of sodomy was "confused."[7] To avoid confusion, we must read all the extant sources carefully, with context, voices, and language in mind, and distinguish patterns from exceptions that illustrate variety in same-sex relations. Michel Rey, who published five articles on the Parisian subculture between 1982 and 1994, read just one series of records and generalized imprudently about identity and community. The documents in this volume, which Rey did not read, show why we must continue to review and revise his conclusions.[8]

The police of Paris arrested thousands of males they called sodomites (from the name of the city destroyed in Genesis 19) before 1750 and pederasts (from the Greek words for "love of boys") after 1750, in both cases regardless of age.[9] Over the course of the century, different types of practices produced different types of documents that include different types of evidence about same-sex relations.[10] From 1723 to 1765, decoys entrapped men on the grounds of the Luxembourg and Tuileries palaces, royal enclaves where the police had no jurisdiction, and in other locations where they did. Sodomites spoke more freely about their sexual interests and adventures to covert agents inside the gardens, before arrest, than they did to officers outside the gates after arrest. For two years, 1748 and 1749, dozens of men named by other men confessed their misdeeds and fingered more men in return for immunity. In the last decade of the Ancien Régime, one of the forty-eight commissaires who preserved public order in the twenty quarters of the city was responsible for surveillance of pederasty throughout the capital. From 1780 to 1783, commissaire Pierre Louis Foucault questioned men arrested by inspector Louis Henri Noël more or (often) less fully, and they answered more or (mostly) less frankly.[11] From 1783 to 1789, commissaire Charles Convers Desormeaux challenged men arrested by Noël or his colleague Jean François Royer Desurbois to explain themselves without interrogating them in the same way.[12] They did not tell him the whole truth and nothing but the truth about themselves, let alone everything we would like to know about them today, but their statements, exacted and recorded in custody, provide remarkable testimony about sexual relations between men in pre-Revolutionary Paris.

The two cartons of Convers Desormeaux's papers from 1785 contain more cases than his (incomplete) papers from the other six years combined.[13] The 221 dossiers include two types of relevant documents: 169 reports of routine arrests made by Desurbois in the course of his regular rounds in suspect places and 40 reports of nocturnal patrols that involved both officers, who typically visited some of the same locations on the Right Bank.[14] Both types of reports begin with formulaic language (reproduced in #1 and #18 only), followed by the inspector's account of the arrest (summarized) and the prisoner's statement (indented and reproduced verbatim). They conclude with the commissaire's verdict (abbreviated). Judging from the writing, a single clerk produced most of the reports at Convers Desormeaux's residence on place Maubert.[15] We can see that he made more than a few mistakes in spelling and grammar, but we cannot tell whether he recorded the inspector's, prisoner's, and commissaire's words accurately, without omissions or additions, not to mention alterations to standardize or euphemize language. In the end, we know nothing more about the heads, hands, and hearts of Parisian pederasts than what the extant sources reveal through intrusive and intensive scrutiny. The reports from 1785 document several voices, which we must study separately and attentively to understand what they do and do not tell us about same-sex relations in this place and time.

THE INSPECTOR'S ACCOUNT

According to Desurbois, the men he arrested did not just happen to walk through suspect places at suspect hours by chance. They loitered (*roder*) or, more specifically, cruised (*raccrocher*, used intransitively) there and revealed their criminal intentions through signals, comments, and actions. Some exposed themselves and pretended to urinate or defecate. Many accosted or, more specifically, picked up (*raccrocher*, used transitively) others by asking about the hour or chatting about the weather. They talked, walked, sat down together, discussed sex between men, and agreed on what they wanted to do, then and there or elsewhere and later. This scenario sounds familiar from the 1720s, when sodomites routinely shoved their hands into the breeches and stuck their tongues into the mouths of men they desired—or at least tried to do so. In 1785, some pederasts used their hands but none used their tongues in this way. Many individuals rejected verbal and physical advances, but others touched or stroked themselves or another man, on or through the breeches or with genitals exposed.[16] Some masturbated, independently (*respectivement*) more often than reciprocally (*réciproquement*), on the spot, but more went off to a tavern to drink or dine, to an alley to have sex, or to one or the other's room "to amuse themselves more comfortably" (#98). A small number offered bribes, resisted arrest, or even tried to rouse a crowd against the police, and a large number escaped capture.

The inspector told the commissaire not only what he had seen and heard himself but also what his observers, mentioned in thirty reports, told him they had seen and heard (or at least thought they had seen and heard).[17] The inspector employed the verbs "seemed" and "appeared" repeatedly. The observers noted common patterns and noticed differences that made some men look more obviously guilty than others. A dozen were "dressed in the costume of men given over to this vice" (#19): round hat, *catogan* (hair tied back with a ribbon), wide cravat, rosettes (instead of buckles) on shoes, and sometimes earrings or perfume.[18] Many walked arm in arm, and several hugged.[19] Some incriminated themselves through gestures and others through remarks. One suggested, "Let's go someplace else to amuse ourselves because there are spies going by" (#6). More than a few men accosted "spies," who did not, or at least Desurbois did not, recount their conversations after the fact, as decoys did in the 1720s.[20] He did repeat some specific sexual propositions and revelations.[21] He also added information, from memory or police records, about dozens of men he labeled "known pederasts": nicknames, companions and associates, cruising habits, sexual interests, previous arrests.[22]

The police observed some men on the prowl, often more than once, without arresting them (if only because of circumstances), and they arrested more men for seeking than for having sex.[23] Desurbois assumed that strangers had no business conversing and consorting with each other in the evening in locations frequented by pederasts. If they did so, like two who left the Tuileries together "without, however, seeming to know each other" (#36), they were obviously up to no good. The inspector made one reference to "those of this type" (#87) and thought that several men had the figure, tone, or manners of pederasts (#53, #70, #79), without explaining what he meant by these words.[24] He noted that one pederast "surrenders himself to this vice by taste" (#59) but did not suggest that all pederasts shared a distinctive "taste." At the same time, he was never surprised when such men returned to the Tuileries and other suspect places. Desurbois believed that his prisoners, whether he recognized them or not, whether they talked or touched, hoped "to surrender themselves to their pleasures" (#123). He made no comments about their pleasures and offered no insights about their desires. Given his orders, he focused on specific behavior that, based on his experience, revealed criminal intentions, without wondering or at least worrying about more abstract issues. As far as he was concerned, men who talked and walked like pederasts were pederasts, and solicitation typically led to ejaculation, either on site or, more likely, offstage.

THE PRISONER'S STATEMENT

After Desurbois delivered a prisoner, Convers Desormeaux asked the man to take the oath to tell the truth and then to state his full name, age, place of birth, occupation, and address.[25] With this information in hand, the commissaire read the inspector's account to him, or at least explained the charges against him, and asked the prisoner "how long he has been given over to pederasty and by whom he was debauched" (#28). The clerk recorded this question only in formal interrogations, but, judging from language repeated in the statements, he must have heard some version of it routinely.[26] For the sake of convenience I have divided the prisoners into two groups, but not men who did or did not have sex with men, since we do not and cannot know for sure what really (or might have) happened in many cases. Some prisoners lied or at least concealed as much as they revealed, but the police could not identify all who did so, and neither can we. My groups, rooted in the records, are men who denied or confirmed that they had deliberately participated in sexual contact with men or at least intended to do so. We might as well call these groups no-men and yes-men. This division, based on what they said rather than what they did, is not intended to distinguish two types of men. On the contrary, it is my objective to demonstrate that any such categories are problematic because of obfuscation and ambivalence in the 425 statements from 1785. To that end, in what follows, I include more rounded than precise numbers and abundant examples of exceptions to patterns that should not be mistaken for something more simple and stable.

Some 150 prisoners declared that they were not given over (*adonner*) to pederasty, the debauchery of men, or the vice of liking men.[27] They often said so toward the end of their statements, as if by way of conclusion. Sixty more stated or implied as much in other words, which deserve study. No-men contradicted Desurbois and exculpated themselves by normalizing their intentions and behavior before arrest. According to them, they walked from here to there with some specific objective or simply strolled for pleasure, "like everyone" (#203/Perrot).[28] They had no other design and did nothing wrong. They did not know this or that spot was suspect and sought shadows or corners only to urinate or defecate, as many Parisian males did. They made nothing more than small talk with strangers and had longer conversations with people they recognized by sight, if not by name.[29] They did not respond to men who touched them, did not discuss sex, did not welcome or accept propositions or invitations. They even had innocent explanations for wearing conspicuous rosettes on their shoes.[30]

No-men claimed that they did not loiter, but we should linger over their statements, and not only because a dozen prisoners at first denied but then confirmed the charges against them, without any recorded menaces or promises from Convers Desormeaux. Many no-men had been accosted by pederasts, for the first time or more than once.[31] Three did not (or at least said they did not) understand what these men meant.[32] Some expressed aversion at the time or after the fact, for the commissaire's benefit. Others, however, acknowledged curiosity about "men who amuse themselves together" (#1/Juillien). One insisted that he had played along with a stranger who propositioned him and shoved his hand into his breeches only in order "to have him arrested" (#123/Rome), but two others went further. They informed the men who had accosted them that they did not like women and thereby invited them to proceed. "To see how far this man would go," Collin told a stranger that "if he found a man who pleased him well, he would lend himself to this debauchery" (#179). Petit told a stranger that "others put it into him, and he puts it into men" and "went with this man to his place to see what he wished to do" (#129). He later assured Convers Desormeaux that he had done so only in jest.[33] We do not know what these two, one married and the other single, would have done if Desurbois had not intervened.

More than a few no-men admitted verbal or even physical contact with pederasts, and some of them admitted misconduct. Unlike Mitraff, who declined to drink a bottle of wine with a man because he did not know him (#209), they engaged in conversations, listened to propositions, allowed others to touch them, or walked off with them, without always adding that they went their separate ways. Jacquet acknowledged that "he was wrong to walk at night with a man he does not know" (#123).³⁴ Bertre realized that it was not appropriate for him to take a man by the arm "although he does not know him" (#109). Mussard walked arm in arm with a stranger who stroked him, but he was not "given over to the vice of liking men" (#119).³⁵ Bucher let a man stroke him but "does not know how he had this weakness," since "he is not given over to the vice of liking men and has never surrendered himself to it" (#204). Frade let a man stroke him but "did not do anything" (#147). Taillardant let a man stroke him but did "nothing *else* wrong" (#110, my emphasis).³⁶ Baillet confessed as much but noted that "he did not do likewise to him" (#117). A stranger shoved his hand into Besson's breeches, and "to tell the truth, he . . . allowed it, but he is not given over to pederasty and has never surrendered himself to it" (#167). Chauveau allowed a stranger to masturbate him, but "he neither touched nor wished to touch this man" (#142). These examples suggest that some men who did not reject pederasts outright thought—or at least thought they could vindicate themselves by suggesting—that they could endure talk and allow touch, just once or now and then, without giving themselves over to pederasty, as long as they did not reciprocate.

A stranger asked Thirion if he wanted to amuse himself (*s'amuser*), but he "understood this man's intentions" only after he stroked him through his breeches. Thirion told him that he "practiced a vile trade" but also gave him some coins to buy bread (#168). Although one man threatened to file a complaint (#12/Desgrignons), most men accosted by men took the experience in stride, without taking offense at the time or expressing aversion later. LeBeau had known the man arrested with him for a year (#24), and Ramard had known the man arrested with him for a day, though the man in question said they had known each other "for a very long time" (#31). In any event, LeBeau and Ramard did not know if the others were given over to pederasty. We cannot read their minds, but we can wonder if they did not care or just did not care to say, if only for their own sakes.³⁷ DuChesne assumed, from his remarks and costume, that Pajot "was suspected of bad morals," but he walked and talked with him anyway (#59). Pouteau, on the other hand, dropped an acquaintance whom someone "reproached for being given over to this vice" (#209). We cannot assume that others who distanced themselves from pederasty reacted to pederasts in the same way.

The no-men, in the end, do not fit a single simple profile: the innocent immigrant or native Parisian who happened to be in the wrong place at the wrong time and did not understand that he was the object of solicitation. They do not constitute a homogeneous group, if only because they revealed more or less about themselves and attempted to exculpate themselves in more than one way. Some of them did not adopt the terminology in the commissaire's leading questions but mentioned knowledge, desires, or actions that confirmed the inspector's suspicions about them. They may sound confused, and some did contradict themselves, but much of the confusion has more to do with differences in the ways in which pederasts and police spoke about sex between men. The police regarded all prisoners as probable pederasts, but many no-men and yes-men specified what they had or had not done or wanted to do without labeling themselves.

Turning to the two hundred yes-men, let us begin with the basic information requested by the commissaire: name, age, place of birth, occupation, and address. A modest number had nicknames based on place of birth, appearance, or occupation, and five of them had female nicknames: The Little Female Wigmaker (#17/Bernard), The Holy Female Savior (#17/Picot), The Big Female Gilder (#23/Le Tourneur), The Woman from Lyon (#69/Compagnat), and The Countess of Seven Points (#215).[38] Only a fifth of the men were natives of Paris. The others, like so many Parisians, immigrated from the environs of the capital, in the Ile-de-France, or from the provinces, with or without sexual experience with men under their belts.[39] The massive majority of these prisoners were workingmen. Around a fifth of them were unemployed for shorter or longer lengths of time.[40] Many of the teenagers, servants, and assistants lived with parents, employers, and masters. Others lived in (furnished more often than unfurnished) rooms in boardinghouses throughout the city.

The complex subject of age requires more detailed attention. The men in question range from eleven to sixty-six years old (#61/Camus, #210/Hoart).[41] The ages of these individuals are significant, to be sure, but less significant than the ages of pairs of males who had or at least hoped to have sexual relations. The words "old" and, especially, "young" merit further scrutiny, but we cannot quantify them.[42] What is more, we do not know the ages of the observers accosted by some pederasts or of the many men who escaped arrest. In a dozen cases the men Desurbois arrested together turned out to be friends or at least acquaintances rather than strangers, which does not mean they could not have had sexual histories or intentions. In another dozen cases it seems possible or probable that the men arrested together wanted to have sex, though one or both denied it. In another dozen cases it seems clear from one or both statements, combined with the inspector's account, that the men wanted to have sex or did so. In the last two groups, the difference in ages ranges from two years (28 and 30) to forty-five (18 and 63). Most of the pairs involved older and younger males, as in other cultures and centuries, and half of them involved teenagers. At the same time, some involved males whose ages differed by no more than five years.[43] The difference between 13 and 18, of course, is more significant than the difference between 33 and 38. Given the limited evidence, not to mention questions about the numbers themselves, we need a longitudinal analysis of patterns across the century in order to formulate meaningful conclusions on this score.

Analysis of cohabitation provides another way to investigate pairs, but we must remember that many workingmen shared rooms and even beds without having sex.[44] We must look for cases in which men lived (*vivre*) rather than resided (*demeurer*) together and cases in which partners or strangers did more than just snooze and snore together. Liber, 34, lived "in the crime of pederasty with" 24-year-old Merillat.[45] Gréant, 36, "sometimes surrendered himself to pederasty with comrades he slept with" (#60).

More than a hundred men responded to Convers Desormeaux's leading questions by admitting that they had been debauched (*débaucher*) into and/or were given over to pederasty.[46] They often said so toward the beginning of their statements, as if to frame and link their comments about events in the past and present. We do not know how many, if any, would have used the words "debauched" and "given over to" if Convers Desormeaux had not used them himself, and we cannot assume that they had the same connotations for the commissaire and the prisoners. He assumed they sought men because they were given over to pederasty, but some assumed they could have sexual contacts without being given over to pederasty.[47] Several noted that they did so just once, "very rarely" (#167/Ribot), or "only from time to time" (#180/Camus).[48] Three stated ambiguously that they did not have a "confirmed" (*décidé*) taste for men (#78/Belloy, #90/Gout de la Brande, #155).

More than a few statements of prisoners who did not use the phrase "given over to pederasty" also exhibit ambiguity. Dozens of men admitted encounters without acknowledging an ongoing interest or history. They "surrendered themselves [*se livrer*] to debauchery" or at least intended to do so, in the Tuileries or elsewhere, or said as much in other words, which themselves deserve study. They applied this language to a variety of scenarios: letting a man touch him (#129/Loulié, #182, #206/Voutancia), touching him in return (#191/Gouy), and so forth. Many others confessed more vaguely that they had "amused themselves" with men, without always explaining what they did together.[49] Two men did not understand the word (#192/Descourty,

#200/Sacqueney), and one guessed that "amusement" involved masturbation (#180/Lehardelay).

Whether or not they used Convers Desormeaux's words, some prisoners traced their interest in males back to sexual exploration with playmates and schoolmates of their own age.[50] One of them declared that he had acquired it "without knowing what it was" (#144/Tonnere). More remembered specific encounters as turning points in their personal histories. Many of them had been debauched in their teens or twenties, whether many years or several days before, by other youngsters or adults whom they knew or by strangers who presumably differed from them more often in age than in class.[51] The adverb "presumably" is necessary here because only two individuals mentioned the age of the men, both "around forty," who had debauched them when they were seventeen and twenty-one years old (#84, #197).[52] Most of the debauchers, like most of those they debauched, came from the working classes. The exceptions include a modest number of clergymen, noblemen, and employers.[53]

Some yes-men noted what happened (masturbation more often than penetration), but none explained in so many words how it felt or what it meant to be debauched, in the passive voice.[54] Did they experience it as an act or process, as a sexual initiation or transformation that involved their heads as well as their hands? Since we know nothing more than what the prisoners told the commissaire, we do not know whether they considered themselves debauched by their first encounters, no matter what happened or did not happen, or only if they ejaculated. We also do not know how many encounters over what length of time it took for them to consider themselves "given over," or how much we should make of the difference between those who said sex with another man happened to them and those who said they surrendered themselves to it. Some had sex more than once with the men who debauched them, and some of these men told them where to go and what to do. Cosse, 26, not only debauched the 18-year-old Fussy "into the vice of amusing himself with men" but also "taught him how to accost men to amuse himself" (#36). Most men, unfortunately, did not talk much more about how they learned to operate in the subculture than they did about their sense of themselves.

Whether they acquired their taste sooner or later, overnight or over time, passively or actively, and learned the ropes from mentors or on their own, more than a few yes-men had this much in common: Judging from what they revealed about themselves, they had an exclusive and enduring interest in men. Everyone assumed that men desired one sex or the other, not both.[55] A dozen no-men mentioned wives or prostitutes to vindicate themselves.⁵⁶ A few men on the prowl asked strangers if they had a mistress or girlfriend to determine whether they were available.⁵⁷ In the 1720s many sodomites assured decoys that they did not like women, to disclose their desire and enhance their chances. In 1785 at least one man said so in earnest rather than in jest (#146).⁵⁸ Did he consider himself, and should we consider him, similar to or different from the men who avoided their wives, in one case because she was ill (#34/Roumier) and in the other case because he did not want any more children (#46/Rouyer), or the men who avoided women altogether because of lack of money (#109/Papelard) or fear of disease (#78/Belloy)? As far as we know, pederasts did not make distinctions based on their reasons for choosing men over women, but we should not ignore this evidence of diversity.

Only two yes-men had wives, and both of them acknowledged that marriage had not changed them.⁵⁹ A modest number insisted that they had reformed, if only to avoid arrest or rearrest after imprisonment. Lefevre "had this penchant but does not give himself over to it anymore" (#13), and Despan used to pay for sex but "has not amused himself at it for about three years" (#90).⁶⁰ Just as many, however, admitted that they had relapsed. After the police summoned and chastised him, Monneret declared that "this does not happen to him anymore" and that "he senses the full horror of it all," and yet he masturbated with a stranger (#155).⁶¹ Daillant "continued to surrender himself to pederasty" not only after he was debauched but also after he was released from prison (#67). Pederasts captured in 1785, unlike sodomites questioned in 1748–49, did not list as many of their sexual companions as they could remember. They had sex, more often than not, with men they did not know, more or less frequently, not only because of opportunities in urban spaces but also because of decisions they made about management of their desires, which they never discussed in so many words.⁶² We do not know how much differences in the frequency of encounters mattered to them, in their own minds, though they presumably assumed it mattered to the commissaire. After all, more than a few assured him that this time was the first or informed him that the last time was months or years ago.

Yes-men admitted that they participated in sexual relations with men, voluntarily and intentionally, or at least that they intended to do so, but what did they do? Less than half of them "consummated the crime" through anal intercourse, in the active or passive role or both.⁶³ Six teenagers played the passive role, but three of them also played the active role. Seven men in their thirties played the active role, but four of them also played the passive role, which no one feminized.⁶⁴ The absence of stigma might make us wonder why men, throughout the century, almost always specified which role or roles they played.⁶⁵ In any event, the numbers do not suggest a simple pattern.⁶⁶ More than half of the yes-men declined propositions involving penetration or mentioned nothing more than (independent much more often than reciprocal) masturbation.⁶⁷ Like Le Clerc de Piervalle, they did not have "the inclination to consummate the crime in the rear" (#28). Like Le Plat and Laurent, they took "it only as far as masturbation" (#211) and had not "taken things further" (#11). We do not know how many Parisian males masturbated, as children and/or adults, but it seems likely that many of them did, in private more often than in public. Many of them presumably did not take it as seriously as clergy concerned about the sin of Onan (Genesis 38:9) or as doctors concerned about the health of future husbands.⁶⁸ The inspector and the commissaire applied the same label to all of them, but it is not obvious that pederasty meant the same thing to men who had anal sex and men who masturbated themselves more frequently than they masturbated each other.

None of the yes-men explained what made them risk arrest by seeking partners in public spaces instead of pleasuring themselves alone in their rooms, but more than half of them mentioned money, as an incentive or benefit, without using the word "prostitution."⁶⁹ More received than disbursed cash for sex. A man offered money to the unemployed 18-year-old Le Vise de Montigny, and he "consented to everything he said but, however, without having surrendered himself to this vice" (#111). A man promised to procure Michel, then unemployed, "to someone proper who would give him money," and this offer "made him yield" (#166). More than a dozen others, most of them out of work, cited indigence.⁷⁰ Some of these individuals may not have had sex with men if they had not needed money, but we do not know if men who expected and accepted payment had a different sense of themselves than men who did not.

The inspector included all the men he arrested in one category, based on their misconduct and his assumptions, but the prisoners insisted on distinctions. Given the extensive evidence of variety among yes-men, it would be imprudent to assume that they shared a common sense of identity that made them feel connected among themselves and different from others.⁷¹ A few men made remarkable and atypical suggestions about consciousness. Picard, debauched into and given over to this vice "at a very young age," declared that "it is in his blood" and that "he is not the only one" (#75).⁷²

Toussaint, who identified himself as an "apprentice hairdresser and pederast," maintained that he had been given over to it "since he has known himself."[73] Cassina, who had promised to correct himself, invoked not only "habit" but also "temperament" (#97). These three did not, unfortunately, explain what they meant. We do not know how many, if any, others thought the same thing or felt the same way without saying so. More than a few expressed themselves much less clearly. What can we say about the man who admitted that he had "an inclination for this debauchery without being wholly given over to it" and that he had "surrendered himself to it sometimes"?[74] Did he not know how to make sense of his desires and actions? Or did he just try to make himself sound less rather than more culpable to the commissaire?

The police reports from 1785 document tradition and transition as well as common patterns and remarkable variety in the Parisian subculture. Men who desired men had options, in public spaces and private places, and they made choices, before and after arrest. Some wore distinctive attire, had female nicknames, enjoyed anal intercourse, sold their sexual services out of necessity, articulated some sense of difference, and so forth, but most did not. Men arrested as pederasts, if only for imputed intentions, denied or confirmed the charges against them and accepted or rejected the commissaire's language. We do not always know for sure who did or expected to do what with whom. We do know that the heuristic distinction between no-men and yes-men collapses under scrutiny because they did not constitute coherent groups. No-men who admitted masturbation and yes-men who acknowledged nothing more than masturbation had much in common, no matter what words they used. The commissaire suggested the same label to all prisoners, but they responded with their versions of their own histories, including and excluding details for their own reasons. He applied a homogenizing category that ignored their diversity and, in more than a few cases, fluidity. They invoked individual experience that demonstrated the category's instability as well as the men's agency in the urban marketplace.

THE COMMISSAIRE'S VERDICT

After the prisoner dictated his statement, the clerk read it back to him and made any corrections and additions, which warrant further study.[75] The commissaire checked the man's pockets for evidence and asked him to sign his name, which more than a few could or would not do.[76] Convers Desormeaux challenged two individuals after their statements (#12/Desgrignons, #209/Mitraff) and recorded his objections within parentheses just twice (#87/Pitot and Pélican). In eleven other cases he staged confrontations between prisoners who had contradicted each other.[77] Some changed their stories, but others did not.

The commissaire knew that some men lied and most men tried to influence his decision by revealing and concealing information. The most flagrant liar, who had accosted observers, declared that "he does not know what the Tuileries are and did not enter there. He is not given over to pederasty and does not know what we mean" (#25).[78] Prisoners asserted that it was the first or last time, that they did it rarely, only with strangers, never for money, that they did not consummate the crime, and so forth. A man who had been warned to avoid suspect places suggested that it was all right for him to return to them "because he does nothing wrong" (#125) there. Another man who had been exiled from Paris suggested that it was all right for him to remain in the city because he could not "make a living in the provinces" (#80). Many used apologetic terminology. They mentioned the "misfortune" to have been debauched or the "weakness" to have surrendered themselves to debauchery. One, and only one, boldly if not brashly insisted that "he does nothing wrong but to himself" (#75).[79]

Convers Desormeaux referred several prisoners to the lieutenant general of police because of their status (#38/Saint-Clément, #90/Gout de la Brande, #97/Cassina) but judged the others himself.[80] Like the inspector, he considered prisoners not innocent but guilty—or at least more likely guilty than not. He obviously considered the circumstances of place and time, what the men had said and done before arrest, what they had stated after arrest, and any criminal history. The commissaire did not release all no-men and detain all yes-men. He locked up some men for nothing more than alleged intentions and let others go despite ocular evidence against them, all of which merits scrutiny. He rarely explained himself but noted that he released one teenager because of his youth (#213/Ratier) and detained two adults in part because of their suspect outfits (#39/Rozier, #64). In one case Convers Desormeaux actually changed his mind, or at least his verdict, after a man pleaded that prison would cost him the job that allowed him to support his parents (#37/Pruneau).

It is difficult to explain why the commissaire sentenced every single prisoner as he did and even more difficult to explain what the police hoped to accomplish in the long run. They assumed that older males corrupted and converted younger males, despite abundant evidence of other patterns in their own records, but they endeavored only to control or at least contain the problem without attempting to purify the capital. The traditional penalty, death by fire, remained on the books, but the magistrates executed no one for sodomy alone after 1750.[81] Pederasts spent weeks, months, or sometimes years in prison, but not life, and many of them returned to suspect places after they did time. The police attempted to preserve public order and manage the subculture through information, intimidation, and imprisonment throughout the century. After an interruption in the extant records in the summer of 1786, they arrested only men caught in the act—that is, for what they actually did as opposed to what they allegedly intended to do. We have no documentation, unfortunately, about this change in practices of surveillance or about the others that preceded it.[82]

CONCLUSION

One man told Convers Desormeaux that a soldier in the guard had told him "to deny everything and nothing would happen to him."[83] Why did half of the men arrested by the inspector ignore this advice and tell the commissaire some version of the truth, shorter or longer, more or less coherent, with or without names and dates? None of the yes-men attempted to exculpate himself by expressing interest in women, and more than a few of them used no apologetic terminology. Did they speak as frankly as they did because they considered masturbation (as distinguished from penetration) and prostitution (especially out of necessity) less serious, offensive, and criminal than the police did? Did they appropriate, even if they did not articulate, the right to use their bodies as they pleased? The documents from 1785 provoke more questions than they answer.

At the same time, the commissaire's papers contain many internal clues and external links that deserve study. The unnamed man with a white muff who picked up Bertin (#33) and Cassegrain (#41), debauched Eugé (#44), and "consummated the crime" with Chevanne (#32) turned out to be a 36-year-old haberdasher, Jean Vacossin, who denied everything when he was arrested in

1786.[84] A man on the cul-de-sac (dead end) des Quatre Vents had sex with and gave money to several teenagers (#97/Baillaux, #176/Dumas and Carié); tipped one, who recognized him as a pederast, for delivering a letter (#176/Brondel); and informed another that he could earn money in the Tuileries (#180/Lehardelay). This Knight of Malta may have been a military officer. The police reports from 1785 include many references to men in the Paris guard, French Guards, and infantry and cavalry regiments.[85] Some pederasts enlisted to avoid prison, and some soldiers were expelled from the army for pederasty. The military—like other sexually segregated institutions, such as schools and monasteries—allowed males to explore sexual desire within structures that sheltered them. This topic, like relations between masters and servants, must be researched in multiple series of records across the century.[86] The same applies to connections between Paris and Versailles, mentioned in multiple documents from 1785. The twelve miles of road between the city and the palace carried traffic in both directions. Courtiers sought sexual adventures in the gardens in Paris, and pederasts sold sexual services in the gardens at Versailles. The taste for men did not trickle down from noblemen to workingmen. Masters, journeymen, apprentices, assistants, servants, and more created a flourishing subculture of their own in the capital.

After forty years of archival inquiry into the subject, we should address sexual relations between men in eighteenth-century Paris from the bottom up, not from the top down. The works of clergy and jurists, of enemies and advocates of Enlightenment, and of novelists and satirists tell us nothing about the real lives of real men who desired men in this place and time.[87] As far as we know, they thought (or at least talked) not about ancients, Scripture, nature, statutes, and scandals but about the pursuit of pleasure in the city that allowed more liberty in practice than in principle, well before the National Assembly decriminalized sodomy in 1791.[88]

POSTSCRIPT

The Policing Male Homosexuality in Eighteenth-Century Paris database under construction at Colorado College may include as many as ten thousand names in the end and will provide reliable answers to complex questions discussed above. It will allow us to perform multivariable quantitative and qualitative analysis of police records from the 1720s through the 1780s, to follow men through space and time, and to assess change as well as continuity over the course of the century.

The project website (https://coloradocollege.website/phs/) includes a comprehensive bibliography on same-sex relations in early modern France, background essays, and more. Visualizations under development include interactive maps of Paris and France.

Documents

JANUARY

1. **Sunday, 2 January 1785, 8:30 pm**
At 8:30 pm on Sunday, 2 January 1785, at our residence and before us, Charles Convers Desormeaux, barrister[1] in the Parlement[2] [as of 1762], royal councilor,[3] and commissaire of the Châtelet of Paris,[4] appeared S.[5] Jean François Royer Desurbois, royal councilor and police inspector, who told us that by virtue of the orders he carries, he had just arrested two men suspected of pederasty, observed since around 6:00 loitering on quai des Orfèvres in the most suspect manner, picking up men, and pretending several times to make water [urinate]. He conducted them before us to have a report of their arrest drawn up and signed. /Desurbois/

Louis Le Tellier, around 30, native of Dieppe (Normandy), domestic, lived chez his master S. Brebion, goldsmith and jeweler, on rue des Orfèvres.
    He admitted he was on quai des Orfèvres since around 6:00, took several turns there, and stopped several times. He remained there after leaving the evening service at the Sainte-Chapelle[6] because he was waiting for his masters, who had gone to dine in the city. He had a key for entering [their house] only through the kitchen, which is very dark and has no fire. He spoke to just one person, who asked him what time it was, to whom he replied it was 6:45. He did not have any bad intentions and is not at all given over to the vice of liking men. /Letellier/
C: W&R

Nicolas Hyacinthe Juillien, 21, native of Verdun (Lorraine), journeyman printer, worked chez S. Desaint on rue Saint-Jacques and lodged at the Providence boardinghouse on rue aux Fèves.

To tell the truth, he walked on quai des Orfèvres and stopped there twice, but he spoke to no one, and no one spoke to him. It is true he leaned on the parapet to look down to the edge of the water. He had heard it said it is a spot to which men who amuse themselves together make their way, but he looked there only out of pure curiosity, without design, and is not given over to that vice. /juillien/
C: W&R

2. Tuesday, 4 January 1785, 8:30 pm

I: A man loitered on quai des Orfèvres and below, next to the Seine, "in the spot called the Mousetrap" (La Souricière),[7] where he unbuttoned his breeches and "made a show of masturbating" before two men. He grabbed one's hand to place it on his genitals, but both rejected his advances.

Jean Louis Gagné, 29, native of Versailles (Ile-de-France), journeyman papermaker, unemployed since the end of August, orderly at the Hôtel-Dieu[8] until two weeks ago, lodged at the Grenada boardinghouse on rue de la Parcheminerie.

He was debauched into the crime of pederasty nearly five years ago, when he was in Versailles, by S. Aubert, unbeneficed +Lazarist[9] priest+ at the church of Saint-Louis,[10] who administered his first communion and debauched him in S. Aubert's room. They masturbated independently. The first time they did it was in the parlor of the Mission in Versailles, in the evening, when he went there to receive S. Aubert's instructions for taking his first communion, around eight years ago.[11] He continued with S. Aubert in this way for two or three years and then saw him more rarely. He did not amuse himself with any other person in Versailles. Denis, with whom he slept at the Hôtel-Dieu, where he was also an orderly in the Saint-Denis ward,[12] with the status of convalescent, informed him that men amuse themselves with men below quai des Orfèvres. He, the deponent, went to that spot this evening to amuse himself if he found someone there. It is the first time he has gone to that spot. Denis told him he went there often and amused himself there, but he has never been there with him. /U/
C: P

3. Wednesday, 12 January 1785, 8:30 pm

I: Three known pederasts loitered and took turns on quai des Orfèvres. One loitered frequently there and in other suspect places. Dessous had been arrested on 20 February 1782[13] and exiled three weeks later. Jean Bourquin had been arrested in the Mousetrap on 21 November 1784, warned, and released.[14]

Pierre Mérigot, 55, native of Villeneuve-Saint-Georges (Ile-de-France), disabled noncommissioned officer, worked and lived at the Royal Military School.[15]

 Coming back from faubourg Montmartre [9th arr.], he recrossed the Pont au Change and then the sidewalk on quai des Orfèvres to return to the Military School. He was arrested there. He took no turns there, only passed by, did not speak to anyone, and had no design but that of going home. He has never been given over to the debauchery of men. /merigot/
C: W&R

Jean Etienne Dessous, 33, native of Paris, clerk[16] of Messire[17] Fauconnier, former magistrate in the Cour des Aides,[18] lived with his father, who had various business interests, chez the earthenware maker on rue Coquillière.[19]

 He admits that he was arrested around two years ago for the same reason for which he was arrested today and that he was exiled. He was coming back from rue de Vaugirard and passed along quai des Orfèvres to go to rue Basse des Ursins. /Dessous/
C: P

Jean Bourquin, 46, native of Longwy in Lorraine, wigmaker, shaved the sick at the Hôtel-Dieu and lived in the Saint-Denis ward there.

 He has the misfortune to be given over to the crime of pederasty. He was debauched into this vice around twelve to fifteen years ago by another wigmaker's assistant whose name he does not recall. He has amused himself at this crime several times with men he encountered in the streets, whose names he does not know. He was with some of them with this object in a tavern at one corner of the street [rue d'Enfer] on Ile de la Cité near the Pont Rouge. Sometimes they encountered each other at the Mousetrap. Around four months ago he consummated this crime for the last time in the passive role with a man whose name he does not know, under a stone archway between the watering spot below quai des Orfèvres and the Pont Neuf. But he has

never known the names or addresses of the men with whom he surrendered himself to this crime. /Bourquin/
C: P

4. Thursday, 13 January 1785, 8:00 pm
I: A man loitered on quai des Orfèvres, accosted a man in a gray jacket, went down to the Mousetrap with him, stayed there for several minutes, came back up, took some turns, and went back down. Another man took more than thirty turns, accosted an observer, and told him he had come to this spot for several days "because he finds men there who oblige him. He needs thirty-six sols this evening."

Jean Louis Blondeau, 21, native of Chelles (Ile-de-France), unemployed pastrymaker's assistant, lodged in a furnished room chez Gaucher on rue Saint-Germain-l'Auxerrois.
 He went down to the watering spot below quai des Orfèvres to do his business but saw that another man had followed him and came back up to go away. He knows this spot is suspect for finding men given over to the vice of liking men, which vice he has a horror of. /Blondeau/
C: W&R

Elie Le Leu, 23, native of Versailles (Ile-de-France), unemployed wigmaker's assistant, arrived in Paris from Martinique[20] on 6 January and lodged at The White Beard on rue de la Vannerie.
 He was coming back from faubourg Saint-Jacques [5th/14th arr.] and returning to his lodging on rue de la Vannerie. He passed along quai des Orfèvres because his route went that way and stopped there without doing anything wrong there. He spoke to a man there who is a client of S. Becquinet, wigmaker, for whom he worked as an assistant last Sunday. This man recognized him and asked him if he would return to work for Becquinet next Sunday. He did not walk on the quay, and he was not found doing anything wrong when he was arrested. He did not speak to any other person and has nothing more to say. /X/
C: P

5. Friday, 14 January 1785, 8:00 pm
I: Four men loitered on quai des Orfèvres in the most suspect manner. A French Guard[21] had been there since 6:00 pm. A man in a blue cloak took seven to

eight turns, accosted him, and conversed with him. A water carrier, a known pederast, took two turns and accosted a man at the entrance to the watering spot. The fourth man took twelve or fifteen turns.

Louis Michel Patard, 19, native of Fontainebleau (Ile-de-France), French Guard, lived at his company barracks on rue de Babilone.[22]

He was walking on quai des Orfèvres while waiting for a prostitute who had made a rendezvous to meet him there. He came there at 5:30 pm with no other design. He asked the man in a cloak he met on the quay what time it was. This gentleman told him, then suggested that they drink a bottle together and observed to him he is quite young. He asked him which barracks he is from, asked him several questions about the person he was waiting for, and often stared at him. They were talking together when he, the deponent, was arrested. Another man, with a [workingman's] apron, whom he had seen take more than two turns on the quay, was also arrested there. This man also came to stare at him, and the deponent was ready to slap him,[23] since he is not given over to the vice of liking men. /Loui michael patar/
C: W&R

Pierre Patrice Boyère, 30, native of Paris, haberdasher and ironmonger, lived at 56, rue de Viarmes. He wore a cloak.

Coming back from a porcelain vendor's store in La Rapée [12th arr.], the vendor, named Le Royou de Roy, who accompanied him, entered a house at the New Market[24] and told him to keep going and he would rejoin him. The deponent took two turns on the quay. A soldier in the regiment of French Guards accosted him and asked him what time it was. He told him it was 7:30. He conversed with the soldier, even walked with him, and told him, since he told him he was pressed to return to the barracks, that he still had time to drink a bottle of wine, but without suggesting that he [the soldier] drink it with him or that he [Boyère] pay for it, and without having any intention to do so. As he was discoursing with the soldier, they were arrested. He does not know why this was suspect. He had no intention in remaining there other than waiting for the porcelain vendor and conducting him to his, the deponent's, place. He is not at all given over to the vice he is suspected of. /Boyere/
C: W&R

Antoine Baffle, 48, native of La Pillière near Besse-en-Chandesse in the diocese of Clermont in Auvergne, water carrier, lived on rue des Moineaux in Butte Saint-Roch (1st arr.).

He passed along quai des Orfèvres to go to Saint-Jean de Latran[25] to buy shoes. He saw them putting people leaving the guard post into a carriage, went back to see what it was, and was arrested. He does not know why and is not in the least given over to the vice he is suspected of. /U/
C: W&R

François Etienne Chedete, 40, native of Chaillot (16th arr.), journeyman painter, unemployed for a week, lived chez a tobacco vendor on rue du Temple, next to the monastery of the Fathers of Nazareth,[26] where he had worked as a doorman until 1 October.

He took two turns on quai des Orfèvres because the man dressed in a cloak, who was also arrested, came to stare at him. He passed along the quay to go from his place to rue Dauphine. He saw a soldier in the regiment of French Guards, but it is false that he stared at him. He has never been given over to the vice he is suspected of. /chedete/
C: W&R

6. Tuesday, 18 January 1785, 7:00 pm
I: A man picked up a 9-year-old child but then told him he was "too little." He picked up someone else, and they entered the stoneyard at the Comédie Française.[27] He undid his breeches and masturbated the other man, who escaped arrest. Another man lowered his breeches in the Mousetrap and made propositions to an observer. When he noticed other observers, he suggested, "Let's not stay here. Let's go someplace else to amuse ourselves because there are spies going by."

Louis Simon, 45, native of Troyes in Champagne, domestic of Mme de Loubon on rue Saint-Jacques near Saint-Benoît.[28]

He came from seeing one of his friends on cour des Fontaines and went away to his employer's residence. He entered the stoneyard at the Comédie Française to do his business but did nothing wrong. He did not speak to or amuse himself with anyone. /X/
C: P

Jean Charles Salmon, 28, native of Chatou (Ile-de-France), domestic of the baronne de Martin, lived at her residence on rue d'Anjou in the Marais (3rd/4th arr.).[29] He had his hair pulled back in a ponytail, ribbons on his shoes, a round hat, and a cane in his hand.

Around two years ago he amused himself with the comte de Garspern from Brittany[30] in his room in a boardinghouse on rue du Champ-fleuri near rue de Baudoin, on the basis of the promises he [Garspern] had made to him to do him a favor. He amused himself several times there. While masturbating he attempted several times to consummate the crime of pederasty with him, in the passive role, but it always hurt him too much. He also amused himself several times with men who picked him up on quai de la Vallée. It is true he went down to the Mousetrap this evening and met a man there to whom he said they could not do anything because spies were passing by. /Salmon/
C: P

7. **Wednesday, 19 January 1785, 8:00 pm**
I: A one-eyed man loitered on quai des Orfèvres, went down to the river, and accosted a water carrier who loitered there. After they masturbated independently under one of the archways, he came back up, went back down, and followed someone else. Another man loitered on the quay from 5:00 to 7:30 pm in the most suspect manner.

Thomas Lallement, 36, native of Estricq (?) in the diocese of Metz in Lorraine, domestic chez S. Coutavoz, doctor, lived at his residence on rue du Fouarre.

It has happened to him around five or six times with men. He was debauched into this vice by young folks when he was still a boy. He has been married for a year. Today, having drunk a bit, he in truth amused himself with a water carrier he met down by the river under quai des Orfèvres. /lallement/
C: P

Michel Jacques Butin, 52, native of Meulan-sur-Seine (Ile-de-France), doorman of the marquis de Saint-Georges,[31] lived at his residence on rue Gérard Beauquet near Saint-Paul.[32]

Today he went to dine with his wife, who is a maid of the marquise de Sinéty[33] in the Palais Royal,[34] and with other domestics in the household. Having drunk more than usual, he went to pay a visit in faubourg Saint-

Germain [7th arr.]. In coming back he amused himself on quai des Orfèvres by watching men who were fishing in the river, but without any bad intention. He is not given over to the vice he is suspected of and did not know this spot is suspect. /Butin/
C: W&R

8. Thursday, 20 January 1785, 8:45 pm
I: Two men appeared to masturbate independently in the stoneyard. Another man, a known pederast, loitered every evening in suspect places, this evening on quai des Orfèvres in the most suspect manner.

Claude Richomme, 16½, native of Paris, student worker chez Messire Le Masson, attorney[35] in the Châtelet,[36] lived with his father, limonadier,[37] on rue d'Enfer Porte Saint-Michel.

For a week he has been going to walk in the evening among the stones near the Comédie. He was there this evening and was accosted by the other man arrested with him, who told him he had been a soldier, but they did not do anything. This man told him there were men there who had offered him money. Since he has been going to this spot, he, the deponent, has indeed seen men committing indecencies there in front of him. Three days ago others tried to talk to him and called to him, but he did not respond. /Richomme/
C: W&R

François Ferdinand Sanzwoell, 16½, native of Paris, journeyman joiner, lived and worked with his father on rue des Boucheries in faubourg Saint-Germain (6th arr.). He had been a soldier in the Rouergue regiment for nearly a year but did not reenlist.

Passing near the Comédie Française, he encountered the man arrested with him, whom he does not know, who urged him to pass through the stones and told him he came there often and had seen a chevalier de Saint-Louis, who had shown him some money. They stayed there for a long time, watching people, but they did nothing and did not amuse themselves together. /Sanzwoell/
C: W&R

François Bourdelet, 30, native of Paris, journeyman engraver, lived on rue des Marmousets on Ile de la Cité.

He passed along quai des Orfèvres but did not speak to anyone there. He consummated the crime of pederasty in the active role twice, around a month ago, with a gentleman he does not know, at his place on rue des Petits Augustins, number 26. This gentleman met him on quai de Conti and conducted him there. He was debauched into this vice around eight to ten years ago. He surrendered himself to this debauchery with seven or eight different persons, always in the active role, but does not know any of them. He met them on quai du Louvre and went either to their places or to spots where they wished to lead him. He was arrested for this debauchery four years ago on the Pont Neuf and released.[38] He passed along quai des Orfèvres this evening with the intention of finding someone with whom he could amuse himself. /Bourdelet/
C: P

9. Friday, 21 January 1785, 8:45 pm
I: A man loitered on quai des Orfèvres, accosted a man, went down under the third archway in the Mousetrap with him, and appeared to try to stroke him. They came back up and went to a tavern on rue Dauphine. When they left, the first man hugged the second and made a rendezvous with him on Sunday, then returned to the Mousetrap.

Etienne Servault, 21, native of La Flèche in Anjou, laundryman, lived in Grenelle (7th arr.) near the Military School.

He went near the Palais [de Justice][39] this evening to find his colleague Leblond, whose carriage was in the square opposite the Palais. In passing along the parapet on quai des Orfèvres, he met a young man unknown to him, who told him he was from Versailles. He, the deponent, went down under an archway to do his business. Then this young man went down, approached him, tried to stroke him, +and told him it was fine weather for getting an erection [*se bander*], to which the deponent replied yes+. Then this man went back up, and he, the deponent, went back up and found this man again, with whom he went to drink two mugs of wine in a tavern. He does not know on which street. When they left, he came back to quai des Orfèvres and went back down to the edge of the watering spot with Brandin, butcher's assistant, who was going to have his horse drink. He lives chez S. Cornu, butcher. He planned to ask Brandin for money to borrow. He took the hand of the man he drank with when they left the tavern but did not hug him. He did arrange to meet him on Sunday, at his place on rue des Fossés de M. le

Prince, where he told him he lives, near the office of the *capitation*,⁴⁰ where he, the deponent, told him he would find him on Sunday at 3:00 pm. /U/
C: P

10. Monday, 24 January 1785, 9:30 pm
I: The police caught a man on the Half-Moon⁴¹ in the act of {masturbating himself} having himself masturbated by another man, who escaped arrest. Lacroix, a known pederast {who has already been in Bicêtre⁴² and exiled}, loitered in the Coal-Box (La Charbonnerie).⁴³

Claude Marchal, 47, native of Neufchâteau in Lorraine, clerk of the Farms⁴⁴ at the Saint-Michel barrier,⁴⁵ lived on rue Saint-Louis in the parish of Saint-Louis (4th arr.) on Ile de la Cité.

As he was coming back from La Haute Borne, he passed along the Half-Moon at the Saint-Antoine gate,⁴⁶ and a young man presented himself before him. As he was making water, this man placed his hand on his penis,⁴⁷ and he was arrested at once. He is not inclined to this vice. /Marchal/
C: W&R

Lambert LaCroix, 42, native of Paris, day laborer, lived on rue du Faubourg Saint-Antoine at the corner of rue Amelot.

He was debauched into the crime of pederasty twelve to thirteen years ago by Levasseur, who made children's toys, who lived in faubourg Saint-Laurent [10th arr.] at the time. He consummated the crime in the passive as well as active role with several persons, among others, within the last seven to eight months, with Camort, soldier in the regiment of French Guards in La Courtille [19th arr.]. He, the deponent, sometimes pays for his eau-de-vie [brandy] and gives him a coin worth twelve sols, and one worth twenty-four sols to go on guard.⁴⁸ Also a hairdresser whose name he does not know. He, the deponent, brought him to sleep with him, gave him supper, and gave him twenty-four sols. Also another man whose name he does not know, who told him he is a glazier, whom he, the deponent, brought to sleep at his place after meeting him in the Sugar Loaf tavern in La Courtille. /U/
C: P

11. Tuesday, 25 January 1785, 7:45 pm
I: A young man, a known pederast, loitered on quai des Orfèvres.

François Gaucher, 21, native of Thennelières near Troyes in Champagne, former shoemaker's assistant, for the last twenty months domestic of the surgeons at the Hôtel-Dieu, lived there.

He passed along quai des Orfèvres to go from the Hôtel-Dieu to rue Mazarine. He took no turns on the quay and had no bad intention. He is not at all given over to the vice he is suspected of. /francois gaucher/
C: W&R

I: 8:00 pm. Laurent, called Raimond, a known pederast on record, who consorted with Buquet,[49] cruised every evening in the Tuileries and other suspect places, this evening on quai des Orfèvres.

Guillaume Raimond Laurent, 25, native of Paris, former tailor's assistant and domestic, haberdasher for the last year, lived with his mother, also haberdasher, on rue du Chantre.

It is true it has happened to him several times to go to the Tuileries in the evening and to have conversations there with men given over to pederasty, but he surrenders himself only to independent touching and masturbation with them. He has not taken things further. The same thing has happened to him on the boulevards, but he does not know the names of any of these men. He has never received money for this or given any. He has sometimes paid for cider for some of them. He was debauched into this vice by Jean, groom at the abbey of Saint-Germain[-des-Prés],[50] when he, the deponent, was twelve years old. Jean is dead. He amused himself once with Allain, who sets gemstones at his place on rue Saint-Louis near the Palais. Chez Allain he saw a soldier in a blue uniform with white braids [French Guard]. He knew from Allain that they arrest people for this. He was last in the Tuileries last week and met no one there. /Laurant/
C: P

12. Wednesday, 26 January 1785, 7:30 pm
I: A man with long hair in a gray jacket, with his breeches unbuttoned, amused himself in the Mousetrap with a man who escaped arrest. Two known pederasts, who loitered "habitually" on the quays, spoke to men who passed them on quai des Orfèvres.

François Jobin Desgrignons, 40, native of Paris, clerk in the civil section of the Châtelet, lived on rue Jean Pain Mollet in the parish of Saint-Merri (4th arr.).

He went down to the edge of the water under des Orfèvres this evening to do his business. While he was there a man indeed loitered around him and placed his hand on his shirt in back, but he sent him away and told him, "Back off. I'm going to make a complaint about you."

Pointed out to him he is not telling the truth at all, since he was seen and observed for some time with this man, with whom he amused himself and masturbated, while this man fondled him in back. Called on to tell us the truth and asked for how long he has amused himself with men, who are those with whom he has amused and amuses himself, and the places where he amuses himself.

Replied he never amuses himself with anyone and did not amuse himself at all with the man he does not know, who escaped, whom he threatened with making a complaint. /X/
C: W&R

Denis Colle, 49, native of Molay in Burgundy, baker at the Petites Maisons,[51] lived there.

He indeed took two turns on quai des Orfèvres and spoke to a man he met on the parapet there, who told him the weather was fine, to which he, the deponent, replied yes, it was like a summer day. He then went his way and was arrested. Before he and this man spoke, they simply looked at each other. He, the deponent, took two or three turns on the quay but without any bad design. He is not inclined to the vice he is suspected of and arrested for. +Then he said that, to tell the truth, he has had the weakness to amuse himself with men on the parapet of this quay. He was debauched into this vice around fourteen years ago and has gone down below the quay several times. He does not recall the time he amused himself the last time. He went on the quay this evening with the design of finding someone there to amuse himself with there but did not meet anyone.+ /Colle/
C: P

Mathieu Cujat, 34, native of La Souterraine in the diocese of Limoges (Limousin), manual laborer, lodged chez Mme Petit, who rented rooms on rue de la Tacherie.

He came back from working on rue du Bac and passed along quai des Orfèvres in returning to his inn. He bent down to empty his shoes and in addition stopped once to piss and was arrested. He has been [there?] only once or twice this year. When he was arrested, he was returning toward the

Pont Neuf to hear the singers. He amused himself with a man only once, four years ago, on the boulevard that leads to the Saint-Antoine gate. He amused himself again more than two weeks ago with another man, a wigmaker's assistant, under the archways below quai des Orfèvres. He was debauched into this vice three or four years ago by an abbé[52] whose name he does not know, at an intersection in the direction of rue Saint-Martin. /U/
C: P

13. Thursday, 27 January 1785, 6:15 pm
I: A man loitered on quai des Orfèvres, accosted a "child" who was doing his business there, and suggested that they go down below. The "little boy" did not reply, pulled up his breeches, and fled. The man followed an observer down to the Mousetrap and accosted him. He exposed himself, pretended to urinate, and claimed he could not do so because of his strong erection. After both men went back up and came back down, he asked the observer, "Do you want to jerk me off [*branler*]?"

Jean Baptiste Lefevre, 43, native of Clermont in Auvergne, in Paris for two and a half months, innkeeper, lived on rue Galande opposite rue Saint-Julien-le-Pauvre.[53]

He has never been given over to the vice of pederasty. It is true he had this penchant but does not give himself over to it anymore. He amused himself several times with men whose names he does not know. He took half a turn on quai des Orfèvres and then went down below. To tell the truth, he said to a man who passed by near him, when he was in a posture to make water, that he could not do it because he had such a strong erection, which was true. It is not true he suggested to anyone to masturbate him. Before going down below he indeed saw a little boy who was doing his business, but he did not speak to him and did not suggest going down to him. /X/
C: P

I: 7:45 pm. A man loitered for a long time on quai des Orfèvres and quai des Augustins in the most suspect manner and fled at the sight of observers. After they captured him and consigned him to a carriage, he escaped. After they recaptured him, he offered them money to let him go.

Malo Duval, 34, native of Angers (Anjou),[54] domestic of Messire Goulet, notary,[55] lived at his residence on rue Saint-Antoine.

At the age of fifteen to twenty he was subject to letting himself be touched by men and touching them but is no longer given over to this and does not know for how long. He was on quai des Orfèvres this evening waiting for Dumaine, domestic, who had entered an earthenware booth at the Marché Neuf to buy a bowl. He went to quai de la Vallée to buy a turkey but did not buy one. He fled because he saw he was arrested and offered money so as not to be conducted before a commissaire. /X/
C: W&R

14. Saturday, 29 January 1785, 6:00 pm
I: Two men loitered in the Mousetrap, accosted men, and accosted each other. One of them, Donison, a known pederast, loitered there daily, today since 4:00 pm.

Charles Charpentier, 28, native of Paris, grocer, lived on rue de Sèvres in the parish of Saint-Sulpice (6th arr.).
 Passing along quai des Orfèvres about 5:30 pm and feeling the need to go, he went down to the edge of the water and set about doing his business. As he was doing so, the man arrested with him, whom he does not know, approached him. He did not know why he approached him in this way and told him, "Just a minute, Sir." This man withdrew. He does not know why this man approached him or that this spot is suspect. As he, the deponent, finished buttoning his breeches, he was arrested. /Charpentier/
C: R

Christophe Donison, 38, native of Le Mans (Maine), domestic, unemployed since 24 December, lived on rue Neuve Guillemain in the parish of Saint-Sulpice.
 He has been given over to the vice of pederasty for only one year. He was debauched by one of his cousins named Louis Darras, who was a French Guard at the time and is currently a domestic of a colonel whose name he does not know, with whom he left [Paris] on the fifteenth of last month. He has indeed been very often, twice or thrice a week, in that spot, where he amuses himself with men +he does not know+. This evening he went to that spot to amuse himself there but had not done so yet. He has never received money to amuse himself and has, on the contrary, given some, but not much. As for his colleague Darras, he did it to make money. /donison/
C: P

15. Saturday, 29 January 1785, 7:30 pm
I: The marquis de Vichy, who had lived with Buquet, called Rag, loitered on quai des Orfèvres and pretended to urinate. He went down to the Mousetrap, pretended to urinate again, and called in a very low voice to an observer, who recognized him.

Abel Claude Marie, marquis de Vichy,[56] 45, native of Ligny in Mâconnais (Burgundy), chevalier de Saint-Louis, lived at 7, quai de Conti.

He, the deponent, indeed went down to the edge of the water to do his business. He might well have made water three or four times because it happens to him often, but he did not call to anyone and did not go down to do anything wrong. He did not know that this spot is suspect and that people do wrong there. Now that he is informed of it, he will not return there.

With regard to Buquet, called Rag, whom we mentioned to him, he made him [a loan or gift of?] 120 livres per month in 1780 to hold him back from the vice of pederasty, to which he said he was given over in order to live. He left for his estate at Montceaux-l'Etoile [Lionnais] on 6 June 1780 and has not heard anything about him since. He never lived with or did anything wrong with Buquet, called Rag. /A., Marquis De Vichy/
C: R

16. Sunday, 30 January 1785, 5:30 pm
I: A younger man, who had loitered in the Mousetrap since 5:00 pm, followed an observer, pretended to urinate several times, and accosted an older man. They went down below and retreated under the archways for a quarter of an hour to amuse themselves together. The older man had his breeches down.

François Jalabert, 35, native of Dieppe (Normandy), tailor, lived on rue de la Vieille Draperie.

He went down to the spot where he was arrested about 5:00 pm to relieve himself and saw a domestic who was washing horses. He walked along the edge of the water, withdrew for several minutes to take cover from the rain, and saw the other man arrested with him come down. He did his business there. He [Jalabert] told him [Charpentier] to beware one man and did not have any other conversation with him. He did not amuse himself with him. He has never amused himself with men. /françois jalabert/
C: P

Pierre Jacques Brillant, 55, native of Paris, lived and worked with his brother, wine vendor, on quai des Augustins.

He had the weakness this evening to go down to the spot called the Mousetrap, where he met the man arrested with him. They accosted each other and withdrew into the entrance of one of the archways, where they amused themselves together. This man fondled and masturbated him, and he also fondled him. This man said to him, "Here come some people." They were afraid and separated. They were arrested immediately. He has been given over to this vice for around twenty years. He was debauched into it by an abbé, son of a wine vendor at The Three Funnels on Montagne Sainte-Geneviève [5th arr.]. For about two years he has been given over to it again. Around a year ago he was robbed of his garter buckles by a man he does not know, with whom he amused himself in this spot. Since then he has returned to this spot at various times and amused himself with men he does not know, but he will not return again. /Briand/
C: P

The commissaire recalled Jalabert and informed him that Brillant had stated that "they fondled each other and amused themselves together."

Briand indeed fondled him, but he claimed he [Jalabert] did not fondle him [Briand]. He was debauched around fifteen years ago by one of his comrades, whom he slept with, whose name he does not recall. He also amused himself last year with Vangron, joiner, +whom he slept with.+ /jalabert/

17. Monday, 31 January 1785, 6:30 pm

I: A man who loitered and took several turns on quai des Orfèvres picked up Picot, called the Female Savior, a notorious pederast, who daily picked up young folks on the quays and boulevards and in other suspect places and procured them to abbés and others. He fenced stolen items for Carton,[57] a notorious pederast, held orgies at his place, bought leaves for several French Guards who were pederasts, and maintained Lacoste, hairdresser, a notorious pederast, for a long time. He had already spent time in prison.[58] Bernard, hairdresser, known as The Little Female Wigmaker, a notorious pederast, loitered on quai de la Vallée in the most suspect manner. He had been maintained by various men, including Modas, chevalier de Saint-Louis, and spent more than a year in Bicêtre for pederasty and procurement.[59]

Pierre François Picot, called The Holy Female Savior, around 50,[60] native of Saint-Germain-en-Laye (Ile-de-France), domestic chez S. Lorlot, chaplain at the Sainte-Chapelle, lived at his residence in the enclosure of the Palais.

He was arrested around two years ago on rue de Bondy and conducted to prison, where he remained three weeks for pederasty, which [charge] was false. He does not know Carton. Then he said he met Carton eight years ago at the Grand Salon.[61] He knew Lacoste from [Lacoste's] dressing his [Picot's] wife's hair. He was debauched into pederasty twenty years ago by the marquis de La Tour du Pin.[62] +He knew and amused himself thirteen years ago with the comte de Buturlin.[63] He has been procured to Saint-Hilaire[64] and men whose names he does not know.+ Since he has been in prison, he no longer surrenders himself to men. He was only passing along the quay today. He no longer surrenders himself to pederasty, has never bought leave for anyone, and does not cruise in any spot. /U/
C: W&R

Jacques François Bernard, called The Little Female Wigmaker, 40, native of Paris, hairdresser, lived on rue de la Calandre.

It is true he was arrested for pederasty around three years ago and was in Bicêtre for a year. He was debauched at the age of seventeen to eighteen by a man whose name he does not recall, who lived in a boardinghouse, but he does not indulge in it anymore. He did know Saint-Hilaire. He only passed along quai de la Vallée. /Bernard/
C: W&R

FEBRUARY

18. Saturday, 12 February 1785, 5:30–11:30 pm
We, Charles Convers Desormeaux, barrister in the Parlement, royal councilor, and commissaire of the Châtelet, went on patrol, accompanied by S. Jean François Desurbois, royal councilor and police inspector, by virtue of the orders he carries, in various spots and on various quays in this city. Passing on quai des Orfèvres, S. Desurbois arrested two men there. He observed one of them loitering on quai des Augustins, where he took several turns, and on quai des Orfèvres, where he was arrested. This man is known to be given over to pederasty, to loiter often in the most suspect places, and to cruise there. The other had been observed loitering and walking for some

time on quai des Orfèvres, where he goes daily, as well as in other suspect places. He was, moreover, already arrested and imprisoned for this crime on 15 September 1784.¹ For these reasons he conducted them to the guard post at the Pont Neuf.²

Jean Baptiste Sébastien Blanchard, 40, native of Auxerre (Burgundy), domestic chez S. Gosse, professor at the collège de La Marche,³ lived at his residence on rue de la Montagne Sainte-Geneviève.

He has been in Paris for eight years but has had the weakness to amuse himself with men for only two years. He has never known those with whom he has amused himself. He has amused himself sometimes in one spot and sometimes in another. He has not amused himself with any man in two months, but he amused himself with a man he does not know past the Chaillot barrier.⁴ He did nothing with anyone this evening and passed along quai des Augustins and quai des Orfèvres without doing anything wrong. /Blanchard/
C: P

Jean Philippe Areintz, 36, native of Châlons in Champagne, domestic of Mme Dufresne, banker, lived at her residence on rue Beaubourg.

He came from his employer's residence and was going to find some syrup on rue du Hurepoix. He passed along quai des Orfèvres to go there. He did not take any turns or do anything wrong. If he looked over the parapet sometimes, it was to see the river. He was indeed arrested and imprisoned on 15 September. He was in the wrong then, but he is not at fault today. /areintz/
C: P

I: Two men, one of them dressed like an abbé, walked arm in arm in the stoneyard.

Théophile Sauvage, 18, native of Béthune in Artois, student, lived at the (Saint-Pierre-) Saint-Louis seminary.⁵

He left there today and was supposed to go sleep this evening in a furnished room behind the Sorbonne.⁶ The other man is the assistant of S. Voisin, limonadier, on rue de la Harpe. He knows him from drinking in his café but does not know his name. They were both seeking to get themselves picked up by prostitutes. /X/
C: W&R

Eustache Robert Vital Boucher, 25, native of Saint-Pierre-de-Cernières in the diocese of Evreux (Normandy), limonadier's assistant at the Café de Monsieur[7] on rue de la Harpe, lived there.

He has known the abbé with whom he was arrested for six months. They went to the fair[8] together this afternoon and were returning for supper when they were arrested. /X/
C: W&R

19. Monday, 14 February 1785, 9:00 pm
I: A man "dressed in the costume of men given over to this vice" loitered in the Tuileries since 6:15 and picked up men in the most suspect pathways.[9] He left the garden with a man who escaped arrest.

Jean Renaud, 27, native of Clermont in Argonne (Lorraine), domestic for four months of the chevalier du Perrier, officer in the dragoons,[10] lived at his residence at 13, rue des Fontaines, near the Temple.[11]

When he arrived in Paris three years ago, he first served in the household of the banker Peixotto,[12] where he remained only four days because the doorman warned him that Peixotto seduced young folks who lived at his place. Then he presented himself to a gentleman, whose name he does not know, on allée du Parfumeur off rue Notre-Dame-des-Victoires, on the third floor. This gentleman made indecent propositions to him, for which reason he did not enter his service. He then served M. de Beauvoir, major in the Cent Suisses [royal bodyguards] and before, for two weeks, Bailly, former personal valet, who came back from the [Caribbean] islands. He left his household because Bailly also made propositions to him. When he left M. de Beauvoir, he served Mlle de Beaumeny, actress at the Opera, for five days, then S. Menion, at whose residence he fell ill, and then abbé Pfaff, whose residence he left on 24 June. He does not go to the Tuileries often. He has been picked up by men several times there but did not respond to them favorably. He was followed every day during Carnival[13] by a man, 36 to 40 years old, who still followed him yesterday. As he crossed the Tuileries this evening, he was accosted by a man unknown to him, who appeared to him to be a domestic, who begged him to walk with him and urged him to take several turns in the garden with him. They talked about Carnival and not other things. He was debauched into pederasty around two years ago by Du Chenu, garde du corps,[14] with whom he consummated this crime chez Du Chenu in Versailles, where Du Chenu conducted him and locked

him in. He does not recall the last time he amused himself since. The man who accosted him in the Tuileries today spoke to him quite casually about this debauchery and took his arm to take a walk. They left together, and the other man escaped at the moment when he, the deponent, was arrested. /Renauld/
C: P[15]

20. **Tuesday, 15 February 1785, 9:00 pm**
I: A man loitered in the Tuileries for at least an hour in the most suspect manner and accosted several men.

Henry Librex, 25, native of Hintowe (?) in Holland (Netherlands), in Paris for eighteen months, domestic of chevalier Van Havre, lived at his residence chez Messire Lefevre Dampierre on rue de l'Arbre sec.

He went to the Tuileries this evening to find a domestic whose name he does not know, whom he has seen sometimes in the garden, who lives on Ile Saint-Louis. In the Tuileries he spoke only to a German domestic he knows by sight from being in the Palais Royal garden together around a year ago and to another domestic, with a hat fringed in silver, whom he does not know, who said good evening to him and asked him how he was. He took a turn with the domestic, who held him with both hands. He usually wears a fringed hat, and this evening he had a plain slouch hat with a ribbon and rosette that belong to him. He tried only once to go to the Tuileries. It is true he stopped there several times, but without design, and did nothing wrong. He is not given over to the vice of liking men. /hendrikcus liebrex/
C: W&R

21. **Wednesday, 16 February 1785, 5:30 pm–12:00 am**
PP: quarters, quays, OP

I: Three men, including one already arrested and released (#14) and another known pederast, took several turns on quai des Orfèvres.

Charles Charpentier, 28, native of Paris, grocer, lived on rue de Sèvres near the barrier.[16]

He came back from buying cheeses on rue Saint-Denis, which he had carried by a man he lost in the courtyard of the Palais. As he passed along the sidewalk, going away to his place, he was arrested. It is true he was arrested

at the end of last month and was released, but he did nothing wrong at all, and he did not take several turns on the sidewalk. /Charpentier./
C: W&R

Simon Guyot, 37, native of Arc-en-Barrois in the bishopric of Conques (Guyenne), clockmaker, lived with his brother, master clockmaker, on rue de Richelieu.

He was coming back from visiting some workmen and a shopkeeper on rue de la Barillerie, from whom he bought a pound [of what?], which he remembered while passing along quai des Orfèvres, when he was arrested. He has never been given over to pederasty. /Guiot/
C: W&R

Nicolas Garet, 30, native of Brouel (?) in Picardy, kitchen assistant chez the vicomte de Blosseville,[17] lived at his residence at 6, rue de l'Université.

He was coming from the Saint-Germain market and going to take a knife to a cutler on the Pont Saint-Michel to be repaired. He made water at the entrance to the courtyard of the Palais and remembered there that he had had a receipt for 102 livres signed by a female fruit vendor and that he needed to have it signed by her husband. He turned back and passed along quai des Orfèvres, where he was arrested. It is true he looked over the parapet after seeing others who were looking. /Garet/
C: W&R

I: 8:00 pm. Five men loitered and cruised in the Tuileries. Two of them "surrendered themselves to pederasty together."

Jean Pierre Bunel, 40, native of Rouen (Normandy), shopkeeper's assistant chez S. Royer, silk vendor, on rue des Déchargeurs, lived chez S. Florence, master joiner, on rue Saint-Jacques at passage des Jacobins.

He has been given over to pederasty for two years. He surrendered himself to it for the first time in the Luxembourg garden with a man unknown to him, who picked him up, with whom he {consummated} masturbated independently. The same thing has happened to him since then with several others unknown to him, in various places, most frequently in the Luxembourg. He went to the Tuileries this evening without any fixed intention and was picked up there by another man, also arrested, who urged him to walk with him and sit down on a bench, where they stroked mutually. Then this

man pressed him to give him something for a drink. Given his repeated entreaties, he gave him a coin worth twelve sols, which did not satisfy him. Insisting on having more, he followed him and pressed him sharply for it until the moment they were arrested. /J. P. Bunel/
C: P

Antoine Piette, 35, native of Paris, dragoon in the Penthièvre regiment, on leave in Paris for half a year, lodged with his brother, gemstone setter, chez S. Lecocq, wine vendor, on rue de Sèvres opposite the Petites Maisons.

He is not given over to pederasty, and it is not true he spoke to anyone in the Tuileries. He only crossed the garden and did not request or receive money from anyone. /U/
C: P

The commissaire recalled Bunel, who reiterated his version of events.

François Gombert, 21, native of Nonaville in Lorraine, in the diocese of Verdun, unemployed kitchen assistant, lodged with his cousin chez S. Létoile on rue Saint-Louis on Ile de la Cité.

Coming back from seeing his sister on rue Saint-Honoré, where she lives, and going to see his brother on rue du Four in faubourg Saint-Germain, he went to cross the Tuileries and found the gate closed. He passed through the courtyards and came out at the Carousel,[18] where he was arrested and does not know why. /f. Gombert/
C: R

Louis Joseph Dutranoy, 27, native of Etroeungt in Hainaut (Belgium), manager of the Artois boardinghouse on rue Beauregard, lived there.

It has happened to him this year to amuse himself with men sometimes in {the Tuileries garden} place Louis XV [de la Concorde], where they masturbated independently. He does not know these men, whom he met in the Tuileries. He went to the Palais Royal garden this evening, where he met the other arrested young man. They went to the Tuileries garden together, then took a turn around place Louis XV and went back to the garden, where this young man accosted other men, to one of whom he said, "There he is, then, Callé." He never amused himself with this young man, whom he knows only by sight, whose acquaintance he made at the Opera ball,[19] but he never wished to go to his place, although he had invited him. He said he gave an écu worth

three livres to each of those with whom he amused himself but never consummated the crime of pederasty completely except for once with a man unknown to him in that man's room in Butte Saint-Roch, where he left a {pair of} silver {earrings} buckle, which he was supposed to bring back to him near the portal of Saint-Eustache,[20] where he, the deponent, was supposed to give him three livres, but this man did not come there. /dutranois./
C: P

Jean Joseph Georges, called Saint-Fermin, 23, native of Herbéviller in Lorraine, in Paris for nine months to pursue a career in theater, lived at The Three Stars on rue Geoffrey Langevin.

He did nothing but enter the Tuileries with the man who just appeared [before the commissaire], whom he met in passing through place Louis XV, whose name he does not know, whom he has seen just once at the Opera ball. In the Tuileries he encountered and spoke to Garnier or Gressier, who asked him if he wished to go to supper with him chez Mlle Tabouret on rue Saint-Honoré. He has never been given over to the vice of liking men. /George/
C: P

22. Thursday, 17 February 1785, 9:30 pm
I: A pederast loitered in the Tuileries since 6:00 pm and picked up men. He accosted an observer, suggested that they go to the Champs-Elysées[21] to amuse themselves, then made a rendezvous with him for the next day.

Louis Michel Alexandre Severet de La Chenaye, 26, native of Rambouillet (Ile-de-France), employee of the Farms, in the transport section in Rouen, in Paris on business for a month, lodged with his brother, master wigmaker, at the old market[22] on rue Jean de Beauce.

Coming back from Chaillot [16th arr.], he entered the Tuileries garden, where he only passed along the central pathway,[23] left, and was arrested as he left. He spoke to no one in the Tuileries, and no one spoke to him. He is not given over to pederasty. /X/
C: P

23. Friday, 18 February 1785, 7:45 pm
I: Letourneur, called The Big Female Gilder, a known pederast and extortionist, loitered on quai des Orfèvres. He had been caught in the act on the Half-Moon some years before and sent to Bicêtre and also prosecuted for theft in 1781.

René Le Tourneur, 25, native of Le Mesnil-Drey in Lower Normandy, unemployed painter and gilder on wood, lodged with his father, day laborer, on rue de la Mortellerie.

He arrived in Paris from Lille, where he spent three years in custody for desertion from the Rohan-Soubise infantry regiment. He was pardoned for this desertion in the last amnesty. He enlisted in that regiment while he was in Bicêtre, where the regiment of French Guards in which he served before had him locked up. Since then he has been imprisoned in the Grand Châtelet[24] on accusation of theft. He left there to be returned to his regiment by the rural constabulary [*maréchaussée*]. He was not on quai des Orfèvres this evening and was arrested when he was near the guard post at the Pont Neuf. He has never amused himself with men. /X/
C: P

24. Saturday, 19 February 1785, 7:00 pm
I: Two men loitered together on quai des Orfèvres. The taller one picked up men there, as well as on quai des Augustins, every evening and went down to the Mousetrap frequently.

Jacques Marie Maurisset, 24, native of Paris, shoemaker's assistant, worked chez Ricard, arrested with him, and lived with his father, master shoemaker, on rue du Cimetière Saint-André-des-Arts.

This evening he went with Ricard to get the cutting tools they had left for repair on rue Galande. Richard urged him to go with him from there to the end of the Pont Neuf, where they charged one sol for a shave, for Ricard to get himself shaved. They passed along quai des Orfèvres, where they were arrested. He, the deponent, does not know why. He had no other intention and did not know this quay is suspect. He is not in the least given over to the vice of liking men. /U/
C: W&R

Pierre Marin Ricard, 22, native of Paris, shoemaker's assistant, lived chez the currier's on rue de la Huchette, on the seventh floor.

He is not at all given over to pederasty and has been married for two years. He passed along quai des Orfèvres only to give what help he can to Ravoisier, his very aged and infirm grandfather, who lives for a fee chez S. Duhamel at the edge of the river opposite the Mint.[25] This evening he brought him ten sols and then went to have himself shaved for one sol at the edge of

the water. He had no other intention and never amuses himself on this quay. He speaks to no one there and only passes by when he needs to. /Ricard/
C: W&R

I: 9:00 pm. Two men loitered in the Tuileries since 7:00 pm and accosted men in the most suspect manner. The taller one finally picked up the shorter one. They took several turns together and joined others suspected of pederasty.

Joseph Antony, 22, native of Bruley in Lorraine, dragoon, enlisted in the Mestre de Camp regiment six months ago but had not joined it because of a broken leg. He left the Hôtel-Dieu three weeks ago and lodged at the Holy Spirit boardinghouse on rue Saint-Etienne in La Villeneuve. He was dressed in a gray levite (a long full robe), wide cravat (neckband), very large hat, and small laced boots.

Before he enlisted, he was personal valet of prince Cardilot, Neapolitan lord, and before that wigmaker's assistant. He is not at all given over to pederasty and was in the Tuileries this evening because he had made a rendezvous at the café on the terrace[26] with the young man arrested with him, whose name he does not know, +whom he has known for only three days,+ and with Lebeau, this man's brother, who did not come to the rendezvous, although he was supposed to come to have supper at his, the deponent's, place with the arrested man. He took three or four turns with the latter and spoke to another man, unknown to him, who accosted him and told him he was a head cook on rue Poissonnière, who took two turns with them. He goes to the Tuileries very rarely. /U/
C: P

Louis LeBeau, 17, native of Reims (Champagne), unemployed limonadier's assistant, lived with his father, employed in the distribution of the *Journal de Paris*,[27] on rue Transnonain. He was dressed in a green jacket, wide cravat, and a very large hat.

He was in the Palais Royal and encountered there his friend with whom he was arrested, whom he has known for a year. They went to the Tuileries together to have a Bavaroise[28] at the café. The other left him and spoke to another person, and he, the deponent, went to do his business. He rejoined his friend, named Antony, +and left at once+. They had no rendezvous in the Tuileries. He has a brother, wigmaker's assistant and soldier. He had no rendezvous for supper with anyone and was not supposed to go to supper chez

Antony or elsewhere with him. He made his acquaintance a year ago at Café d'Yon[29] on the boulevards, where he, the deponent, was then an assistant. He is not given over to pederasty and does not know if the other is given over to it. He said it is he, the deponent, who paid for the Bavaroises they had at the café in the Tuileries, since Antony had no money. /Lebeaux/
C: P[30]

25. Monday, 21 February 1785, 9:00 pm
I: A man who entered the Tuileries about 7:00 pm loitered there in the most suspect manner and picked up men, including one who urinated or at least pretended to do so, in the pathway below the terrace along the Seine. They appeared to stroke mutually, and he then played "what pederasts call cancan,[31] by saying loudly to passersby, "Do you want me to jerk you off for an écu?" He called old men old aunts who should sing [succumb to blackmail] and, displaying his white handkerchief,[32] said, "At the sign of good wine. No need for a shop-sign. Here is my placard."

He then accosted two observers and conversed with them. He told them he sold fruit in the streets of Versailles, liked the active but not the passive role, knows a pederast called The Lovely Female Baker, domestic chez S. de la Lunette, doctor, and likes to amuse himself with French Guards. He resisted arrest, threw a soldier's hat in the mud, and called the sergeant a rascal.

Joseph Petit, 20, native of Versailles (Ile-de-France), sold fruit there, lived on rue de la Paix, and came to Paris today to buy fruit to resell in Versailles.

He does not know what the Tuileries are and did not enter there. He is not given over to pederasty and does not know what we mean. He did not amuse himself and did not speak to anyone anywhere. /U/
C: P

26. Monday, 21 February 1785, 10:30 pm
I: A pederast accosted an older man in the salesroom in the Palais Royal. They walked, went behind the Beaujolais theater,[33] where they apparently touched themselves independently, came back, took three turns under the arcades,[34] and entered the Mechanical Café.[35] The younger man ordered a Bavaroise and small bread roll. The older man, in a blue cloak, ordered a lemonade. They took two more turns under the arcades and parted at the exit onto rue des Bons Enfants.

Jean François Bâtonnier, 20, native of Beauvilliers in Picardy, domestic of Messire Lobestein, barrister in the high court of Alsace, lived at his residence in the Russia boardinghouse on rue Tiquetonne. He was dressed "in the costume of pederasts," with rosettes on his shoes and a very large unfastened slouch hat.

He did nothing but cross the Palais Royal garden from the side on rue des Bons Enfants, where he encountered a gentleman in a cloak whose name he does not know, whom he saw once chez his master, who recognized him, asked him for news of Messire Lobestein, and charged him to give him his compliments. They parted, and he, the deponent, went his way without stopping and left the garden by way of rue des Bons Enfants. He did not enter any shop or café. Then he admitted he entered the Mechanical Café with the gentleman, had a Bavaroise with milk, paid for by this gentleman, who had a Bavaroise with water. Then they entered the salesroom, where this gentleman had accosted him. After leaving the salesroom, they both went to piss at the same time behind the Beaujolais theater. He is not given over to the vice of amusing himself with men. Men unknown to him have made propositions of this nature to him on various occasions in the Palais Royal garden, but he did not accept them. The one this evening did not make propositions to him, and they did not stroke. /Batonnier./
C: W&R

27. Tuesday, 22 February 1785, 8:45 pm
I: Two men loitered in the Tuileries for a very long time in the most suspect manner, accosted each other, took several turns in the most suspect pathways, and left together by way of rue de l'Orangerie.

Antoine Genin de Baudière, 22, native of Moulins in Bourbonnais, bourgeois, lived chez S. Jouhannin, clockmaker, on rue Jacob in faubourg Saint-Germain, near rue des Deux Anges. He used to work for attorneys in the Parlement.

He has played checkers in the café in the Tuileries several times with the other arrested man, whom he found there again this evening. They played a game and then left by way of the Orangery gate.[36] He has known this man for only around two months, from seeing him in the café, but does not know his name, status, or address. They did not walk at all in the garden, which he, the deponent, did not even go down into. He has never surrendered himself to pederasty. /Genin de Baudiere./
C: W&R

Charles Matherne, 26, native of Kircaems (?) on the Arth (Neckar?) river near Mannheim (Germany), chief domestic of the comte des Deux-Ponts,[37] lived at the De la Marque boardinghouse on rue d'Aguesseau.

This evening he went to the café in the Tuileries, where he goes sometimes, and found there the man whose name he does not know, whom he saw the last time in that café and in the Café de Foy in the Palais Royal,[38] where they played checkers together. This man taught him, the deponent, this game. They played this evening and then took several turns together on the terrace where the café is and two or three turns below. He did not speak to anyone else in the garden. When they were arrested the other man was taking him back to rue Saint-Honoré. /Carl Matherrn/
C: W&R

28. Tuesday, 22 February 1785, 9:30 pm
I: A clergyman made his way into a journeyman mason's place to sleep with him, attempted "to seduce him into the crime of pederasty," and offered him twelve livres.

Deposition of Gabriel Guinedou, journeyman mason, who lived on rue des Canettes near Saint-Sulpice.

As he went home this evening, about 8:30 or thereabouts, he encountered the arrested clergyman, who accosted him in rue des Canettes and asked him, "My friend, would you be so good as to give me lodging this evening? I will give you twelve francs." He, the deponent, replied that for that price he would find a better inn than his room. The abbé replied, "What does it matter to you, as long as you earn my money as well as another?" He, the deponent, entered his house, and the abbé entered a moment later and went up. Seeing him, he, the deponent, made a sign to one of his neighbors to come up after them. He was on the landing where he, the deponent, lives, and the abbé, when he got here, asked him, the deponent, if he likes women, to which the deponent replied yes. Then he asked him if he likes men, to which he, the deponent, replied, "I don't hate them. Why should I hate them? They have never done me harm." Then the abbé said to him, "All right, then, give me a kiss," presented himself to embrace him, the deponent, and placed his hand on his breeches, over his parts [genitals], while asking him, "Do you like to f[uck] in the butt?" He, the deponent, pushed him away vigorously

and punched and kicked him, which made him fall into the stairway. He got up and said, "My friend, don't hit me. I'm going to give you twelve francs." He, the deponent, said, "I don't want anything to do with your money" and went down the stairs to detain him and have him arrested. The abbé removed his frock coat and threw it on the stairway. Seeing one of his neighbors on the stairs, he started to shout "Stop, thief! They're murdering me!" He, the deponent, nevertheless pursued him with the help of the neighbor to whom he had made a sign to follow them while coming up. As he saw himself detained by the neighbor, and as he, the deponent, went down to send for the guard, the abbé asked if he could find a way to escape. He was arrested, and he, the deponent, came to make this statement. /U/
C: P because he appeared to have tried to commit extortion

Interrogation

Asked for his first and last names, age, place of birth, status, and address.

After taking the oath to tell the truth, with his hand on his heart, replied he is named Maximilien Le Clerc de Piervalle, 30 years old, native of Montmartre [18th arr.], priest in the diocese of Paris, not beneficed in any parish, says mass at the Oratory on rue Saint-Honoré [no. 145], and lives on the alley off rue du Sépulcre, between the cleaner and the stationer.

Asked how long he has been given over to pederasty and by whom he was debauched.

Replied he has been given over to it for around ten years and took up this taste in the seminaries and collèges [secondary schools]. His passion is to kiss men, suck their part, masturbate them, have himself masturbated, and have his part sucked, but he does not have the inclination to consummate the crime in the rear. He has surrendered himself to these amusements only at his place or in alleys.

Asked with whom he surrendered himself to this debauchery.

Replied he cannot specify the men too well because they never told him their names or addresses, except for a tall young man whose residence he was at in a building that was formerly the Café Dauphin[39] on the new boulevards near rue de Vaugirard. This man sells boxes and candy, occupies the shop that was formerly the Café Dauphin, and has earrings [for sale]. He told the deponent he had consummated this crime with a Polish lord. He, the deponent, paid the young man nothing but has paid others twelve sols and twenty-four sols.

Asked if he goes to surrender himself to this vice in the promenades[40] and public gardens.

Replied no. He has been accused of it by, among others, S. Mernas, building painter, who lives [at no. 26] on rue Saint-Victor opposite Saint-Nicolas [-du Chardonnet], where he has boarded, and yet he does not go there [promenades].

After reading Guinedou's deposition to him, we called on him to respond to it.

Said that, to tell the truth, around six weeks ago he, the deponent, encountered this mason and asked him if he wished to jerk him off. He replied yes, and he went up to the mason's room. When they were there, this mason told him he must first give him some money. He, the deponent, had none then. He suggested that he come to his room and that he would give him some. He accepted, but he, the deponent, took a secluded street and lost him from sight. He, the deponent, found him this evening in rue des Canettes and asked him if he wanted him, the deponent, to go up to his room. He consented, so he went up to the room of the mason, whose name he does not know, on the fifth floor. Once there he, the deponent, kissed him and suggested to him that he jerk him off. The mason asked him for money before doing so. He, the deponent, offered him ten sols, which was all the money he had, and placed them on the table. He was not satisfied[41] with it, grabbed him by the collar, and told him he would leave only if he gave him his frock coat. He then opened his door. After he, the deponent, gave him his brown ratteen [woolen fabric] frock coat, he told him he could leave safely. He, the deponent, left and on the stairs {started shouting, "Stop, murderer"} encountered another man, a friend of the mason, who kicked the deponent in the hips, which made him fall on the stairway, which made him shout, "Call the guard" and "Stop, murderer." Someone advised the mason to place his frock coat and the deponent's hat on the stairs and say it was he, the deponent, who placed them there. The mason had the guard come, and the guard had the deponent arrested.

Asked if he has not already been subjected to reproaches by his superiors for his morals.

Replied that the archbishop of Paris[42] told him three years ago that his creditors had presented memos to him regarding the debts he contracted as well as his morals, without providing other details.

Asked if he has ever been in prison.

Replied no.

We had him searched and found nothing suspect on him.

After his interrogation and his replies were read to him, he said they contain the truth, reaffirmed them, and he signed.

/Leclerc Depiervalle/

C: P

The commissaire recalled Guinedou and told him what the priest had said about him.

Guinedou admitted that the abbé indeed came to his place around three months ago, although he did not know him, and suggested having him enter a household [as a domestic] +and did not make any other proposition to him+. Today he did not receive the ten sols mentioned by the abbé, who has not entered his room recently. He did not leave his frock coat as he said. It was on the stairs, as he fled, that he removed and threw his frock coat. /U/

29. Wednesday, 23 February 1785, 9:00 pm

I: Two men loitered in the Tuileries every evening, this evening since 6:30, and picked up men.

Charles Ponchel, 18, native of Paris, lived and worked with his father, seed vendor, on rue des Moulins in Butte Saint-Roch.

He went to the Tuileries this evening because he was urged to do so by the man arrested there, cobbler, who lives on rue d'Argenteuil, and another friend of this cobbler, who took him there with them, and told him, to persuade him to go there, that they would find men who are of the cuff [pederasts][43] and have a good laugh. From the conversation with these two young boys, he learned that they go to this garden often in the evening. With regard to him, it was the first time he went there. They saw a man there who said to them, in passing next to them, "You are walking, gentlemen. The weather is fine." He, the deponent, replied yes, but it was cold. This man added that there was fine moonlight, to which he, the deponent, replied, "It is good for travel." He then went near the basin[44] to break the ice. His two comrades went to join him there, after also speaking to the gentleman, who is an old man. He does not know what the intentions of the two who took him there were. With regard to him, he had none other than the curiosity they inspired in him to see these debauched men. He is not given over to this debauchery. /Charle Ponchel/

C: W&R

Didier Sibille, 17, native of Paris, cobbler in a street stall on rue de Richelieu, lived with his parents on rue d'Argenteuil in Butte Saint-Roch. He wore a cravat and rosettes on his shoes.

He has been to the Tuileries in the evening several times with Durand, dyer, who lives on rue Saint-Honoré, and Gillet, sculptor, who lives chez S. Cardon on rue des Petites Ecuries, who urged him to go there and to place Louis XV. He never spoke to anyone in these places, and no one spoke to him. This evening he went there again with Gillet and Pouchel, also arrested, who suggested going there to him. He knows from having heard it said that men who amuse themselves with other men go to the garden in the evening, but he has not seen any. He went there this evening to see those men. Pouchel persuaded him to do so. He has never done anything wrong with any man. They took three turns. A man who was there spoke to Pouchel and told him that the weather was fine and that he had lost his watch and given three livres to a man who shared some light with him and found it. /Sibille/
C: W&R

30. Thursday, 24 February 1785, 8:00 pm
I: A man loitered in the Tuileries since 6:00 and masturbated independently with Beaurain, pederast on record, {former personal valet of the comte de Sade[45]} who escaped arrest.

Emmanuel Federitz, 25, native of Toulouse (Languedoc), unemployed tailor's assistant, lived in furnished rooms for tailors on rue des Fossés Saint-Germain-l'Auxerrois.

He is not at all given over to pederasty but has heard that men who are given over to it go to the Tuileries. He went there this evening to see what happens there. He was accosted there by a man unknown to him, who suggested that they amuse themselves together, took him by the arm, and led him into several turns. They did nothing wrong, and he was not found doing anything wrong. To tell the truth, they stopped together three times in the avenue on the terrace along the water. The other pressed him to amuse himself and placed his hand on his breeches, but he did not want to. He had already been accosted in the same way by others in this place in the evening. /U/
C: P

I: 10:00 pm. A man who surrendered himself to pederasty, wearing rouge and a wide cravat, loitered in the Tuileries with another man, who had accompanied him from the Palais Royal.

Charles Voisin, 18, native of Diarville in Lorraine, unemployed domestic, lodged at the Great Monarch boardinghouse on rue Sainte-Croix-de-la-Bretonnerie.

He had the misfortune to be debauched into pederasty around a year ago by a tall, pockmarked upholsterer's assistant chez Mlle la Chapelle of the Comédie Italienne,[46] at whose residence he, the deponent, served at the time. The upholsterer, from rue Taitbout, worked there. They masturbated independently on three different occasions. This evening he crossed the courtyards of the Tuileries with another man whose name he does not know, whom he knew to be a domestic as well, who told him he lived on rue du Champ-fleuri. {He had him do [what?] with him in the garden and told him to come there} He met him in the Palais Royal and urged him to go to the courtyards, where he said he had a rendezvous with a gentleman to whom he wished to procure the deponent, to which end he applied rouge to him and arranged his cravat. This gentleman was not at the rendezvous. As he left, he was arrested. It is the need for money that made him consent to surrender himself to this gentleman, if he had come. The other man led him to believe he would give him some and advised him not to refuse it if he offered him some. /voisin/
C: P

31. Friday, 25 February 1785, 9:30 pm
I: Two men loitered together in the most suspect spots in the Tuileries for at least an hour and accosted several men.

Gabriel Ramard, 26, native of Fontainebleau (Ile-de-France), cook of the marquis de Pleurre,[47] lived at his residence at 12, rue Vieille du Temple. He wore a wide cravat and rosettes on his shoes.

He knows the man arrested with him only as of today. He does not know who directed him to him to find him a position as a cook or meat-roaster, as he is a meat-roaster. He came to find him about 11:00 am, and they went to dine together in La Courtille. They left La Courtille about 7:00 to go to rue du Bac, chez Monproffet, also cook, friend of the deponent. He wanted to introduce the man, whose name he does not know, to him and persuade him to find him a position. They entered the Tuileries, where they took three or four turns. As it was too late to go see Monproffet, they left to go their own

ways home. The man told him he lived at or near the Military School. In the Tuileries they met a man who spoke to them, but he does not recall what he said to him or what he, the deponent, replied. They did not stop with him and did not walk there [together]. He walked next to them, drifted away and returned, and they did likewise. They did not stop in any spot and did not enter any place from La Courtille to the Tuileries. They came by way of rue de Cléry and following streets until place des Victoires[48] and passed under the arcades of the Palais Royal. He does not know if the man arrested with him has been in anyone's service. He told him he had kept an eating house in Saint-Germain and had not had a position since he left it two months ago, after he was there five or six months. In addition, he does not know what they conversed about together, except that he, the deponent, told him if his master left for the army, he, the deponent, could take him with him. He has never been given over to pederasty and does not know if the other man is given over to it, since he has only known him as of today. /Ramard/
C: W&R

Charles Du Jardin, 21, native of La Feuilletière in Normandy, unemployed cook, spent nearly two years as an apprentice of S. Michel, master meat-roaster, on rue Coquillière, then worked as a meat-roaster with S. Berger, restauranteur, for six months, as a domestic chez S. Carnault, on rue de Tournon, for two to three months, and as a tavern keeper on rue des Louviers in Saint-Germain-en-Laye. After mismanaging the business, he returned to Paris on 1 January. He lived at the Military School with his uncle, inspector of buildings.

He has known Ramard, arrested with him, for a very long time. He went to see him today to persuade him to find a position for him. They went to dine together in La Courtille with a coachman from the same household. Ramard paid for him, the deponent. They left there about 7:00 and went to the Palais Royal, where he, the deponent, hoped to see Prévost, officer in the prince's [duke's] household, but he was not there, since he did not see any light in his room. They then went to the Tuileries at nearly 8:00. They walked there with Ramard for around half an hour. They spoke to no one, and no one spoke to them. He is not given over to pederasty and has never surrendered to it. He left the Tuileries to go sleep chez Ramard, who suggested it to him because he, the deponent, told him he had had some problems with his aunt. /Carle dujardin/
C: W&R

32. Saturday, 26 February 1785, 9:00 pm

I: Two men loitered alone in the Tuileries in the most suspect manner and picked up men. One of them, a wine vendor's assistant, picked up a man with a white muff. They sat down on a bench and appeared to masturbate independently. The other, a known pederast, who cruised every evening in the garden, picked up the first man, and they walked with the man with the muff. Another man, a known pederast, had been arrested on 18 July 1782 and spent ten months in Bicêtre.[49] He picked up men in the garden this evening.

Olivier François Le Comte, 34, native of Tilly d'Orceau in Lower Normandy, unemployed domestic,[50] lodged chez S. Villandon in a boardinghouse on rue Platrière.

He has known the wine vendor's assistant arrested with him for a week. He made his acquaintance at the salesroom in the Palais Royal, where he saw him for the second time on Wednesday or Thursday. He found him this evening in the Tuileries, where he, the deponent, accosted him and spoke to him. He went to this garden to walk and has been there four times in the evening in the week he has been in Paris. But he has never spoken to anyone there. He was there last Thursday before going to the Palais Royal and spoke to a gentleman he encountered there. They discussed the weather. He is not given over to pederasty. /le Conte/
C: P

Jean Baptiste Chevanne, 25, native of Méréville near Etampes (Ile-de-France), wine vendor's assistant, unemployed since Shrove Monday (7 February).[51]

He left the service of S. Ancelin, wine vendor at the Temple barrier, for attending a ball at the Good Children [tavern] on rue de Clichy[52] with Levasseur, domestic of the comte d'Espart.[53] He, the deponent, has been given over to pederasty for three years and was debauched into it by a wood turner named Bellanger. He amused himself with Lecomte, arrested with him, just once, a week ago, in the Champs-Elysées, where they went after they encountered each other in the Tuileries, where they found each other again this evening. He, the deponent, spoke this evening to a man with a white muff, whose name he does not know, with whom he, the deponent, consummated the crime of pederasty in the passive role in the Champs-Elysées at the end of October. He wanted to amuse himself this evening, but he, the deponent, did not want to because he had already seen Lecomte, whom he had told to go to one side, and he would go to the other. Lecomte told him he had found a client [*pratique*].[54]

He, the deponent, knows that Lecomte goes to the Tuileries and Palais Royal gardens every evening. He does not believe that he likes to consummate the crime but only to have himself masturbated and to masturbate others. Lecomte was in the salesroom in the Palais Royal with him and pointed out to him a tall man in a blue cloak with gold braid, with his hair curled in ringlets, whom he told him was his friend, who would not be happy if he saw him with another man. He, the deponent, amused himself twice with Desjardins, gilder, on rue de Bourgogne in faubourg Saint-Germain. /U/
C: P

The commissaire recalled Lecomte.
To tell the truth, he has been given over to amusing himself with men for five to six years and has amused himself with several. He has amused himself with several men he does not know in the Tuileries and with another this evening. He has amused himself with the wine vendor's assistant arrested with him just once, this week. He knows a lace vendor in Paris who is from his native region and dresses in a blue cloak with gold braid, whose address he does not know, whom he has seen twice at the salesroom in the Palais Royal but has never amused himself with him and does not know if he is given over to this debauchery. /le Conte/

Alexandre Fraquerre, 36, native of Fraquerre (?) in Auvergne, domestic of Messire Martin de Gibergue, attorney in the Parlement (since 1783), lived at his residence on rue de Moussy.
He has been given over to pederasty for six years and was sent to Bicêtre for ten months for this. He left there nearly two years ago. It is true he accosted four or five men in the Tuileries this evening, but he did not amuse himself. He does not go to the Tuileries often and goes to the Palais Royal very rarely. /U/
C: P

33. Monday, 28 February 1785, 8:15 pm
I: Two men loitered in the Tuileries. One, who cruised there every evening, accosted several men. They finally accosted each other, took six turns, arm in arm, and walked to the Saint-Germain fair.

Pierre Joseph Sébastien Liez, 30, native of Ruremonde in Austria,[55] master pastrymaker, lived on rue du Bac.

He entered the Tuileries this evening and encountered the man arrested with him, whose name he does not know, whom he has known by sight for two to three years but had not seen for two years. He knows him from seeing him as a domestic chez M. de Menars on rue Bergère. They left the Tuileries and went together to the Saint-Germain fair, where he, the deponent, had a brother-in-law with S. Coltard, kitchen assistant, on rue de Bourbon in faubourg Saint-Germain. He goes to the Palais Royal sometimes in the evening. A week ago today he encountered a young man there, journeyman goldsmith, whose name he does not know, who lives in the direction of rue Montmartre. He, the deponent, paid for his Bavaroise at the Mechanical Café. He has the misfortune to have been given over to pederasty since his youth and has amused himself with French Guards, among others Deure, grenadier from the barracks in Nouvelle France [10th arr.],[56] Hébert or Vébert, also grenadier from l'Estrapade,[57] and others whose names he does not recall. He, the deponent, is in the habit of consummating the crime in the active role and pays the men with whom he has relations. He also amused himself once with the young man for whom he bought a Bavaroise in the Palais Royal for what they did in a coach three weeks or a month ago. He has never amused himself with the man with whom he was arrested, whom he knows, however, to be given over to the same vice, who picked up the deponent in the Tuileries, which they left without recognizing each other. They recognized each other only while passing along rue Jacob to go to the fair. /Liez/
C: P

Nicolas Bertin, 21, native of Verdun in Burgundy, domestic of Mme de Manelar, lived at her residence on rue des Bons Enfants.

He made the acquaintance [of the man arrested with him] last summer or fall and then said he is the Carnival reveler at the ball at the Good Children on rue de Clichy, where he, the deponent, was disguised as the wife of the pastrymaker arrested with him, whose name and address he does not know, who was also disguised as a woman. He was debauched into the crime of pederasty on rue de la Marche in Paris last year, by a domestic named Lajeunesse, domestic chez Mme Montigny on rue Saint-Louis in the Marais, in the room of a prostitute of Lajeunesse's acquaintance who lived on rue de la Marche, where they consummated the crime with him, the deponent, in the passive role. He goes to the Tuileries sometimes and made a rendezvous for this evening with Saint-Pierre, domestic of Mme de Siney, who did not come to the rendezvous today or yesterday. He, the deponent, was picked up this

evening by a man with a white muff, whom he did not wish to stop with. He then picked up the pastrymaker without recognizing him. They recognized each other only after they left the Tuileries and were on rue Jacob. He has also amused himself at masturbating with Saint-Pierre. He does not give or receive money. It has been a good two months since he amused himself in the Tuileries with an unknown man. They masturbated independently. /Bertin/
C: P

MARCH

34. Tuesday, 1 March 1785, 9:00 pm
I: A man loitered in the Tuileries for an hour and picked up a man with whom he left by way of the courtyard of the riding school.[1] The second man had been arrested in the same place on 22 February (#27), warned, and released. Another man loitered, cruised, and picked up several men, including an observer, to whom he said, "It's fine weather for getting an erection," and urged him to take him to his place to divert themselves. They left together to go there and do so.

Etienne Roumier, 45, native of Corbigny in the diocese of Autun (Burgundy), cook of the comte d'Ailly,[2] lived at his residence on boulevard Montmartre next to rue Saint-Fiacre.

His wife has been ill for fourteen years, and for that time he has been given over to pederasty, into which he was debauched by a domestic who is dead. He has amused himself several times in alleys with men he does not know. He goes to the Tuileries often and has met men unknown to him there with whom he amused himself. He has never surrendered himself to anything other than reciprocal masturbation. The last time he did it was around two weeks ago. This evening he was picked up in the Tuileries by the man arrested with him, whom he does not know, who spoke to him first about the weather and then entered into conversation about pederasty. He told him he knows the comte de Sparre, who is given over to it, and Levasseur, his domestic, with whom the man told him he had amused himself. They left the Tuileries for him, the deponent, to return to his master's residence and for the other, from what he told him, to go to the Palais Royal. He, the deponent, has also amused himself sometimes in the Palais Royal, but he will never return to these places. /roumier/
C: P

Charles Matherne, 26, native of Hircaems (?) on the Arthe (Neckar?) river, near Mannheim (Germany), domestic of the comte de Deux-Ponts, lived at his residence at the De la Marck boardinghouse on rue d'Aguesseau. He was "full of scents" and wore a wide cravat and rosettes on his shoes.

Coming back from rue de l'Université, he entered the Tuileries and met the arrested man, unknown to him, and spoke with him. He walked around for an hour, with him as well as alone. Another man passed near him and said good evening to him. He is not given over to liking men and has never amused himself with any. It is true he was in the Tuileries this evening, in spite of the injunctions we made to him. /Carl Matherrn/
C: P

The commissaire recalled Roumier.

Matherne told him that the comte de Sparre, his personal valet, and Levasseur, his domestic, are given over to the debauchery of men and that he, Matherne, had amused himself in this way with Levasseur. And it is he, Matherne, who picked up him, Roumier, in the Tuileries this evening. /roomier/

Matherne denied it.

Jean Marchand, 32, native of Coulon in the diocese of Chartres (Orléanais), domestic of Messire Guénard, secrétaire du roi,[3] lived at his residence on rue St-Thomas-du-Louvre.

He was debauched into pederasty around four years ago by Caron, domestic, who now lives in Saint-Germain-en-Laye, with whom he amuses himself when he comes to Paris. He goes to the Tuileries sometimes. He amused himself once in a tavern on rues des Frondeurs with Etienne, domestic, who lives on rue des Prêtres Saint-Paul. He was in the Tuileries this evening and accosted a young man unknown to him there, with whom he conversed about this debauchery. They left to go to their own places. The last one with whom he amused himself is Etienne, twelve to fifteen days ago, and before that it was with Caron, in his wife's room on the fourth floor over a shop on rue Saint-Denis near the Paris gate. /Marchand/
C: P

35. Friday, 4 March 1785, 9:00 pm
I: Two men loitered in the Tuileries for a very long time and picked up men. One, with a white button on his hat, surrendered himself to pederasty and

cruised every evening in the public gardens and near the Comédie Française. The other picked up an observer and suggested that they amuse themselves.

Alexandre Charles Brochet, 33, native of Paris, upholsterer's assistant, unemployed for two years, sold jewelry for children at fairs.[4]

He is not given over to pederasty and did nothing but cross the Tuileries after leaving the Capuchin church,[5] where he arranged the chairs. /brochet/
C: W&R

Julien de Pontez, 41, native of Vannes in Brittany, unemployed domestic, lived, since the beginning of winter, chez his friend Bucher, private coachman, at the Black Head on rue Croix des Petits Champs.

He goes often to the salesroom in the Palais Royal, more rarely to the Tuileries, does not go around the Comédie Française, and has not been there since the beginning of winter. He walked there with a domestic of his acquaintance named François, domestic of a gentleman on rue de la Bourbe. When he goes to the Tuileries, it is only to walk. This evening he only passed along the terrace in coming back from faubourg Saint-Germain. He is not given over to pederasty. /U/
C: W&R

36. Sunday, 6 March 1785, 9:00 pm
I: Two men loitered in the Tuileries since 6:30 in the most suspect manner and pathways. They picked up men, including Garnier, a well-known pederast, and left together, "without, however, seeming to know each other."

Charles Fussy, 18, native of Vauge (Foggia?) in Italy, apprentice doorman chez S. Gelé, lived with his father on rue Saint-Honoré.

He was debauched into the vice of amusing himself with men two years ago during Carnival by Cosse from Provence,[6] whose acquaintance he made at an inn where they both ate. Cosse took him to the Tuileries several times and taught him how to accost men to amuse himself. He has amused himself around a dozen times in all in the Tuileries, with men he met there. Since he last saw Cosse, he has not returned to the Tuileries. He went there this evening in hopes of finding Cosse there, to ask him for the money he owes him. He did not find him there and was accosted by another unknown to him, who stroked him, but he [Fussy] did not stroke him. To

tell the truth, he also went to the Tuileries with the design of amusing himself. /fucy/
C: P

Pierre Badarou, 15, native of Amiens (Picardy), apprentice saddler chez S. Lepine the younger, lived at his residence on rue du Faubourg Saint-Honoré. He wore very long earrings and a very wide cravat.

He was debauched into pederasty around a year ago by Hyacinthe, journeyman inlay worker, whose acquaintance he made on the boulevard, with whom he amused himself many times, who took him to the Tuileries to amuse himself. He has never amused himself there but left with those he found there and went to amuse himself in alleys. In the Tuileries this evening he accosted a man unknown to him, and they touched themselves independently. /badarou/
C: P

37. Tuesday, 8 March 1785, 6:30 pm–12:00 am
PP: quays, Mousetrap and Sofa (Le Canapé),[7] exits of the Tuileries, OP[8]

I: A confirmed pederast, arrested on 23 July 1781, imprisoned, and exiled,[9] loitered for a long time in the Tuileries, accosted a domestic in livery, and conversed with him for a long time. When they left, the domestic escaped arrest.

Jean Nicolas Pruneau, 29, native of Paris, broker for silk vendors, lived on rue du Faubourg Saint-Denis.

He crossed the Tuileries, and as he left the garden, a domestic he does not know asked him what time it was and immediately fled. /X/
C: S&R, after Pruneau informed the commissaire that his detention would cost him his job, by means of which he supported his parents

I: A man loitered in the most suspect pathways for a long time and sat down on a bench, where he was accosted by a man, with whom he spoke with a long time, whom he then left.

Dominique Nicolas Bailly, 22, native of Château Sellier (?) in the diocese of Metz (Lorraine), assistant of S. Michel Martet, master wigmaker, lived at his residence on rue des Nonaindières.

He went drinking with one of his comrades on quai de la Ferraille and from there came to walk in the Tuileries garden about 7:30 pm. He was

accosted by a man he does not know, who suggested to him that they get a drink, which he refused. He sat down on a bench, where another man, also unknown to him, asked him what time it was. [He told him he?] was in a household and was obliged to return to his employer about 8:00 but was free after 9:00 until the next day. He suggested that they go to rue Saint-Louis about 9:30 to have supper together, which he refused. /U/
C: W&R

I: A man, badly dressed but partly in "the costume adopted by pederasts" (wide cravat, large round hat with rosettes, thick *catogan*), loitered for a long time in the most suspect pathways, picked up men, spoke with several others, and appeared to stroke some of them. He finally left with a known pederast who cruised in the garden but escaped arrest.

Nicolas Philippe Champy, 19, native of Versailles (Ile-de-France), soldier in the Soissonnais regiment, on leave for half the year in Versailles, where he lived, lodged on rue Saint-Germain-l'Auxerrois for two sols per night.
    He has been in Paris since yesterday and has not spoken to anyone in the Tuileries garden. Then he said he indeed took several turns and sat down there, and the man he does not know accosted him and spoke to him. He does not know what they said to each other. They left together. /U/
C: P

I: A man loitered and was accosted by another man, with whom he left.

Edme Bailleux, 21, native of Montreuil-aux-Lions in the diocese of Soissons (Ile-de-France), unemployed domestic, lodged with his aunt, domestic chez S. Desvignes, and lived at his residence on rue Clos Georgeau.
    Coming back from rue d'Anjou in faubourg Saint-Honoré, he entered the Tuileries by the swivel bridge[10] as they were going to close the gates. He crossed the garden and was arrested in leaving, at the same time as another man who had stopped him and came behind him. /U/
C: W&R

I: A man loitered for a long time, accosted men, and chatted with several, including an observer to whom he made propositions the latter rejected. He left him and accosted Bailleux, with whom he left.

Jean Carin, (missing number) years old, native of Sainte-Livrade in the diocese of Agen (Guyenne), unemployed tailor, in Paris for three days, lodged near the place de Grève, at a boardinghouse and on a street he could not name.

He went to walk in the Tuileries and sat down on a bench, where he fell asleep. They awakened him to leave. He did not speak to anyone and does not know anyone in Paris. He has no certificate or passport. /U/
C: P

38. Thursday, 10 March 1785, 9:00 pm
I: Two men loitered in the Tuileries and accosted men in the most suspect places. The marquis de Saint-Clément, former musketeer "quite given over to pederasty," already arrested twice, also loitered there. He cruised every evening in the royal gardens and called regularly on a cobbler on rue de Valois, with whom he amused himself, and paid him twenty-four sols each time.

Thierry Defrance, 23, native of Châlons-sur-Marne (Champagne), domestic chez S. Lecaze, first surgeon of the comte d'Artois,[11] lived at his residence on rue Saint-Honoré near the gate (no. 422).

He entered the Tuileries with his friend Monnelle, also arrested, after they were in the Palais Royal, on rue Saint-Avoie, and at the Saint-Germain fair. He had the time to go out this afternoon, but he had no design to do anything wrong. He spoke to no one but Monnelle. In the Tuileries he spoke to a man of his acquaintance who said good evening to him. He, the deponent, is not given over to amusing himself with men. /U/
C: W&R

Claude Monnelle, 30, native of Chaumont-au-Bassigny (Champagne), domestic of the princesse de Chimay,[12] lady-in-waiting of the Queen,[13] lived at her residence on rue Saint-Honoré at the gate.

He went out this afternoon with Defrance, who lives in the same building, and they went to walk, first in the Palais Royal, then at the Saint-Germain fair, near which they drank cider in a café where there are prostitutes. In returning they entered the Tuileries, where they took several turns. He encountered a man he knows by sight to be a cook, who said good evening to him. They intended to return to the Palais Royal when they left the Tuileries and were arrested. They did not intend to go home until 9:00. They had no bad intention, and he is not given over to the debauchery of men. /monnelle/
C: W&R

Louis Denis, marquis de Saint-Clément, 45, native of Montpellier (Languedoc), former musketeer in the first company,[14] lived at the Saint Victor boardinghouse on rue de Grenelle in faubourg Saint-Germain.

He is not at all given over to the vice he is suspected of. He passed through the Tuileries garden this evening to go to faubourg Saint-Honoré. After leaving the garden and judging that it would be closed when he came back, he went back through at once and was arrested in leaving. He does not know why. He did not do anything wrong and did not speak to anyone. It is true he has already been arrested and conducted before the lieutenant general of police,[15] who told him not to be in suspect places at a late hour.[16] He did not think he violated this prohibition in crossing the Tuileries. /X/
C: S&R

39. Monday, 21 March 1785, 6:30 pm–12:00 am
PP: quays, Mousetrap and Sofa, environs of the Tuileries, OP

I: One known pederast loitered in the Tuileries and picked up men in the most suspect manner. Another walked for forty-five minutes in the most suspect pathways and manner.

Pierre Rozier, called Des Roziers, 39, native of Bordeaux (Guyenne), limonadier's assistant, in Paris for eighteen days after five or six years in America (Le Cap in Saint-Domingue[17]), lodged at the Saint Louis boardinghouse on rue Fromenteau.

He has had the misfortune to be given over to pederasty. He went to the Tuileries one other time, on Friday, and today. He walked there since 6:30 but did not amuse himself. He has not amused himself with any man since his return to Paris. /U/
C: P because he was dressed "in the costume of pederasts" and "appeared to have gone to the Tuileries with the intention of surrendering himself to this debauchery"

Louis Doré, 22, native of Paris, tailor's assistant, lived in furnished rooms for tailors chez a locksmith on rue des Vieilles Etuves.

After his work was done, he passed through the Tuileries to go to walk in the Champs-Elysées. After his work he is also in the habit of walking in

the Palais Royal, in the Tuileries, and on the quays. But he has never amused himself with men and is not subject to this vice. Two different persons made propositions of this type to him, but he refused them. /Dorê/
C: W&R

40. Tuesday, 22 March 1785, 9:15 pm
I: A man who loitered and cruised every evening in the Tuileries picked up several men and left with one of them, who escaped arrest.

Louis François Justin Delagrange de Juniac, 16, native of Rennes in Brittany, law student, lived with his father, tax farmer for vehicles of the court, on quay d'Orsay.[18]

He was debauched into the vice of pederasty at the collège de Juilly in Picardy, without, however, surrendering himself to it in that place.[19] He has surrendered himself to it only in Paris, since the beginning of February. Passing through the Tuileries one evening, he was picked up by a man given over to this vice, whom he did not know. They stroked independently in the garden. Since then he has amused himself in the same place with others, all unknown to him, with whom he masturbated independently. He does not know how many times he has surrendered himself to this vice since the beginning of February but thinks it is around fifteen times. Two or three times men with whom he had amused himself asked him for money, but he did not give any. He has not gone to anyone's place and has not taken anyone to his place. During the first days of Lent[20] a fat man dressed in a blue coat, jacket, and breeches, whom he had accosted in the Tuileries, while amusing himself with him, stole from his fob pocket his purse, in which there were two écus of six livres and some change. Since that time he has not carried money when he goes to the Tuileries. Another man with whom he amused himself asked him if he liked to put it in, to which he replied he did not know what he meant.[21] The man told him that if he wished to go to the Champs-Elysées, he would teach him. This evening, having seen a man near a tree in the Tuileries, he accosted him, and they left together to go amuse themselves in Petite rue Saint-Louis, where they were going when he was arrested. He added that he took his ideas about this vice from reading *The Doorman of the Carthusians*,[22] which a domestic in the collège de Juilly had loaned to him. He stated that he had never seen [been with] a woman.[23]
/Lagrange de Juniac/
C: P

41. Wednesday, 23 March 1785, 9:30 pm
I: A man loitered in the Tuileries for at least an hour and a half and picked up a known pederast who typically wore a white muff. He took several turns in the most suspect pathways and accosted men who did not respond to him.

Louis Cassegrain, 42, native of Châteauneuf-en-Thymerais (Maine), clerk of S. Geoffrey, bailiff on horse of the Châtelet,[24] lived on rue du Sépulcre near Saint-Sulpice.

He went to walk this evening in the Tuileries, where he had a rendezvous with Detaure, who also works for Geoffroy, who went to Longchamp. While walking in the garden, he met a man unknown to him with whom he spoke. He does not recall if it is he, the deponent, who spoke to him first or the other way around. They walked together and talked about the cold weather and the small number of people there were in the garden this evening. He did not have any bad design, is not at all given over to the vice of pederasty, and does not usually go to the Tuileries in the evening. /Cassegrain/
C: W&R

42. Thursday, 24 March 1785, 9:15 pm
I: Two men loitered in the Tuileries in the most suspect manner, accosted each other, went to leave by the swivel bridge, which was closed, and then left together by the Orangery gate.

Jean François Brochier, 24, native of Paris, surgery student, lived chez S. Brochier, surgeon, in Gros-Caillou (7th arr.).

He parted with S. Desault, surgeon, at the gate of the Tuileries near the Pont Royal[25] to go chez S. De la Caze, also surgeon, at the Saint-Honoré gate. He crossed the Tuileries garden and stopped near the grand [octagonal] basin to look at a man who staggered and appeared drunk. The man arrested with him accosted him by speaking about this drunk man. In discoursing they went almost near the swivel bridge, which they found closed. For that reason he, the deponent, went by the Orangery gate, where the man accompanied him, while they were still discoursing together, and they were arrested there. He does not know this man and does not know his name or address or where he was going. He does not recall what they discoursed about, but they by no means talked about debauchery with men. He, the deponent, had no bad intention. /Brochier/
C: S&R

Jacques Thibout, 25, native of Orléans (Orléanais), grocer's assistant, lived with his brother on rue des Barres near rue des Jardins, near Saint-Paul.

Coming back from Longchamp, he entered the Tuileries, where he took three or four turns then wished to leave by way of the swivel bridge to go home. The man arrested with him called to him in a pathway. He went to him and asked him what he wanted. He asked him if he was walking. He, the deponent, replied he was leaving. He asked him on which side. He told him it was by the swivel bridge. The man told him, "Me, too." They went together as far as the swivel bridge, which they found closed. They then went through the Orangery gate, all without speaking to each other, neither one nor the other. He, the deponent, had no intention in the Tuileries other than walking. He has never been to the Tuileries in the evening. /J. Thibout/
C: S&R

The commissaire read the depositions to both men, and both reaffirmed their versions.

APRIL

43. Saturday, 2 April 1785, 10:00 pm
I: A man loitered in the Tuileries since 7:30, picked up men, and conversed with them.

Pierre Augustin Antoine LeRouge, 26, native of Pont Sainte-Maxence (Picardy), gemstone setter, lived at the residence of S. Laforge, master lapidary, whose apprentice he had been, chez S. Boudier, candlemaker, on rue du Temple at the corner of rue de Pastourelle, and worked chez S. Labataix, goldsmith, on rue Saint-Martin.

He went to the Tuileries at 7:30 to walk, with the intention of finding some pederast. He had heard it said there are some there. He does not deny that if he had had the chance, he would have amused himself. He spoke to only one person, who told him it was quite cold, and spent a bit of time with him. He made no propositions to him. He knows he was wrong to stay so long. He still earns nothing from his work. He has never amused himself with any man and lives chez his master, where he works. /lerouge/
C: P

44. Sunday, 3 April 1785, 9:30 pm
I: Two men loitered in the Tuileries for a long time in the most suspect manner and picked up men.

Etienne Vandeuvre, 50, native of Salins in Franche-Comté, dishwasher, lived chez S. Trilly, who kept an eating house on rue de Beaune.

He went to the Tuileries to cross the garden and go to the Saint-Honoré gate, where he needed to speak to a man who owes him several sols. He did not stop there and did not speak to anyone. Later he admitted he asked one gentleman what time it was, spoke to another, and pissed once near a tree. He did not go to the Saint-Honoré gate because it was too late. He does not go to the Tuileries often. It is true one of those he spoke to in the Tuileries as he was pissing placed his hand on him. He asked him, "What are you doing?" and he withdrew. He has been confronted several times in this way in the Tuileries in the evening. /U/
C: P

Louis Marie Eugé, 16, native of Boulogne-sur-Mer (Picardy), shoemaker's assistant, unemployed for around a month.

He has been given over to the debauchery of men for only five days, and it is indigence that makes him do it. He was debauched into it by a gentleman with a white muff he met in the Tuileries, who led him into a pathway where they fondled themselves and masturbated independently. This gentleman gave him twenty-four sols. He also amused another gentleman he met another day on quai du Louvre, who gave him twelve sols. Also another he met in the direction of place de Grève, who took him to his room in the direction of the boulevards, gave him twelve sols and money for supper, and wanted to have him sleep with him, but he, the deponent, did not want to. The first of these men wanted to put it into him, but he, the deponent, did not want to. This evening he went to the Tuileries again to earn something. He earned only six sols, which a gentleman gave him to fondle him in the garden this evening. He sought yet another person to earn as much again. /Louis marie Eugé/
C: P

45. Wednesday, 6 April 1785, 8:30 pm
I: A known pederast and a younger man loitered in the Tuileries in the most suspect manner and accosted another man.

Pierre Goran, 27, native of Seiches in Anjou, butler's assistant chez the comte de Crillon,[1] lived at his townhouse on rue de Bourbon in faubourg Saint-Germain.

He was debauched into pederasty and does not recall by whom but knows it is a young man from Seiches, when he was in Angers. He has amused himself in Paris with several persons whose names and addresses he does not know, once in the Tuileries around a month ago. He has never consummated the crime and has surrendered himself only to independent masturbation with those with whom he has amused himself. He goes to the Tuileries sometimes, but it is not always with the intention of amusing himself. He entered the garden this evening, on his way back from rue des Lombards, and took two or three turns there. He was accosted by another man unknown to him, who told him he is a hairdresser and suggested to him that they go amuse themselves in his room or a tavern, but he, the deponent, did not want to because he needed to return to his place. /X/
C: P

Jean Baptiste Du Villard, 16, native of Versailles (Ile-de-France), apprentice wigmaker, enlisted in the regiment of the Dragoons of the Pyrenees as of 17 March. He lived with his father, intendant (household manager) of the comtesse de Lupé,[2] at her residence chez S. Villeminot, bed and bath merchant, on rue de Bourgogne in faubourg Saint-Germain.

Today is the third time he has gone to the Tuileries in the evening and was persuaded to do so by Leroy, former domestic, currently unemployed, who lodges chez S. Ourlier, who rents rooms on rue des Ciseaux. He, the deponent, went to Leroy's room, where they both fondled themselves and Leroy masturbated in his, the deponent's, presence. He could not do likewise because it hurt him. Leroy took him with him chez the chevalier de Silvie[3] to seek some syrup at the Avignon boardinghouse on rue Fromenteau, where S. de Silvie amused himself with Leroy in the deponent's presence. They masturbated, hugged, and fondled themselves. The chevalier de Silvie also hugged him, the deponent, and gave Leroy six livres. In the Tuileries yesterday he met a man unknown to him, in a white jacket, who wanted to lead him off with him, but he did not want to. He has amused himself with Leroy two or three times in his room. Leroy made a rendezvous with him for yesterday and today in the Tuileries and promised to loan him three livres but did not come. /Duvillart/
C: P

46. Wednesday, 6 April 1785, 9:15 pm

I: A known pederast loitered in the Tuileries in the most suspect manner and picked up men, including one he tried to fondle in front and back, who appeared to resist.

Dominique Claude Rouyer, 37, native of Malaumont near Commercy in Lorraine, grocer, lived on rue Pagevin.[4]

He was debauched into pederasty ten years ago by Lefevre, master candlemaker on rue Mouffetard. He consummated the crime in the passive role some months ago with a stranger on the new boulevards. He has never committed it in the active role. He went to the Tuileries this evening with the design of amusing himself and met a man there, unknown to him, who suggested that they amuse themselves, but he did not want to. He surrenders himself to this debauchery because he does not wish to see his wife anymore, out of fear of making her bear children. He already has four. /D Rouyer/
C: P

I: 10:00 pm. A pederast amused himself in the Mousetrap with a man who escaped arrest.

Nicolas Charles Cellier, 52, native of Verneuil-sur-Marne (Champagne), managed the White Pigeon boardinghouse on rue des Deux Ecus and lived there.

He went down below quai des Orfèvres to do his business. He was alone there and did not speak to anyone. Then he admitted that while he was in that spot, a man unknown to him came down after him and asked him if he wished to show him his rear end, which he did. To tell the truth, they fondled themselves and masturbated. It is the first time this has happened to him, and he has lived in Paris only since 13 March. /Cellier/

The contents of his pockets included a letter addressed to him signed Des Roches, whom he identified as Nollan, called Des Roches,[5] who resided with Blanchard, called chevalier de Monchevreuil, deserter, in Château Thierry, where they were regarded as pederasts. Cellier visited them just once and never amused himself with them.
C: P

47. Thursday, 7 April 1785, 7:30 pm–12:00 am
PP: quays, Mousetrap and the Sofa, environs of the Tuileries, OP

I: 9:15. Beaurain, "inveterate pederast," arrested and imprisoned more than once,⁶ exiled on 2 June 1783, continued to surrender himself to pederasty. He cruised in the Tuileries every evening and escaped arrest repeatedly because "he knows all the observers and takes precautions to avoid them."

After 9:30. Two known pederasts loitered and picked up several men, including observers whom they asked for money.

Claude Baurain, 50, native of Calais (Picardy), cook of M. Mabile, commissaire of war⁷ and administrator of the *vingtième* tax⁸ in Rouen, lived at his residence on rue de la Chaussée d'Antin.

It is true he was imprisoned twice in Bicêtre for pederasty and was released with an order of exile. It is true he has been given over to pederasty for more than twelve years, and this passion rules him to the extent he cannot rid himself of it. /baurain/
C: P

Jean Toussaint LeClerc, 27, native of Evreux in Normandy, shoemaker's assistant, lived chez S. Audrot, master shoemaker, on rue de Jouy. He had been arrested and released in the Champs-Elysées on 22 April 1781.⁹

He has been given over to pederasty for around five years and has surrendered himself to this debauchery in the Tuileries several times with men unknown to him. He has not consummated the crime in the passive role but consummated it in the active role three or four times in the Champs-Elysées but does not know any of the people with whom he had relations. He earned around nine livres from this from various persons. He often goes to the Tuileries in the evening. /Leclerc/
C: P

Louis Marion, 15, native of Clermont in Auvergne, wigmaker's assistant, lived chez S. Daste, master wigmaker, at the Boulainvilliers market.¹⁰

He did nothing but cross the Tuileries and was accosted by a man unknown to him, who tried to place his hand on his breeches and offered to give him three livres to put it into him from behind, but he refused him. He is not given over to the vice of liking men. /U/
C: W&R

48. Friday, 8 April 1785, 10:30 pm

I: A known pederast, associate of Thomas and Hutin, loitered in the Tuileries and took several turns with a man.

Louis François Gabriel Bellat, 19, native of Paris, tailor's assistant, unemployed for four months, and soldier in the Mantes battalion for four months, lodged chez Bourguerelle, who rented rooms on rue de la Vannerie.

    He entered the Tuileries at 7:00 pm to walk and met a man unknown to him, who said to him, "The weather is fine." They took two or three turns together. This man talked to him about the debauchery of men, but he, the deponent, is not given over to it. This man suggested taking him to a gentleman in Butte Saint-Roch who would give him money, which he refused. He has never surrendered himself to this debauchery but often goes to gambling dens, where he wagers. /Bellat/
C: W&R

49. Sunday, 10 April 1785, 9:15 pm

I: A man loitered in the most suspect manner and places in the Tuileries and picked up men, including a known pederast, with whom he took several turns. When they left, the other man escaped arrest.

Jean César Robin, 59, native of Asnan in Nivernais, bourgeois, lived at 17, rue de Rohan, on the seventh floor.

    For the last three months he has had the weakness to surrender himself to pederasty sometimes in the Tuileries garden, on occasion with persons he meets there and does not know. He does nothing but masturbate men and have himself masturbated by those with whom he amuses himself. Coming back from the Champs-Elysées this evening, he entered the Tuileries garden by the swivel bridge. He walked and found another man, who accosted him, told him he was given over to this vice, suggested that they amuse themselves together, even placed his hand on the deponent's breeches, and asked him, "Do you have an erection?" He suggested that they go to one of their rooms, which he, the deponent, did not accept. They left together and were arrested in leaving. /Robin/
C: P

50. Monday, 11 April 1785, 9:00 pm

I: A man loitered in the Tuileries for a very long time in the most suspect manner and picked up a man with whom he walked and chatted for a long time. They stroked together.

Paul Miller, 27, native of Fort-Louis-du-Rhin near Strasbourg (Alsace), shoemaker's assistant, lived chez S. Lucien d'Ardivillers, shoemaker on Grande rue de Passy in Passy (16th arr.).

Coming from Passy to Paris, he entered the Tuileries, where he met a man with whom he walked and sat down on a bench. This man placed his hand on his breeches. It is he, the deponent, who accosted him by asking him what time it was. This man suggested to him that they amuse themselves and go to his room. He said yes, and they left together, but it was to get a laugh out of it that he, the deponent, told him he would gladly go to his place. It is true they walked arm in arm. /Paul muller/
C: P

I: 10:00 pm. A man loitered and cruised daily in the Tuileries as well as the Champs-Elysées.

André Cendre, 36, native of Paris, haberdasher's assistant, lived chez S. Brison, haberdasher, at 5, rue des Lavandières Sainte-Opportune.

He went to take some fabric samples to M. de la Vaupallière in faubourg Saint-Honoré and passed through the Tuileries and then the Champs-Elysées. He has never been given over to pederasty. Then he said he was given over to it when he was young and was debauched into it at the age of ten years by a painter {and consummated the crime several times}. He has not surrendered himself to it for several months. He goes to the Tuileries almost every evening and has not been in the Champs-Elysées for six months until today. /cendre/
C: P

51. **Wednesday, 13 April 1785, 9:45 pm**
I: A man who often loitered in the Tuileries in the evening picked up men.[11]

Martin Mariot, around 30, native of Monsaufray (?) in Limousin, lackey of the vicomte de Carbonnières,[12] lived at his residence at the Rennes boardinghouse.

He went to the Tuileries this evening, walked for a long time there, and spoke to a man with a lemon-colored collar, who asked him if he was walking and if he was looking for someone to amuse himself with. He, the deponent, went away. He is not given over to pederasty and has never surrendered himself to it. /U/
C: W&R

52. Thursday, 14 April 1785, 8:30 pm
I: A man loitered on the boulevard, stopped several times, picked up men, and went down to rue Amelot near the Coal-Box and came back up on the boulevard several times.

Louis Etienne Roux, 29, native of Pecqueuse, near Chevreuse (Ile-de-France), former domestic, bourgeois, lived chez the sister of Messire Brullé, attorney, on rue Cloche Perche.

He went to walk on the boulevard and went down and came back up several times. He did not accost anyone or speak to anyone, and no one spoke to him. He had no bad intention and is not given over to the vice he is suspected of and arrested for. /Roux/
C: W&R

53. Friday, 15 April 1785, 9:30 pm
I: A known pederast, "with the tone and manners of it," and two other men picked up an observer on boulevard Saint-Antoine. They chatted about pederasty and "their various tastes in this type of debauchery." They made a rendezvous on the boulevard this evening to go to one of their places to have "a party of debauchery" and urged the observer to join them. One man was arrested when he showed up at the rendezvous, and another escaped arrest.

Joseph LeComte, 21, native of Versailles (Ile-de-France), unemployed kitchen assistant, lived at The Bell on rue de l'Arbalète.

As he passed along the boulevard, he was accosted by a man unknown to him, who asked him what time it was and where faubourg Saint-Honoré is. He replied he does not have a watch and does not know where faubourg Saint-Honoré is. He has never been on the boulevard. Today is the first time he passed that way, and he is not given over to pederasty. /U/
C: P

54. Saturday, 16 April 1785, 7:30 pm–1:00 am
PP: quays, environs of the Comédie Française, OP

I: 9:00 pm. A man loitered in the Tuileries and picked up a man with whom he sat down on a chair.[13] They appeared to masturbate independently.

After 10:00 pm. A man followed an observer down to the Mousetrap, undid his breeches, bared his rear end, and said, "Put it into me." After the observer went back up to seek assistance and came back down, he again showed his rear end and said, "I don't have an erection."

Pierre Gossin, 30, native of Châlons in Champagne, cook of the marquis de Pronleroy,[14] lived at his townhouse on rue du Bac.

He has never been given over to the vice of liking men, is married, and has a child, and his wife is pregnant. He goes to the café in the Tuileries sometimes. He went there this evening believing he would find S. Surgius and S. Patin, both head cooks. They were not there, and he was returning when he was arrested. He did not stop or sit in the garden and did not speak to anyone. /Gossin/
C: W&R

Raphael Nicolle, 56, native of Paris, porter at the central market, lived chez the glazier on place Maubert.

He went down to the spot where he was arrested to do his business and was arrested after doing so, but he did not do anything wrong and was not with anyone in that spot. He was coming back from taking a letter to the main postal office on rue Platrière[15] that Mme Avelin, his landlady, charged him with. Then he said that, to tell the truth, he did not come from taking the letter to the main postal office. He was walking on quai des Orfèvres when he went down under the archways but is not given over to the vice of liking men. /U/
C: P

55. Sunday, 17 April 1785, 9:30 pm
I: A man took several turns on quai des Orfèvres, went down to the watering spot, appeared to position himself to do his business, walked along the water as far as the Pont Neuf, came back along the water to the Mousetrap, entered one of the archways, repositioned himself, left, and went as far as the fifth archway, where he again lowered his breeches.

Alexandre le Maître, 22, native of Paris, third clerk of Messire Semillard, notary, lived at his residence on rue Montmartre.

He did not walk at all on quai des Orfèvres and did not pass along there. When he left the Comédie Française, he came back by way of rue Saint-André-des-Arts and the Pont Saint-Michel. He entered the Palais, felt the urge to do

his business, and went to the watering spot at the end of quai des Orfèvres, where he wanted to go about doing his business. A man came by, which made him withdraw and go down below the quay. This man followed him. He went as far as the archway under the Pont Neuf, where this man followed him. He, the deponent, came back along the edge of the water to the archways at the end of the quay on the side of the Pont Saint-Michel. He set about doing his business at the entrance of one of the archways, and this man came there. He, the deponent, withdrew and entered the second archway, where he did his business. During this time, this man turned about several times around and before him. He then came back up and was arrested as he did so. He did not speak to the man who followed him, who did not speak to him. He had no bad intention in going down to this spot and is not given over to the vice he is suspected of and arrested for. He did not know this spot is suspect. /Lemaitre/
C: W&R

56. Tuesday, 19 April 1785, 9:30 pm
I: A pederast known as the Abbé, who went to the gardens every evening to pick up men "with effrontery," picked up several, including an observer. He placed his hand on his breeches several times and asked him if he had an erection. He finally suggested that he go to his place and put it into him. He played the passive and active roles. He told the observer they should leave separately rather than together. Another man loitered in the Champs-Elysées in the most suspect manner.

Jean Edme Deroche, 34, native of Ervy-le-Chatel in the diocese of Sens (Champagne), parish priest of Dixmont in the same diocese, in Paris since Friday, lodged chez S. Joigny at the Abbeville boardinghouse on rue Neuve Saint-Merri.

He went to walk in the Tuileries this evening. To tell the truth, he was debauched into pederasty when he was young {at the seminary in Sens}. He surrendered himself to masturbation with other young folks in the seminary of Sens and sometimes since, but he has never consummated the crime. He has known for three years that men given over to this debauchery go to the Tuileries garden in the evening. He even went there three years ago out of curiosity to amuse himself. This evening he went there and met a man with whom he, the deponent, indeed stroked through his breeches. They did not do anything else and did not masturbate. /Deroche/
C: S&R

François Marie Antoine Deschamps, 17, native of Paris, former grocer's assistant in Saint-Germain-en-Laye, unemployed for two months, lodged chez Mme Debrie, silk stocking washer, on rue des Vieux Augustins.

He went to the Champs-Elysées this evening to walk. It is the third time he has gone there since he has been in Paris, but without doing anything wrong and without any bad intention. He is not given over to the vice of liking men. This evening in the Champs-Elysées he met a prostitute who spoke to him and suggested to him that they amuse themselves, which he refused. He sent her on her way and continued to walk. /Deschamps/
C: W&R

57. Wednesday, 20 April 1785, 9:30 pm
I: A young man loitered in the Tuileries and picked up men, including a known pederast two days in a row. Yesterday they agreed to sleep together and left together. When they left together today, the other man escaped arrest. Another man loitered on quai des Orfèvres since 8:00 pm, took at least twenty turns, pretended to urinate, and went down several times to the watering spot adjacent to the Mousetrap. He loitered there very often and had suggested to an observer there the day before that they amuse themselves.

Pierre Louis Turbot, 16½, native of Gif near Chevreuse (Ile-de-France), former jockey[16] of Constance, prostitute, bootblack, lodged at the boardinghouse operated by a woman on rue Soly.

He was released from Bicêtre on Monday to be treated with gall-nuts.[17] He was in the Tuileries yesterday evening to wait for Antoine, coachman, who lives on rue Montmartre near the sewer.[18] Yesterday in the garden he accosted a man unknown to him, who told him he was a shoemaker, who took him to dine at an inn on rue de Rohan and then to sleep with him in his room. He masturbated him, the deponent, while he masturbated himself. He was there because he did not have the money to pay for his lodging. He does not know if Antoine is given over to pederasty. Although he was unemployed when he, the deponent, had no money, he gave him some. It is Antoine who told him one could earn money from this in the Tuileries. This evening he returned to the Tuileries, where the man from yesterday told him he would be at 8:00. He indeed found him, and they were leaving together when he, the deponent, was arrested. /U/
C: P

Philippe Jacques Jean Prévost, 43, native of Paris, bootblack on the Pont Neuf, lived on rue de la Calandre near the Palais.

He went on quai des Orfèvres, and, to tell the truth, it happened to him to amuse himself in pederasty with men in the Mousetrap. He was debauched into it three or four years ago in that place by a gentleman he met there. He has surrendered himself to this around twenty times, but without consummating the crime. He has only masturbated those with whom he amused himself, who masturbated him. He does not know any of those with whom he amused himself. /U/
C: P

58. Thursday, 21 April 1785, 9:15 pm
I: A wigmaker's assistant, a known pederast who loitered in the evening in the Tuileries and Champs-Elysées, loitered this evening in the most suspect manner and pathways in the Tuileries. He picked up men, including one he took by the arm to walk with. They conversed about pederasty and agreed to go to the first man's room "to have it put into him." When they left the garden, the second man escaped arrest.

Jean Baptiste Richeux, 22, native of Paris, assistant of S. Gosse, wigmaker, lived at his residence on rue des Moineaux in Butte Saint-Roch.

On his way back from his mother's place on rue de Grenelle in faubourg Saint-Germain, he entered the Tuileries, where he walked and was accosted by a man unknown to him, who said to him, believing he knew him, "There you are," and asked him what time it was. This man told him he lived on rue des Moulins in Butte Saint-Roch and took him by the arm. They left together to return there. This man asked him if he had a mistress, to which he, the deponent, replied yes. To tell the truth, he was debauched into pederasty three or four years ago in Thionville, when he was a solder in the Queen's Regiment, by another soldier. He consummated the crime in the passive role with several soldiers in that regiment as well as the Lionnais and Agenois regiments, in which he also served, including one in the last regiment named La Geroflée.[19] He has also consummated the crime in the passive role, during the eight months he has been in Paris, in a tavern on rue de Beauvais, with a grocer's assistant who lives in faubourg Saint-Honoré at the corner of rue d'Anjou. To tell the truth, he had promised the man he met in the Tuileries this evening to go to his room to have him put it into him, but he was not sure he would be there. /richeux/
C: P

I: 10:45 pm. A man sat alone on a chair in the Tuileries.

Louis Pierre Bigot, 25, native of Chevreuse (Ile-de-France), sailor and journeyman mason, lived chez Mme Leclerc, laundrywoman, on rue de Longchamp in Chaillot.[20]

He was debauched into pederasty six weeks ago by a young man, cowherd in Passy, whose name he does not know. He has consummated the crime in the passive role several times in the Champs-Elysées and has also consummated it in the active role in the Champs-Elysées and Tuileries but does not know any of the persons with whom he has relations. He received at most two louis to do it with the persons he had relations with, some of whom give him three livres, others twenty-four, twelve, and six sols. He did not meet anyone in the Tuileries this evening and did nothing. /U/
C: P

59. Friday, 22 April 1785, 8:00 pm–1:00 am
PP: quays, place Louis XV, Champs-Elysées, exits of the Tuileries, OP

I: 9:00 pm. Picart, domestic of an attorney on rue du Coq Saint-Jean, pederast who "surrenders himself to this vice by taste, in either the active or passive role," cruised very often in the Tuileries, took men he picked up there to his place, and had them sleep with him.

9:45. Pajot, pederast on record for a long time, "made a profit from his obligingness" (*complaisance*), held parties with rich folks, and cruised in the royal gardens and suspect places. He was suspected of subjecting men to extortion and was connected with Saint-Hilaire, Herque,[21] and other known pederasts on record. This evening he loitered alone then picked up men, including one with whom he left.

François Picart, 43, native of Amiens (Picardy), domestic of Messire Ades, barrister, lived at his residence on rue du Coq Saint-Jean.

He was debauched into pederasty only a week ago, on quai du Louvre, by a man unknown to him he met there, who went to sleep with him, the deponent. They masturbated independently. He has amused himself only with this man. Coming back from dining this evening with Violette, his cousin, haberdasher on rue Saint-Dominique in Gros-Caillou, he passed through the Tuileries garden and found the same man who took him by the arm and suggested that they go drink of mug of wine. They left to go do it,

and he, the deponent, was arrested, at the moment when he left with this man and another he was with. /picard/
C: P

Louis Pasquier DuChesne, 27, native of Paris, wine merchant in Abbeville (Picardy), in Paris for nearly two weeks, lodged with his father, haberdasher and buttonmaker at the Gold Chain on rue des Fossés Saint-Germain-l'Auxerrois.

He does not know S. Pajot, with whom he was arrested, whose name he knows only as of today. Wednesday and today they found themselves next to each other at the Comic Medley theater[22] on the boulevard and conversed together about the show and the performance of the actors. They parted in leaving. Today they found themselves by chance in a café on the boulevard, where S. Pajot struck up a conversation with him. They went on the boulevard, while talking, as far as rue de Grammont. S. Pajot told him he had business at the Louvre[23] and was going there and urged him, the deponent, to go to the Tuileries to wait for him. He would go rejoin him there. He, the deponent, went there and sat down on a bench, where S. Pajot came to rejoin him. They walked together along the river, where Pajot had told him to go. After they whistled to signal closing, they left and were arrested in leaving. +Pajot told him he lives in faubourg Saint-Germain and would take him, the deponent, part of his way back because he took the Pont Neuf to return to his place. From his remarks and his costume he guessed Pajot was suspected of bad morals.+ As they left, they were arrested. {They did not have any suspect conversation together} He, the deponent, did not have any bad intention and is not given over to liking men. He got married six months ago or thereabouts. /Duchesne/
C: W&R

Charles Pajot Doricourt, 24, native of Nancy (Lorraine), threadmaker, lived with his father and sister chez the first hosier on the left on rue du Faubourg Saint-Martin. He wore rosettes on his shoes, a wide cravat, and earrings.

He is not at all given over to pederasty. He made the acquaintance of S. Duchesne, arrested with him, three or four days ago at the Comic Medley theater, where they found themselves seated near each other. They found each other again today in a café on the boulevard and went on the boulevard as far as the Saint-Denis gate.[24] He left Duchesne to go to the Louvre, where he had something to do. After doing what he had to do there, he went to the Tuileries garden, where they had made a rendezvous. He found him there on a bench,

and they took a turn or two. When the gates closed, they left and were arrested, but he does not know why. /Pajot/
C: P

60. Saturday, 23 April 1785, 10:00 pm

I: A man loitered in the Tuileries and picked up men, including one who was there daily, with whom he conversed about pederasty. He said he was not in the garden to amuse himself because of the moonlight.[25] Two other man loitered separately, sat down on chairs near each other, and left together by the riding school gate.

Joseph Gréant, 36, native of Trélon in Hainaut (Belgium), domestic chez S. de Valliers, inspector of the [royal] weapons manufactory in Maubeuge,[26] in Paris with his master, lodged at the Holy Spirit boardinghouse on rue Neuve des Petits Champs.

He came back from [Little] Poland [8th arr.] with Lajeunesse, domestic, whose address and master he does not know, though he believes them to be in faubourg Saint-Germain. Lajeunesse is his school comrade and is named Roussy. {He goes by [this name] in the Tuileries} He has sometimes surrendered himself to pederasty with comrades he slept with, the last time with Ledoux, also domestic in Maubeuge. They masturbated independently. When he was in the Tuileries, on a bench, a man unknown to him came and sat on the end of the same bench, conversed with him about the fine weather, and added that it was not good for getting an erection. He told him, "So be it." They went away together. /greant/
C: W&R

Louis Philippe, 22, native of Paris, former clerk of an attorney in the Parlement, doing nothing presently, lived chez widow Philippe on rue Saint-Germain-de-l'Auxerrois. He wore a wide collar and rosettes on his shoes.

He left the Boston [card game] gambling den on rue des Fossés de M. le Prince, where he goes to play, and entered the Tuileries to go to sleep with a banker's clerk, on rue Saint-Nicolas in Chaussée d'Antin, who had accustomed him to going to gambling dens, with whom he has slept for three weeks. Having lost his money in gambling and feeling sad, he sat down in the Tuileries. The man arrested with him came loitering around him, approached him, and struck his feet several times with his own without saying anything, then sat down and told him the weather is quite fine this evening.

He, the deponent, replied curtly, "It's true." The man remained seated for a long time, got up, gave him another kick, and then walked. He, the deponent, got up to go away. The man followed him, and they were both arrested. He, the deponent, thought it was his parents who had him arrested because he gambles. He is not given over to the vice of liking men. /Philippe/
C: W&R

Roch La Pérouse, 25, native of Draillaint in Savoy (Italy), kitchen assistant of M. Anisson du Perou, lived at his residence on rue des Orties near the Louvre.

He goes to the Tuileries from time to time. To tell the truth, he was debauched into pederasty around four years ago by Lapierre, domestic, who lived then, like himself, chez S. Rivière on rue de la Chaussée d'Antin. He has amused himself with other persons, sometimes in the Tuileries with persons unknown to him. When he wants to amuse himself with someone he has found, he makes water near a tree. To tell the truth, he picked up the man arrested with him by brushing his foot with his own after taking a turn around him. He then sat down near him and told him the weather was fine this evening. The man replied yes. He does not know if he is also given over to this vice since he did not have any other conversation with him. He wanted to amuse himself with this young man, who did not respond to his signals. He, the deponent, followed him when he left, and they were both arrested. /U/
C: P

61. Monday, 25 April 1785, 9:30 pm
I: A man and the "child" seated next to him in the stoneyard had their breeches unbuttoned and their penises protruding. The man had his penis "in a state of erection" and appeared to touch the child's penis.

Nicolas Camus, nearly 12, day laborer, orphan, lodged chez Carton, who rented rooms on rue Neuve Saint-Médard. He ran errands at the Comédie and on rue des Cordeliers.

This evening he sat down on a stone near the Comédie Française and fell asleep there. The man arrested with him woke him up, sat down near him, and told him he would give him money for his supper and lodging if he wished to amuse him. He unbuttoned his, the deponent's, breeches and fondled his penis +and buttocks+. This man also unbuttoned his breeches and pulled out his penis, which he had him, the deponent, fondle. He wanted to buttfuck [*enculer*] him, suggested it, +and had him sit on his knees to that

end+. He, the deponent, did not want to. It has already happened to him to amuse two other men among the same stones. One gave him twelve sols and the other twenty-four sols. /U/
C: P

Louis Dorgny, 33, native of Darçon in Franche-Comté, kitchen assistant of the vicomte de Virieu, lived at his residence in the Luxembourg palace.[27]

He goes very often in the evening to the stones that are near the Comédie Française. This evening, to tell the truth, he found the man arrested with him asleep on a stone. He approached, woke him up, and told him he would give him something for supper and lodging if he wished to amuse him. The young man responded yes, and he, the deponent, led him in farther, where he, the deponent, undid this child's breeches and fondled his penis and buttocks. To tell the truth, he suggested to him that he buttfuck him, and the young man kneeled on the deponent's knees for that purpose, but he, the deponent, got no further. He, the deponent, also undid his breeches, and the young man fondled his penis. It is the first time he has had this weakness. /loui dornier/
C: P

62. Wednesday, 27 April 1785, 9:15 pm

Deposition of Marie Barbe LeClerc, called the Desired Woman, and Charlotte Brouard, both prostitutes, who lived in the same house on rue du Bourbon in Villeneuve.

Around three years ago, when Leclerc lived chez S. Capron, limonadier, on rue Neuve des Petits Champs, a man came to her place and told her he practiced the same trade she did. She did not understand what he meant. He explained it her and told her he put it into men in the rear or the mouth, received whipping from those who wanted to give it, and for six francs, one could do all one wished with him. He urged her to procure him among her acquaintances and promised to divide with her what he would earn. After this he came back every day to know if she could procure someone for him. One day there was a man at her place when he knocked at her door. When she told the gentleman who was with her what the other man wanted, he desired her to have him enter. He did not wish to believe that there were men who thought that way. The other man entered and declared to the gentleman, whom he believed to be a pederast, that he would do with him all he wished. He unbuttoned his breeches, uncovered himself in front as well as in back. The gentleman told him that was enough, did not want to touch him, dismissed him, and gave him nine livres, of which he gave four livres and ten sols to her, LeClerc. He told her he had accumulated assets in this trade, made investments that produced income, and even found himself at a party with abbés and had it put into him from behind by a dog. In the last three months this same man has gone frequently to see Brouard, shared the same confidences with her, and urged her to procure men for him to hold parties at her place. She asked for payment in advance and told him she would give half of it back. He told her, like Leclerc, that he had had it put into him from behind by a Great Dane and at a prostitute's place. He had recently contracted an illness from kissing a woman while another man put it into him, the deponent, from behind. By dint of solicitations and to get rid of this man, she, Brouard, promised him to seek a man for him for 8:00 pm. He came twice yesterday to assure himself she would keep her word. He came back twice more today, at 11:00 am and 5:00 pm, and finally came at 7:30 to have this party. He took the precaution of detaching one curtain from her bed to place it in front of the door, then had her prepare pomade [for lubricant], while sounding her out if the one he would have to do with had a real thick one. He said he did not have a very wide one, then pushed the bed to the back of the alcove and placed his watch in the pocket of his short jacket.[28]

Interrogation

Asked for his first and last names, age, place of birth, status, and address.

After taking the oath to tell the truth, replied he is named Mathurin Augustin Capriny, around 35, native of Paris, bill-broker, lives in Paris chez Mme Dumas on rue Montmartre near rue Notre-Dame-des-Victoires.

Asked how long he has been given over to pederasty.

Replied he has known prostitutes with whom he contracted illness, and, in this state, could not see other women. His imagination[29] was aroused through libertinage, and, through the passions, he has given himself over, for several years, to mutual stroking with men, but he has never consummated the crime, although he has often been on the verge of consummating it. He has even very often paid to see men amuse themselves with women. It is true he once received money from a prostitute for stroking with a man and that because he had his imagination aroused and he desired to be a prostitute [*fille d'amour*].

Asked if it has not happened to him to reside with a woman and, during this time, to have himself inhabited from behind by a man.[30]

Replied no, but he often said so out of imagination.

Asked why he went today to the prostitute's place where he was arrested.

Replied it is as a result of his aroused imagination. He believed he would find a man there with whom he would amuse himself, but he believes he would not have amused himself.

Asked if it is not he who urged this prostitute to procure him a man at her place.

Replied yes, and there is no horror that his imagination did not make him devise, which he did not carry out.

Asked if he has had such parties with men chez other prostitutes.

Replied yes.

Asked if he has told several of these prostitutes that he put it in, had it put into him in the mouth and the rear, had himself whipped by men, and lent himself to all they wished.

Replied yes.

Asked if he also told them he had had it put into him by a Great Dane.

Replied yes, but it is, however, not true.

Asked if, when he was at the place of one of the prostitutes, where there was another man, he, the deponent, uncovered himself and displayed himself nude before this man, in front as well as in back.

Replied yes.

Asked if this man gave him nine livres, of which he turned four livres and ten sols over to the prostitute.

Replied no. It is the prostitute who received the nine livres and handed four livres over to him, the deponent, as a prostitute.

After his interrogation and his replies were read to him, he said they contain the truth, reaffirmed them, and he signed. /Caprini/
C: P

MAY

63. Tuesday, 3 May 1785, 11:00 pm

I: A man loitered in the Tuileries and accosted men. He sat down next to one below the terrace of the Feuillants[1] and suggested to an observer that they go to his place to have it put into him for an écu. He preferred to amuse himself in the garden because men had subjected him to extortion several times when he went to their places.

François Haranger du Beauceron, 19, native of Hauterive-le-Bourgeois near Châteauneuf in Thymerais (Maine), day laborer, lived chez Mme Gaillard, who rented rooms on rue du Champ-fleuri.

He was debauched into pederasty around two weeks ago by the chevalier de Besenval, officer in the Swiss Guards,[2] who met him on the Sablons plain [in Neuilly-sur-Seine] and charged him to take a letter to his residence and wait for the person. He waited there, and S. de Besenval arrived, had him taken up to a room on the sixth floor, sent away his domestics on duty, locked himself in with the deponent, had him undress until completely nude, washed his body with a sponge, masturbated him, and had himself masturbated by the deponent. He had placed a hunting knife out of its sheath on the table and shown him a bag of gold he said he would give him but gave him only thirty sols. He, the deponent, returned twice to the chevalier de Besenval's place on rue de Caumartin, between a wigmaker and a limonadier, where they again masturbated independently. S. de Besenval gave him twelve sols each of these two times. He, the deponent, went this evening to the Tuileries, where S. de Besenval had made a rendezvous with him but was not there. He met another man there who offered him three livres to go have supper and sleep with him. He was arrested in leaving to go there. It is the need of money that obliged him to give himself over to this vice, but he has not committed the crime. He has amused himself only with the chevalier de Besenval. /U/
C: P

64. Wednesday, 4 May 1785, 10:30 pm
I: A man loitered from 8:00 to 10:00 pm in the most suspect pathways in the Tuileries, accosted men, and pretended to urinate a number of times.

Guillaume Potier, 30, native of Signé (?) in Maine, breeches maker's assistant, unemployed for three weeks, lodged chez S. Huet, tailor, on rue Jacob opposite rue Saint-Benoît.

He went this afternoon to see André, domestic chez S. Vicq on rue du Four in faubourg Saint-Germain, to entreat him to find him a position as a domestic. He has almost always been one. After leaving him he crossed the Pont Neuf and followed quai du Louvre past the Pont Royal to take rue des Saints-Pères. He did not enter the Tuileries and is not given over to the vice of liking men. Then he said that, to tell the truth, he was debauched into pederasty by a man who is dead. Since then he has amused himself with persons he does not know. If he had found someone respectable this evening, he could have amused himself. /U/

C: P because he was already on record as a pederast and was "dressed in the costume of pederasts"

65. Saturday, 7 May 1785, 8:00 pm–1:00 am
PP: Champs-Elysées, Cours de la Reine,[3] stone port,[4] site of the Colosseum,[5] place Louis XV, Tuileries, quays, OP

I: After 9:00. A man who loitered in the Tuileries every evening for two weeks and surrendered himself to pederasty there had been expelled by the guards on 4 May.[6] He cruised in the Champs-Elysées yesterday and again today.

10:00 pm. Another man loitered for more than an hour in the Tuileries in the most suspect manner, accosted a man, struck up a conversation, made remarks about pederasty, and named "various notorious pederasts."

Pierre Légal, 20, native of Mayenne (Maine), unemployed wigmaker's assistant, lodged chez Bauche, who rented rooms on rue de la Mortellerie.

He arrived from Tours and has been in Paris for only three weeks. He was debauched into pederasty in Nantes by Gougère, wigmaker's assistant, with whom he worked in the same shop. He goes very often to the Tuileries in the evening. He was there yesterday evening and left at 10:00 with a man he does not recognize. He then went to sleep with another named Antoine, on rue des Fossés Saint-Germain-l'Auxerrois. He was indeed expelled from the Tuileries garden by the guards last Wednesday. He was picked up in plain daylight within days of his arrival in Paris, in a billiard parlor on quai de la Ferraille, by Dieu, printer on a street that leads into rue Saint-Victor. He amused himself with him out of need. Dieu introduced him to Aubert, cook in a collège or seminary on rue Saint-Victor,[7] with whom he amused himself out of obligingness in a tavern on the same street last Thursday. He has amused himself various times with both of them. It is Dieu who informed him that men cruise in the Tuileries and advised him to go there. He came to the Champs-Elysées this evening with Antoine, and they separated. Antoine told him he would come back. /U/

C: P

Simon Perrault, 28, native of Nogent-le-Roy in Beauce (Orléanais), unemployed domestic, lodged chez a man who rented rooms chez a master cooper on rue Montmartre, near the referral office for domestics.[8]

He indeed walked in the Tuileries garden. A man he does not know accosted him there and suggested that they share a bottle of wine. They left but did not drink one. He is not given over to pederasty. /U/
C: W&R

66. Monday, 9 May 1785, 11:00 pm
I: A man loitered in the Tuileries since 8:15 in the most suspect places and manner, accosted several men, and pretended to urinate several times. He made remarks about pederasty to a man seated on a bench and told him he lived on rue Dauphine, with his own furniture.[9]

René Jouan, 27, native of Noyen-sur-Sarthe (Anjou), independent tailor, lived at the Orléans boardinghouse on rue Dauphine, on the fifth floor in the front.

In going home from rue d'Aguesseau, he went through the Tuileries and met a man there unknown to him, who asked what time it was. This man spoke to him about pederasty and told him he was a goldsmith and lived on quai des Orfèvres. It has already happened to him to meet men in the garden who passed a hand over his breeches. Three years ago, Orlan, personal valet of a merchant, who lived at the Three Bishoprics boardinghouse on rue des Filles Saint-Thomas, made him offers, at his place, to surrender himself to pederasty with him. He did not accept these offers. Orlan stroked him only through his breeches. It has never happened to him to surrender himself to anything in this vice, and he has never been given over to it. He has been married for eighteen months and lives with his wife, who has already had a child, who died. /rene joüan/
C: W&R

67. Tuesday, 10 May 1785, 9:45 pm
I: Daillant, pederast on record, had been arrested and imprisoned on 12 July 1784.[10] Since his release he loitered and cruised in the Coal-Box, as he did today.

Sébastien Daillant, 36,[11] native of Paris, journeyman building painter and soldier in the Paris regiment, lived with his mother chez S. Blanville, smelter, on rue des Jardins.

It is true that he has continued to surrender himself to pederasty since his release from prison and that he surrendered himself to it chez and with Toussaint, wine vendor, on rue de Charenton, with +whom he has slept several times at his place, opposite rue Traversière or rue Saint-Nicolas. He made Toussaint's acquaintance two years ago when they were on the Half-Moon on boulevard Saint-Antoine.+ And yesterday at the place of a man whose name he does not know, whom he met in the Coal-Box, who lives on rue Saint-Honoré. He does not recall which building. They consummated the crime, with him, the deponent, in the passive role. This man, moreover, made a rendezvous with him for this evening on boulevard Saint-Antoine. He also knows Prelaut, clockmaker near the Saint-Antoine gate, to be a pederast. He urged him, the deponent, to go see him at his place. He was debauched into this crime in Versailles by a priest in the parish of Notre-Dame, whose name he never knew, around eighteen years ago. Since that time he, the deponent, has continued to surrender himself to this vice. /dalliant/
C: P

68. Tuesday, 10 May 1785, 11:30 pm
I: Two pederasts loitered in the Tuileries, accosted each other, sat down on chairs next to each other in one of the darkest spots, and appeared to masturbate independently.

Pierre Beaujar, 25, native of Saint-Brieuc in Lower Brittany, domestic, unemployed for a week, lodged in a furnished room at The Royal Hunt on rue du Sépulcre.

He went to walk in the Tuileries garden this evening and met the man arrested with him, whom he does not know, whose name and address he does not know. He asked him what time the Tuileries closed. They sat down next to each other but did not touch each other. They did not talk about the debauchery of men, to which he, the deponent, is not given over. As the gates were closed, the man urged him to leave with him by the gate to cul-de-sac de l'Orangerie and told him he just needed to go around on the quays to go to rue du Sépulcre. They were arrested as they left. Then he said he has surrendered himself to amusing himself with men only with Séraphin, domestic, who slept with him in Cambrai and Rouen, when he, the deponent, was a domestic of M. de la Ballegrie, captain in the Boulonnais regiment, and Séraphin was a domestic chez S. Martigny, officer in the same regiment. /Beaujant/
C: P

François du Doigt, 28, native of Beauvais (Ile-de-France), domestic chez S. de la Barchette, secretary of M. de Veimerange, intendant of the army,[12] lived chez Barchette on rue Neuve des Mathurins in Chaussée d'Antin.

He went to walk in the Tuileries this evening on the way back from errands. He sat down there, and the man arrested with him passed around him several times, then sat down near him. He asked him what time it was, and he, the deponent, told him it was 9:45. This man then asked him when they closed the garden. They conversed about the cold. The man told him he was cold because he was from America, which is a very warm country. He, the deponent, heard 10:15 strike and, seeing it was quite dark, decided to leave by way of cul-de-sac de l'Orangerie. The man came with him, in spite of the fact he said he lived in faubourg Saint-Germain and he, the deponent, told him that his route was to leave by the gate on the side of the Pont Royal. They were arrested as they left. They did not talk about the debauchery of men, to which he, the deponent, has never been given over. /francois dudoigt/
C: W&R

69. Thursday, 12 May 1785, 10:00 pm
I: A man loitered in the Tuileries and accosted several men, including an observer. The former offered to amuse himself with the latter in his room for three livres. Mallard, a known pederast, already imprisoned on 3 December 1783, loitered in the garden and masturbated a man he had picked up.

Henry François Nicolas Jameau, 25, native of Abbeville (Picardy), journeyman playing card maker and grenadier in the royal regiment of Picardy, in Paris for nearly a month, lodged chez Lefevre, innkeeper, who rented rooms on rue Sainte-Anne in Butte Saint-Roch.

He entered the Tuileries and met a man he accosted. To tell the truth, he, the deponent, asked him for three livres to amuse himself with him at pederasty. It is indigence that made him do it. It is the second time he has gone to the Tuileries. He has surrendered himself to the vice for only ten to twelve days. He does not know any of those with whom he has amused himself. He amused himself once in the Tuileries, a week ago Monday, with a man who did not give him anything. /Jamot/
C: P

Charles Antoine Mallard, 43, native of Paris, unemployed domestic, lived chez the spurrier on rue Saint-Honoré opposite the Assumption.[13]

He was in the Tuileries this evening and took two or three turns in a pathway. As he was making water, a man approached him and tried to stroke him. He, the deponent, withdrew. He knows they pick up men in the garden. He went there only to pass through and walked because it was still early. /malard/
C: P

I: 11:00 pm. A man known by the name of The Woman from Lyon, who prostituted himself and held parties, loitered on the Sofa.

Laurent Compagnat, 29, native of Saugues in Forez, limonadier's assistant, worked and lived at the Mechanical Café in the Palais Royal.

He left his place of work at 9:30 pm to go to his brother's place on rue Montmartre and then went to see a doorman on rue de Tournon but did not go there. To tell the truth he has amused himself with men several times when he had the chance to do so. He has been given over to this vice for nine years. He was even given over to it when he was in his native region, before coming to Paris, where he has been for fourteen years. Of all those with whom he has amused himself, he knows only Compiègne, who lived chez S. Lefou, surgeon, on rue du Faubourg Saint-Denis. /U/
C: P

70. Friday, 13 May 1785, 8:00 pm–1:30 am
PP: northern boulevards,[14] Coal-Box, planned streets between rue Basse du Temple and La Courtille, Petite rue Saint-Nicolas, rue Saint-Fiacre, small streets and cul-de-sacs off the boulevards, OP

I: After 9:00. A man loitered on the boulevard du Pont aux Choux during the week, went down to the Coal-Box, and tried to pick up men there. Yesterday he loitered for a very long time in the most suspect manner and accosted passersby.

11:00. A man "dressed in the most obvious costume" (rosettes on shoes, wide cravat, hat), with "the tone and figure of pederasts," loitered on boulevard Montmartre in the most suspect manner. Two other men also loitered there in the most suspect manner, insulted passersby, called them female rivals,[15] and threatened to strike them with rods.

Pierre Pilard, 22, native of Meudon (Ile-de-France), boarded chez S. Roland on rue Culture Sainte-Catherine.

He sometimes goes to walk on the boulevard after class, while waiting for supper. He did not accost anyone, did not have any bad intention at all, and does not know anyone in Paris but S. Roland's other boarders. /X/
C: W&R

Nicolas François Bertheaume, 26, native of Argentan in Normandy, worked as a day student to educate himself chez Messire des Issarts, notary,[16] and lived at 6, rue Françoise.

He was waiting for a woman with whom he had made a rendezvous at 11:00 on the boulevard. /X/
C: W&R

Louis Paillot, 22,[17] native of Paris, unemployed postilion, lived on rue de Vendôme. He had been arrested and imprisoned on 13 December 1780 for attempting to debauch "a thirteen-year-old child."[18] The royal order for his exile was issued in February and revoked in December 1781. He continued his misconduct and was arrested again in June 1783, warned, and released.

Antoine Barthélemy, 21, native of Riom in Auvergne, unemployed grocer's assistant, lived at the Bordeaux boardinghouse on rue Geoffroy Langevin.

Both[19] said they have known each other for two or three days and then said three years and, furthermore, gave a very poor account of their conduct. /U/
C: P

71. Tuesday, 17 May 1785, 11:00 pm
I: Two men entered the Tuileries one after the other, accosted each other, and loitered and picked up men in the most suspect manner. One of them picked up a tall man with whom he conversed for a long time. The other picked up and conversed with a tall man dressed in blue.

Antoine Simon Mielot, 17½, native of Paris, pinmaker, lived with his father, master pinmaker, on rue des Boucheries in faubourg Saint-Germain.

At 3:00 pm today he went with Le Cocq, with whom he has been friends since the age of six, to walk first on the new boulevards, then on boulevard du Temple. They entered Café d'Yon and Café Alexandre,[20] where they drank beer. They then entered the Tuileries by the Orangery gate, crossed the garden, and sat down on chairs. He, the deponent, made water near a tree, while Le Cocq walked on, which obliged him, the deponent, to whistle at him. He did

not speak to any other person in the Tuileries garden and has never amused himself with men. To tell the truth, two men suggested it to him under the arcades of the Comédie Française.[21] He is not subject to this vice. /Mielot/
C: W&R

Alexandre Louis Le Cocq, 18½, native of Paris, saddler, lived and worked with his father, master saddler, in the courtyard of the Saint-Germain fair.

He walked with Mielot this afternoon on the new boulevards, in the Luxembourg, and on the boulevard du Temple. They entered Café Alexandre, where they drank four bottles of beer, which he paid for. They then came by way of place Louis XV to the Tuileries garden, which they entered by the Orangery gate. They crossed the garden and sat down on chairs. A man who passed by accosted him by asking him what the drums were that someone was beating. He told him it was the signal for return to barracks. During this time Mielot went ahead, which obliged him, the deponent, to whistle at him. He is not given over to the vice of liking men. /LeCoq/
C: W&R

72. Thursday, 19 May 1785, 10:45 pm
I (Noël): A pederast loitered in the Tuileries and picked up men, including one to whom he made remarks about pederasty.

Louis Henry Lefevre, 33, native of Saint-Cloud (Ile-de-France), former novice sailor, gardener's assistant, in Paris for six months, without work for several days and without a residence.

He has been given over to the vice of pederasty for two years. He gave himself over to it on the ship *The Hero*[22] with other sailor comrades.[23] Since he returned to Paris, he has amused himself with several men unknown to him at the edge of the river on the La Rapée side. He does not have a sol and went to the Tuileries this evening in hopes of finding someone who would give him some money. He met a young man there with whom he talked about this debauchery, who suggested to him that he go sleep with him. As they left together to go there, he was arrested. /Louis Henry Lefebvre/
C: P

73. Friday, 20 May 1785, 10:45 pm
I (Noël): Two men loitered in the Tuileries, accosted each other, sat down on chairs near each other, appeared to stroke, took several turns in the darkest pathway together, sat down several times, and left together.

François Sabat, 20, native of Aurillac in Auvergne, unemployed kitchen assistant, lodged at the Little Burgundy boardinghouse on rue Neuve des Bons Enfants.

He had nothing to do and went to walk in the Tuileries. He and the man arrested with him, whom he does not know, approached each other, and he, the deponent, asked him what time it was. They chatted about various things. They did not make any propositions about debauchery to each other. The man arrested with him told him he comes from Bordeaux, has been in Paris for two weeks, +intends to learn the trade of confectioner+, and lodges near the Palais Royal. They left the Tuileries to go to the Palais Royal. He, the deponent, has never surrendered himself to the debauchery of men. He did not request and does not have certificates from the masters at whose residences he has lived. /U/
C: P because he picked up the other man,[24] was unemployed, and had no certificates

Jean Louis, marquis de Mânes, native of Saint-Jean-d'Angély (Saintonge), in Paris for the first time, for three weeks, lodged at the Artois boardinghouse on rue Montmartre. He wore a wide cravat and rosettes on his shoes.

He went to the Tuileries this evening without any design and did not know in the least that this place is suspect. While he was there, the arrested man accosted him and asked him what time it was, then asked him various questions intended to reveal where he, the deponent, is from, how long he has been in Paris and what he has done, and where he lodges. He, the deponent, responded very vaguely. Having told him, among other things, that he came from Bordeaux, the man told him he is from Bordeaux. They took several turns and sat down twice. The man told him he does not like to remain in pathways where there is light. When he, the deponent, said he was going to leave and go to the Palais Royal, the man said he would accompany him. They left together, and they were arrested, but he does not know why. /le marquis demanes/
C: W&R

74. Saturday, 21 May 1785, 8:30 pm–2:00 am
PP: exits of the Palais Royal, quays, stone port, place Louis XV, exits of the Tuileries, OP

I (Noël): 10:15. Two men loitered separately in the Tuileries, picked each other up, sat down on a bench, walked, and left together. Another young known pederast frequented the garden and other suspect places and cruised there.

10:45 Two other men loitered, and one picked up the other. They amused themselves together and masturbated independently under a tree. One said "very loudly that he had quite a strong erection." When they left, the other man escaped arrest.

Antoine Joseph Badar, 31, native of Douai (Flanders), wigmaker's assistant, unemployed since his arrival in Paris a few days ago, lodged chez Mme Lefevre, who rented rooms on rue de la Tannerie.

Coming back from Neuilly, he entered the Tuileries, and sat down. The man arrested with him took several turns before him, then sat down near him, told him he appeared quite tired, asked him where he is from and how old he is, and discussed various matters. The other went to make water near the gate, and he, the deponent, waited for him. They left together to go to their own places. He has never been in the Tuileries except for today. They did not do anything wrong. /badar/
C: P

Jean Seron, 35, native of Paris, employed in the library of the marquis de Juigné,[25] lived at his residence on rue de Thorigny in the Marais.[26]

He came back from walking in the Champs-Elysées and entered the Tuileries. He sat down on a bench where the wigmaker's assistant arrested with him was. He, the deponent, spoke to him first and believes he began by telling him it was around 9:00. They had a very vague conversation, but it had nothing to do with debauchery. He, the deponent, is not at all subject to debauchery with men. /Séron/
C: W&R

Philippe Claude Noël Garon, called Parisian, 18, native of Paris, unemployed shoemaker's assistant.

He went to the Tuileries to walk and goes there every evening. He met a man there who suggested he go with him to his place to sleep. He, the deponent, did not accept. They left at the same time to go to the Palais Royal, where this other man wanted to take him. He is not given over to the debauchery of men. /garon/
C: P

François, chevalier d'Abzac,[27] 35, native of Lunerac (Lusignac?) in Périgord (Guyenne), nobleman, master of the horse at the large royal stables in Versailles,[28] lived there and lodged in Paris on rue Jean Saint-Denis.

He went to the Tuileries garden this evening and was accosted there by a man unknown to him, with whom he conversed, but nothing bad happened. He senses it was an indiscretion on his part to stop with a man he does not know in this place in the evening. He has never surrendered himself to the debauchery of men. /le chevalier d'Abzac/
C: W&R

75. Wednesday, 25 May 1785, 10:00 pm
I (Noël): One known pederast, known by the name of the Fat (or Pregnant) Woman, loitered in the Tuileries and accosted another, with whom he walked for a long time. Judging from their conversation, he had a rendezvous in the garden. The one who was arrested was also a known thief, had been subjected to criminal proceedings twice, detained in Bicêtre twice, and exiled. He was closely connected with Carton, Joret, and Chauffour, notorious pederasts and thieves.[29] Back in Paris, he was back in the Tuileries and on the boulevards.

Jacques Louis Picard, 28, native of Paris, unemployed tailor's assistant, arrived in Paris from Dijon last Saturday and lodged chez widow Denis on rue du Faubourg Saint-Jacques.

It is not true he is given over to the debauchery of men. Then he said he cannot say since when he has been given over to this vice or who debauched him into it. He is not the only one. He does nothing wrong but to himself. He gave himself over to it at a very young age, and it is in his blood. He was debauched into it by a priest in the parish of Saint-Benoît. /piccare/
C: P

76. Thursday, 26 May 1785, 11:30 pm
I (Noël): One pederast masturbated independently with another in one of the darkest pathways in the Tuileries.

Jean Maurice, 43, native of Châteauneuf in Thymerais (Maine), domestic chez S. Roche, silk fabric vendor, lived at his residence on rue des Mauvaises Paroles.

He was debauched into pederasty three or four years ago by Saint-Louis, also a domestic, when they both lived chez S. Guyon on rue des Deux Portes Saint-Sauveur. He does not know his current address. Since that time he has amused himself with several persons unknown to him, whose residences he went to, one on rue Saint-Denis. [He] does not know where the others [live]. He went to the Tuileries this evening with the design of amusing himself and

met a man there dressed in a black jacket, with a round wig, who approached him, the deponent, while he was making water near a tree. They amused themselves together. He does not know this man, whom he had never seen. /maurice/
C: P

77. Friday, 27 May 1785, 11:00 pm
I (Noël): A man loitered in the Tuileries for forty-five minutes in the most suspect manner, picked up men, and made "the most indecent remarks about pederasty" to them.

Jean Baptiste Barat, 22, native of Nevers (Nivernais), tonsured cleric in the diocese of Bourges and musician at the collegial church of Saint-Ursin in Bourges,[30] lived there. In Paris since last Sunday, he lodged one night in faubourg Saint-Martin, has had no place to stay since, and spent last night chez abbé Duguet, music director at Notre-Dame.[31]

He was debauched into pederasty at the age of seven by Father Cheullot, canon of Nevers, who lives there and is currently in Paris. He has amused himself at this vice several times, with, among others, Mercier, secondhand dealer in Bourges, with whom he slept and consummated the crime in the active role. Since he has been in Paris, he has consummated this crime only once, with a prostitute whose name he does not know, who picked him up in the Tuileries, where he put it into her from behind on a bench.[32] He gave her twenty-four sols, which was all the money he had. Then he said he did not sleep chez abbé Duguay last night. He was there in the afternoon and told him he had no money. S. Duguay gave him three livres. He spent thirty sols on dinner. The twenty-four sols he gave the prostitute were the rest of the écu. He then slept on benches on quai de la Ferraille. Today he only ate some bread for one sol and three apples that cost him three liards and drank a decoction for one liard, which makes in all two sols, which he had. Having nothing more, he went to the Tuileries this evening and was accosted there by a man who suggested to him that they go and sleep [together] to surrender themselves to pederasty and led him to believe he would earn some money from it. The [need] for money made him consent. In leaving he was arrested. /Barat/
C: P

78. Monday, 30 May 1785, 10:30 pm
I (Noël): Two men loitered separately in the Tuileries, accosted each other, took several turns in the pathways with the most foliage, sat down next to

each other, walked again, and finally left together. They told each other they were going to have a Bavaroise in the Palais Royal.

Antoine Valérien de Jowe, 24, native of Montpellier (Languedoc), subdeacon in the diocese of Paris, by permission of the bishop of Montpellier,[33] and canon of Embrun, lived in Montpellier and lodged at the Richelieu boardinghouse on rue de Richelieu for the last month.

He went to the Tuileries for the second time this evening about 8:30. Several moments after he entered, he saw he was followed by the man arrested with him, whom he does not know, which made him change pathways. This man followed him and came {to stare at him} to accost him and said to him, "Monsieur abbé, is it not you with whom I had supper several days ago at a lady's residence?" He, the deponent, replied while walking, "No, sir." The man continued to follow him and, several moments later, came to stare at him and told him, "It's indeed you, Monsieur abbé. Upon my word, it's you. I'm not mistaken. I don't have the honor to know you." He, the deponent, turned back to go away. The man still followed him and, a bit later, said something to him that he, the deponent, did not understand. He told him testily and very loudly, "Sir, I don't understand you. There must be a great resemblance between me and the abbé you spoke about, to explain why I cannot look around without having you behind me." The man told him not to speak so loudly and added, "Yes, you resemble him very much." He, the deponent, told him, "I'm leaving." The man took him by the arm and asked him where he was going. He replied he was going to the Palais Royal, and the man suggested to him that they take some refreshment there and urged him to take a turn on the side where the facilities for men[34] are located. He, the deponent, said he did not have time. The man said they reduced the pathway by half. They were indeed at some distance. They returned to leave, and in leaving they were arrested. He does not know why. Nothing wrong took place between him and the man. The man only said to him, in addition, that he would be delighted to make his acquaintance. /De jouve/
C: W&R

Charles Joseph de Belloy, 34, native of Auchonvillers in the diocese of Amiens (Picardy), chevalier de Saint-Lazare,[35] former musketeer in the first company, lived chez S. de Bourget on rue du Champ-fleuri.

He indeed accosted in the Tuileries the abbé arrested with him, whom he took for abbé Servins, of his acquaintance. It is likewise true he spoke several times to the arrested abbé and suggested that they go to have

something in the Palais Royal. After speaking with this abbé, after realizing he was not S. Servins, [he persisted] with the intention of chattering with him and walking while laughing and chatting. Sometimes he joked and jested with young folks as with women because he no longer wishes to amuse himself with women, for fear of contracting illness. But he does not have a confirmed taste with [for] men. /Belloy/
C: W&R

79. Tuesday, 31 May 1785, 6:00 pm–1:00 am
PP: northern boulevards, Coal-Box, planned streets, rue Saint-Nicolas, rue Saint-Fiacre, cul-de-sacs and small streets off the boulevards, OP

I (Noël): 8:30. A man loitered on the boulevard in the most suspect manner and accosted men, with whom he appeared "to seek to have a good time." He surrendered himself to pederasty, cruised very often in the Tuileries, Luxembourg, and other suspect places, and slept with men he picked up, at their places or his own. He was connected with others given over to this debauchery and had already done time in Bicêtre.

After 10:00. A man with "the manners of men given over to pederasty" loitered on boulevard du Pont aux Choux, went down to the Coal-Box, and masturbated independently, with his breeches down, with a man who escaped arrest.

Jean Etienne Cochois, 20, native of Paris, florist, lived on rue Saint-Martin opposite rue au Maire, between the haberdasher and the ironmonger.

He was debauched at the age of ten {to twelve} by his brother and was detained in Bicêtre around eight years ago. He renounced pederasty eight years ago. He returned to Paris from Provence eight months ago. It is true he spoke to a man he does not know on the boulevard. /U/
C: P

Urbain Ancelin Joseph Gautier, 38, native of Lens in Artois, unemployed postilion, lodged chez a man who rented rooms, whose name he does not know, on Vieille rue du Temple.

He did not walk on the boulevards. As he was doing his business, a young man he does not know, who also appeared to be doing his business next to him, stretched out his hand onto his parts. He got up, and this young

man then took his hand by force. Then he said, "One does not walk on the boulevard" [without reason?], and said he is leaving tomorrow for his native region. /U/
C: P

JUNE

80. Wednesday, 1 June 1785, 7:30 pm
I (Noël): Bidault, nicknamed Sheep's Head,[1] exiled on 19 December 1784, did not leave Paris.

Jean Baptiste Etienne Bidault, 33, native of Paris, parish of Saint-Hilaire (5th arr.), unemployed journeyman binder, sold songs and lodged chez Mme LaRose, who rented rooms on rue de la Tannerie.

    He was notified on 24 December about the royal order that exiled him thirty leagues from Paris.[2] At the time he was in the hôtel de La Force prison,[3] where he had been detained since 13 November.[4] He remained in Paris for fear of not being able to make a living in the provinces. /Bidault/
C: P

81. Wednesday, 1 June 1785, 10:00 pm
I (Noël): A man loitered in the Tuileries every evening and picked up men. He left with one on 30 May to sleep with him.

Jean Baptiste Le Duc, 30, native of La Chapelle-en-Serval (Ile-de-France), domestic, unemployed for three and a half months, lodged in a furnished room chez S. Piot, wine vendor, who rented rooms on rue Sainte-Marguerite in faubourg Saint-Germain.

    For three days he has gone to the Tuileries in the evening. He passed through the garden to go to the Saint-Honoré gate, to the place of a girl whose name he does not know, who, he believes, mends stockings, with whom he had business [or is involved?]. She is currently in the country. The day before yesterday he met a man unknown to him in the garden who told him he is a women's hairdresser and did not know where to go to sleep. He, the deponent, took him to sleep at his place, and he went away the next day at 7:00 am. He, the deponent, gave him forty-eight sols because he said he needed red powder

and had no money. This hairdresser went to find some at a hairdresser's shop in the abbey of Saint-Germain, where he, the deponent, is learning to dress hair, and told him, "If you wish to come take a turn we'll drink a bottle of wine," but he was not there. He, the deponent, went to the Saint-Denis gate to visit his sister, Catherine le Duc, wife of S. Monnier, public writer, and went from there by way of the boulevards to the Tuileries, where he found the hairdresser. They did nothing wrong together, even while sleeping together. He is not given over to pederasty. +Since he met the hairdresser, he has consummated the crime of pederasty with him in the active and passive roles.+ /U/
C: P

I: A man loitered in the Tuileries and picked up a man. They masturbated independently.

Jean Augustin Marinot, 20, native of Colombes (Ile-de-France), earthenware worker, lived chez Mme Hanort on rue Saint-Dominique in Gros Caillou (7th arr.).

He entered the Tuileries this evening and was accosted there by a man who suggested that they amuse themselves. They sat down on a bench, where this man tried to stroke him, which he, the deponent, did not want to allow. He was then accosted by another man, who also made propositions to him. The first man was dressed in a silk vest and silk moiré breeches the color of blackthorn. He does not know the color of his jacket. It is the first time he amused himself in this way. /marino/
C: P

82. Friday, 3 June 1785, 10:45 pm
I: A man loitered in the Tuileries since 9:15 in the most suspect manner and accosted a well-dressed man. They took two turns in the most suspect pathways, stopped near a tree, and appeared to stroke. One said he was afraid, and the other told him "not to fear anything" because he, far from causing him pain, would give him pleasure. Another man loitered since the same time and accosted some abbés, then a man with whom he talked about pederasty.

Louis Dominique Raimbaut, 19, native of Paris, journeyman chez S. Thierry, master dyer, lived at his residence on rue Saint-Dominique in faubourg Saint-Germain.

Coming back from visiting his father, kitchen assistant at the Nicolai boardinghouse on rue d'Anjou in faubourg Saint-Honoré, he entered the Tuileries at 9:45 or thereabouts and only crossed the garden. He did not stop there at all and did not accost or speak to anyone. He is not given over to the debauchery of men. /Raimbaut/
C: W&R

Jean Marie Denot, 29, native of Paris, porter at the central market, lived on allée du Corroyeur off rue Sabot.
When he left Nicolet's,[5] he followed the boulevards and crossed the Tuileries garden to go home. In the garden he met a man unknown in him who conversed with him and suggested to him that they drink a bottle of beer. He has never been given over to the debauchery of men. Men unknown to him have made propositions to him, which he has never wanted to accept. /denot/
C: W&R

83. Saturday, 4 June 1785, 8:00 pm–1:00 am
PP: environs of the Comédie Française, exits of the Tuileries and Luxembourg, quays, OP

I: 10:30 pm. A man came from the Luxembourg, took several turns under the arcades of the Comédie Française, and accosted passersby. Two others, one of whom escaped arrest, loitered under the arcades, took several turns, went to the Luxembourg, came back, and joined the first man. They took several turns together, arm in arm.

Pierre Joseph Grosdemonge, 34, native of Fresse in Franche-Comté, cook, unemployed for around four months, never employed in Paris, lived at the White Rose boardinghouse on rue Saint-Germain-l'Auxerrois.[6]
He went to walk under the arcades of the Comédie Française this evening. The arrested man and another, whom he does not know and has never seen, passed by him and said good evening to him. He walked with them, but without any bad intention. He is not given over to the vice of liking men. /grodemonge/
C: P

Charles Portier, 22, native of Paris, journeyman building painter, lived with his parents on cul-de-sac des Quatre Vents in faubourg Saint-Germain.

He debauched himself into pederasty two years ago with young folks he does not know. He knows to be given over to pederasty: Levasseur, The Woman from Provence, and a domestic whose name he does not know, who lives on rue de la Harpe. One of those with whom he has amused himself is a domestic whose name he does not know, who lives at the Tours boarding-house on rue du Paon, with whom he was in the Luxembourg this evening and under the arcades of the Comédie Française, where they found Monge, arrested with him. He has known him for three months, when Monge was a kitchen assistant chez S. Putot, who kept an eating house on rue des Quatre Vents, where he remained around a month and which he left three weeks ago. Since then, judging from what he told him, he had another job for two weeks. He has gone to walk with Demonge several times in the Luxembourg garden and under the arcades of the Comédie Française but has never amused himself with him. He walked with Demonge again this evening under the arcades, arm in arm. He knows that The Woman from Provence and Levasseur, stationer,[7] have squandered a lot of Demonge's money and taken objects from him. /portier/
C: P

The commissaire recalled Grosdemonge and read Portier's deposition to him.

To tell the truth, he was debauched into pederasty by The Woman from Provence, with whom he amused himself. To tell the truth, The Woman from Provence and Levasseur have squandered his money. He has also amused himself with Levasseur. /grodemonge/

84. Monday, 6 June 1785, 11:00 pm

I: A wigmaker's assistant loitered in the Tuileries in the most suspect manner and picked up men, including one with whom he took several turns and another, a known pederast, with whom he talked about pederasty. He suggested that they have supper and sleep together.

Etienne Foujat, 17, native of Linières in Berry, unemployed wigmaker's assistant, lodged chez Mme Similar, who rented rooms on rue de la Vannerie.

He was debauched into pederasty around a month ago, in the Tuileries garden, by a tall, well-dressed man around forty years old, who masturbated him and had himself masturbated by him, the deponent. This man promised to give him money but did not give him any. He went to the Tuileries this evening [and spoke?] to three different men. One of them, whom another

called chevalier, proposed to him that he go have supper with him in the Palais Royal, but he, the deponent, was arrested in leaving. It is the need of money that made him go to the Tuileries this evening. /fougeat/
C: P

85. **Tuesday, 7 June 1785, 11:00 pm**
I: Two men sat next to each other in the Tuileries, separated to cruise, and accosted a taller man. They spent more than an hour in a dark spot, where they appeared to masturbate and hug each other. After they took several turns, the tall one hugged the others "with so much affection" that passersby remarked, "There is a gentleman who loves these young folks very much, since he kisses them so." One of the shorter ones received money from the tall one and walked off on the terrace of the Feuillants. The other one left with the tall one.

Pierre Regnier, 19, native of Belleville (19th/20th arr.), wigmaker's assistant, unemployed for a month, lived on rue {Phélypeaux with his mother} de Bretagne across from the Enfants rouges market (no. 41).

He passed through the Tuileries this evening to go to the d'Aguesseau market.[8] He did not speak to anyone there. He does not know the man arrested with him and did not speak to him in the Tuileries. He wears rosettes on his shoes[9] and breeches because he does not have buckles but is not given over to pederasty. /U/
C: P

Jean Bailly, 39, native of Paris, personal valet of abbé de Perochet, lived at his residence at the Brige boardinghouse on rue Basse du Rempart.

He went to the Tuileries at 7:15 this evening and read there until 9:30. He then took two or three turns alone and did not speak to anyone. He does not know the man arrested with him and did not speak to him in the Tuileries. He saw him only in leaving. He does not know why he was arrested and is not given over to pederasty. /Jean Bailly/
C: W&R

86. **Wednesday, 8 June 1785, 10:15 pm**
I: A man loitered in the stoneyard and accosted and fondled a young man, 15 to 16, who urinated behind a work shed. The younger man fled as they left. The older man resisted arrest and attempted to rouse "the public."

Pierre Humbert Droz, 43, native of Neuchâtel in Switzerland, clockmaker, lived in the cour du Prince in the enclosure of the abbey of Saint-Germain-des-Prés.

He went to walk this evening near the Comédie Française and needed to make water. He went among the stones and found a little boy, to whom he said one could not go through that way. As he came back, he was arrested. He is not given over to pederasty. He defended himself because he did not know why they arrested him, even though they said they arrested him in the king's name. /S. P. Humbert Droz/
C: P

Jean Verdier, 16, native of Saint-Amand in Auvergne, domestic of Mme Delorme, lived at her residence on rue Saint-Nicaise.

While he made water in the stones near the Comédie Française, the man arrested with him came near him, fondled him for a long time, asked him how he wanted to amuse himself, said he did not have an erection, and told him they had to go elsewhere because the guard arrested people there. As they left this man was arrested. He, the deponent, fled and was arrested a little while later. He did not know what the man wished to do with him. He is the first man who touched him and made such propositions to him. /Verdier/
C: W&R

The commissaire recalled Droz and read Verdier's deposition to him. Droz denied the allegations and added that "even if he had done and said what Verdier says, there would have been no great harm in it.[10] Then he said he did not wish to amuse himself in that spot." The clerk wrote that Verdier declined to sign, but he must have meant Droz, since Verdier signed again.

87. Thursday, 9 June, 8:30 pm–2:00 am
PP: northern boulevards, Coal-Box, planned streets, small streets off the boulevards, quays, OP

I: 9:30. A man arrested, warned, and released on 8 November 1784[11] continued to loiter and seek "good luck" on the boulevards and in the Coal-Box.

Jean Cholette, 28, native of Tours (Touraine), journeyman glazier, lived at the Adam pavilion in faubourg Saint-Germain.[12]

He was going from his place to faubourg Saint-Denis to seek work and only passed along the boulevard. /U/
C: W&R

I: 10:00. A known pederast cruised on the boulevards and in the Coal-Box. He accosted a man on boulevard du Pont au Choux. They chatted and went down together to the Coal-Box, behind the wall along rue Amelot. They masturbated, standing, with their breeches down, with another man who escaped arrest.

10:15. A man who cruised frequently in all the suspect places, specifically in the Tuileries, went home with young folks, liked to consummate the crime of pederasty in the active role, and paid those who obliged him. He was known as Pointed Jerome "to all those of this type [*genre*] who frequent the gardens and suspect places." This evening he loitered for a long time on the boulevard and struck up a conversation with a young man. They went down to the wall in the Coal-Box and fondled independently. The first man had his breeches down, and the second man escaped arrest.

After 11:00. A man with long rings in his ears and "full of scents" accosted another man on the boulevard and went down to the Coal-Box with him. They spent a good half a quarter hour in a hole [in the ground] with their breeches unbuttoned and masturbated independently. One resisted arrest, which allowed the other to escape.

11:15. A man who surrendered himself to this debauchery accosted a man near a dairy stand under a tent on boulevard du Pont aux Choux. They talked, walked, stopped next to the parapet, masturbated independently, and parted.

François Maugrat, 28, native of Senoncourt in the diocese of Besançon (Franche-Comté), quarrier, worked for Regnard and lived in the warehouse of a quarry near Ménilmontant.

He was accosted by a man he does not know who wished to strike up a conversation with him. This man tried to fondle him more than once and took hold of his parts, but he pushed him away. /U/
C: P

Vincent François Pitot, called Pointed Jerome, more than 50, native of Morlaix in Brittany, former mayor (1774–75) and lieutenant of police of Morlaix, then banker in Paris, currently without a position, lodged chez Quelon, joiner, in the Temple.

So as not to make water on the boulevard, he went down to the spot where he was arrested. A man unknown to him approached him as he made water (which is contrary to the truth since he had already struck up a conversation with him on the boulevard), stopped near him, and said to him, "It's after 9:00." He replied, "It's past 9:00." He said nothing more, did nothing wrong, and cannot prevent a man from speaking to him. He denied amusing himself and said he would deny it anyway, even if there were a hundred witnesses. He added that he is in the greatest indigence and, in going to prison, he will at least not lack bread. /X/
C: P

Charles Pélican, 26, native of Villers-le-Sec in the diocese of Châlons (Champagne), domestic of the marquis de Bausson, major general,[13] lived at his residence on place des Vosges.[14]

He came from rue de Popincourt, and it was his route to pass the spot where he was arrested. He did not speak to anyone and was not with anyone (which is a lie since S. de Desurbois arrested at the same time the other man he was with, who escaped only because of Pélican's resistance and violence). Then he said he went to this spot to look for prostitutes there. /U/
C: P

Nicolas Albin, 55, native of Montbard (Burgundy), soldier in the Paris guard, lived on rue des Jardins Saint-Paul.

He denied speaking to anyone, walking and stopping near the parapet, and amusing himself. /U/
C: R in the custody of Etienne Biot, corporal of the Paris guard posted at the Saint-Antoine gate, who was instructed to conduct him before their commander, "who will decide his fate"

88. Saturday, 11 June 1785, 11:15 pm
I: A man loitered in the Tuileries since 9:30 in the most suspect places and manner, picked up several men "with effrontery," and pursued one for a long time.

Jacques Joseph Eve, 27, native of Paris, music master, lived chez a hatter on rue Royale Saint-Antoine.

He went to the Tuileries this evening, as he goes there sometimes, to walk, but he did not stop or speak to anyone, and no one spoke to him. To

tell the truth, he knows the well-covered pathways where he walked are suspect, but they are not when one does nothing wrong there. He does not have the defect[15] of liking men and had no bad intention. /Eve/
C: W&R

89. Sunday, 12 June 1785, 12:00 am
I: A man loitered in the most suspect places in the Tuileries and picked up men, including an observer with whom he tried to stroke. He suggested that they go amuse themselves in an alley outside the garden. Another man also loitered and picked up men, including an observer with whom he conversed about pederasty.

Pierre Dupré, 63, native of Paris, sold matches and tinder and lived chez S. Lasseret on rue des Lionnais.

He was debauched into pederasty at the age of twenty by Carilliers, who is dead. He has not amused himself with men for around two years. Having had a drink, he had the idea to go to the Tuileries this evening to see what was happening there. He accosted a man there with whom he talked about this debauchery. He left with him, to tell the truth, with the design of going to amuse himself in an alley, but he was arrested in leaving. /U/
C: P

Jean Naudin, 27 or 28, native of Bellême in Perche (Maine), tailor's assistant, worked for S. Hubert, master tailor, on rue Saint-Martin and lodged in a boardinghouse on rue Jean de l'Epine.

He went to the Tuileries this evening to walk. He goes there from time to time. He has been given over to the debauchery of men since his youth, in his native region, but has not surrendered himself to it since 18 April. He has been in Paris for many years. He asked a man he met in the Tuileries if they whistled for closing. They then walked together, but without doing or saying anything wrong. /U/
C: W&R

90. Monday, 13 June 1785, 8:30 pm–4:00 am
PP: southern boulevards,[16] Comédie Française and environs, OP

I: 10:45. A known pederast, who cruised every evening here and in other suspect places, picked up several men under the arcades of the Comédie

Française and chatted with one of them for a long time as they walked along the stones. When he realized he was about to be arrested, he threw himself on a woman who passed by with her husband and shouted "to arouse the populace."

Pierre François Gout de la Brande, 44, native of Pons in Saintonge, priest in the diocese of Saintes, doctor of the collège de Navarre,[17] former canon of the cathedral of Tours, had lived at 25, rue de Tournon for more than a year.

He has been given over to the debauchery of men since the time he was in secondary school. He goes to walk around the Comédie Française in the evening. When he meets some man, he amuses himself with him. He does not, however, have a confirmed taste for this. This evening he was accosted by a man who tried to stroke him, which he refused. He likes women more than men. Seeing that several persons were ready to fall upon him and arrest him, he in truth grabbed a woman who was near him to shelter himself from those who wished to arrest him. /X/
C: Conducted to the lieutenant general, who ordered him released after verification of his identity

I: Around the same time, in the same place, two men loitered in the most suspect manner and picked up men to whom they made "propositions about pederasty."

Jean Auberger, 17, native of Paris, apprentice chez S. Mercier, royal binder, on rue de Beauvais near the Louvre, lived in a boardinghouse on rue Saint-Jean de Beauvais.

He was taking his route when he was arrested. He did not walk either under the arcades or near the Comédie Française or among the stones and did not speak to anyone. /U/
C: P

Jean Guillaume Despan, 50, native of Toulouse (Languedoc), former shopkeeper in Cap Français in Saint-Domingue, in Paris for a lawsuit, lodged chez Breton, who rented furnished rooms on rue de Vaugirard near rue des Fossés de M. le Prince.

He has been given over to pederasty on occasion since his return to Paris. He was debauched into it when he was in secondary school. He was much given over to it three years ago and paid men who lent themselves to him but

does not know any of them. He has not amused himself at it for about three years. As he went home this evening and passed under the arcades of the Comédie Française, he was accosted by a man with whom he surrendered to this vice three years ago, to whom he gave money at the time. This evening he suggested that they walk, but he, the deponent, said he gave this up three years ago. As they talked, he, the deponent, was arrested, and the other man escaped. /Dispan/
C: P

91. Thursday, 16 June 1785, 10:45 pm
I: A young man loitered in the Tuileries with the marquis de Soyécourt,[18] a notorious pederast, a week ago, in the most suspect manner, and again tonight, since 8:30, in the most suspect pathways. They sat down on a bench in the "pathway of sighs," where they appeared to fondle themselves. After an observer disturbed them, they went to one of the alleys near the terrace of the Feuillants and masturbated independently. They left together and parted in the courtyard of the riding school. The marquis returned to the garden. The young man ran off and, as he was arrested, tried to conceal money in his fob pocket. An older man loitered in the most suspect manner and picked up a man to whom he made remarks about pederasty and with whom he stroked.

Alexisanne Le Gendre, 18, native of Angers (Brittany), law student, clerk boarded with Messire Gelhay, attorney in the Parlement, had lived at his residence on rue du Four in faubourg Saint-Honoré for eight to nine months.

He left his attorney's place about 8:00 this evening and went to walk in the Tuileries, at first on the terrace on the side of the water, where he was accosted by a tall man unknown to him, who wished him good evening. He replied he did not have the honor to know him. This man said that this made no difference and that he wished to make his acquaintance in walking with him. They walked together, and this gentleman took him, the deponent, by the arm, and asked him many questions about his situation, family, fortune, and what his father had given him. He, the deponent, did not wish to tell him the truth and told him that his father lives in the provinces, that he has an uncle, haberdasher, in Paris, and, +however, that his father is S. Legendre, broker, who lives on rue de la Chaussée d'Antin, opposite rue des Mathurins.+ He, the deponent, also asked him some questions about his situation, but he told him nothing except that he lives not far from the Tuileries and is going to leave for his estate in Picardy. This man had them sit down on three different benches, and on the

last one he tried to stroke him, the deponent, who told him to stop because it was very indecent. He, the deponent, got up to leave. The man followed him as far as the passage of the courtyard of the stables, where, in parting, he asked him, the deponent, if he would come to walk in the Tuileries again. He replied he knew nothing about it and would not promise to do so. He started to run to return to his father's place for supper, since it had struck ten. He has never walked with this gentleman on other days and is not given over to the debauchery of men. Around a [missing word] ago he had a more or less similar encounter in the Palais Royal garden with a man who tried to speak to him, but he refused it. The man today did not talk to him at all about this debauchery before he tried to stroke him. /Legendre/
C: W&R

Jean Guillaume Guillaumet, 52, native of Paris, sold small wares and canes in the streets and lived on rue du Faubourg Montmartre.

In the Tuileries garden this evening he met a man unknown to him, whom he had never seen, with whom he walked and talked about the debauchery of men. He, the deponent, told him that at the age of thirteen, in the church in the Temple, a tall man shoved his hand into his breeches and polluted [masturbated] him. He, the deponent, suggested to him that they sit down, and the man did not wish to. He, the deponent, also asked him if he had an erection. He admits that if this man had wanted to amuse himself, he, the deponent, would have had the weakness to masturbate independently with him, but the man did not want to amuse himself in the Tuileries and suggested that they go amuse themselves in an alley. He, the deponent, accepted, they left together to go there, and he, the deponent, was arrested. /guillaumet/
C: P

92. Friday, 17 June 1785, 11:00 pm
I: Two men loitered in the Tuileries for a very long time, picked up men, and talked to them about pederasty. One of them, lame, agreed to go sleep with a man he had accosted. The other had loitered and picked up men every day since Tuesday.

Claude Michelot, 22, native of Leurville near Joinville (Champagne), limonadier's assistant, unemployed for fourteen months, lived in a furnished room chez the wine vendor at The Green Bars on rue de Gesvres.

He went to the Tuileries this evening to walk and met a man unknown to him, accosted him, walked with him, and asked him several questions to find out if he has a special female or male friend. He asked him if he could receive someone at his place. He, the deponent, replied no because his room is too small. The man suggested that he go sleep with him. He, the deponent, replied that he would like to do so. They left together. He, the deponent, was arrested, and the other escaped. He has never amused himself with men. /C Michilot/
C: W&R

Charles Basse, 22, native of Mondovì in Piedmont (Italy), shoemaker's assistant chez S. Louis, lived at his residence on rue Troussevache.

He has gone to the Tuileries garden after his work is finished every day for three or four days {months} to walk until 10:00. This evening he spoke to a wigmaker he met there, with whom he had spoken in the garden several days ago. They did nothing wrong. He, the deponent, is not given over to the debauchery of men and has never surrendered himself to it. /Basso/
C: P

93. Tuesday, 21 June 1785, 8:30 pm–2:00 am
PP: northern boulevards, Coal-Box, small streets and cul-de-sacs off the boulevards, quays, OP

I: 10:00. A man loitered in the Coal-Box in the most suspect manner and accosted an observer, whom he sought to pick up.

10:30. A man who cruised in the Coal-Box and on the boulevards in the evening loitered in the most suspect manner, accosted an observer, and asked him "if there were lots of people out for trade."

11:45. A known pederast caught in the act in cul-de-sac Saint-Fiacre resisted, and the other man escaped arrest.

12:00. A man loitered on boulevard de Richelieu in the most suspect manner, accosted an observer, and asked to go to his place.

Pierre de la Voyepierre,[19] 43, native of Ruelle (Saintonge), lord of Bauzeville and other places, governor and royal lieutenant of the city of Guéret in Marche, lived on rue de Popincourt. At first he "took the tone of a man of importance, said he was a man of rank, and was not taken in the act." Then he "changed his tone and said he did not have a title."

He was on his way home and took some turns because he feared some men he had seen were thieves. /X/
C: W&R

Jean Baptiste Racine, 48, native of Nonileau (?) in Artois, domestic of Mme de Vaux, lived at her residence on rue Pastourelle.

He came from that street and went to meet his employer chez S. de Vaux, her son, on rue Saint-Gilles and took this route to walk a bit, since he was not supposed to call for his employer until 11:00. He did not speak to anyone, then said he did not talk about trade and only asked a man he does not know, "Are there lots of people walking there?"[20] /U/
C: W&R

Joseph Anne Corberon, 26, native of Paris, unemployed, lived chez M. de Harville on rue du Sentier.

He was debauched into pederasty around five years ago in the Palais Royal by a young man he does not know. Since then he has surrendered himself to it several times on the boulevards and in the Champs-Elysées, always with persons he does not know. He has consummated the crime once in the passive role. At the time when he was arrested, he was amusing himself at masturbating independently with a man he does not know. /X/
C: P

Barthélemy Pingan, 41, native of Mortefontaine in the diocese of Senlis (Lorraine), cook chez de Rauque, who kept an eating house, lived at his residence at the England boardinghouse on rue Saint-Honoré.

He spoke to someone he does not know on the boulevard and does not know what they said, but he did not ask him to go to his place. Moreover, he appeared drunk to us. /U/
C: W&R

94. Wednesday, 22 June 1785, 11:00 pm
I: A man loitered in the Tuileries and accosted men. Another loitered in the most suspect manner and picked up men, including one to whom he made remarks about pederasty. They agreed to go amuse themselves.

Claude, comte de Beauharnais,[21] 28, native of La Rochelle (Aunis), officer in the French Guards, lived on rue Notre-Dame-des-Victoires.

He went to the end of the terrace in the Tuileries along the water to see the illumination of the hôtel de Montmorency on the quay. Then he crossed the garden and left through the courtyard of the riding school, but he did not accost or speak to anyone and is not at all given over to pederasty. /le comte de Beauharnais/
C: W&R

Jean Gouldhorn, 37, native of Emden in Prussia (Germany), personal valet of M. de Fitzhemberg, Englishman, lodged at the Royal Park boardinghouse on rue du Colombier.

He went to walk under the trees in the Tuileries garden. A man who passed before him several times accosted him and suggested that he go with him. He told him he had two pretty girls, but they did not talk about the debauchery of men. He is not given over to it. He indeed offered three écus of six livres when he was arrested for them to let him go because he would lose his position if he returned too late. /Gouldhorn/
C: W&R

95. Thursday, 23 June, 1:15 am
I: Daquin, exiled on 20 June 1784, loitered on quai de l'Ecole.

Laurent Daquin, said he had nothing to say and declined to answer any questions. /X/
C: P

96. Thursday, 23 June 1785, 2:00 pm
I: Thomas, son of a domestic, former soldier, upholsterer's assistant, gave himself over to pederasty for several years, played the active and passive roles for pay, cruised everywhere, and staged parties. He loitered in the Palais Royal around noon for several days, picked up respectable men, and followed them until they gave him money.

Jacques François Thomas, 20, native of Paris, parish Saint-Gervais (4th arr.), former soldier in the Artois regiment, unemployed upholsterer's assistant, lived with his mother, married to a domestic of the marquis de Pracomtal,[22] on rue de Grenelle opposite rue de la Chaise.

He has known Toussaint, given over to pederasty, for four years. They have been friends since that time, and they go together every day. A number

of times they have squandered the money that Toussaint earned from this debauchery. He, the deponent, has amused himself only with Toussaint, with whom he has slept three or four times. He was with him in Draveil[23] chez the marquis de Fautereau,[24] who gave five louis to Toussaint, who gave forty livres to him, the deponent, and forty livres to Monin. He, the deponent, gave the forty livres back to Toussaint. /X/
C: P

97. Monday, 27 June 1785, 7:00 pm–2:00 am
PP: environs of the Comédie Française, environs and exits of the Tuileries, quays, OP

I: Two men arrested before picked each other up in the Tuileries. Batteny, arrested in the Coal-Box on 7 September 1784,[25] cruised in the Tuileries and Palais Royal. Badarou, arrested and imprisoned on 6 March (#36), had promised not to frequent suspect places on pain of detention in Bicêtre. Another man loitered in the garden. Another young man, given over to pederasty, loitered habitually in the stoneyard.

Pierre Badarou, 15½, native of Amiens (Picardy), apprentice saddler, lived with his father, locksmith, on rue de Cléry. When he was arrested, he put his earrings in his pockets.

He was in the Tuileries, and the man arrested with him suggested that he go bathe[26] with him. He, the deponent, told him it was too late, but the man insisted and told him it would take them only a quarter of an hour. In leaving to go there they were arrested. Since he left prison, it has happened to him to amuse himself several times, in various places, with persons he does not know. /badaru/
C: P

Camille Cassina, 30, native of Venice (Italy), secretary of the Venetian ambassador,[27] lived at his townhouse on the boulevard near the Saint-Martin gate.
Asked if he had not already been arrested in the act of pederasty on 7 September in the spot called the Coal-Box.
Said yes.
Asked why he said his name was Jean Baptiste Batteny on that date and gives another name today and why, likewise, he has changed his title. The

first time he said he was the ambassador's secretary.[28] What are his true name and title?

Replied that the first time he disguised his name, which is Camille Cassina, and that he is indeed the ambassador's secretary.

Asked why, after promising to correct himself of this vice and not to visit suspect places anymore, he continues in this way. He is seen cruising daily in the Tuileries garden and Palais Royal at night.

Replied it is from habit and temperament, but he hopes he will correct himself of it.

Asked if he picked up the young man arrested with him in the Tuileries this evening and suggested to him that he go bathe with him, with the design of amusing himself.

Replied he indeed suggested to the man that they go bathe together. After some objections the man made, they left to bathe. They were arrested as they made their way. His design was to amuse himself with him and pay him. They had with them a third man he knows from amusing himself with him, whose name he does not know. He was of their party and fled at the moment they were arrested.

After his interrogation and his replies were read to him, he said they contain the truth, reaffirmed them, and he signed. /Cascina/
C: Conducted to the lieutenant general, who had him released

Christian Benevald, 26, native of Elfeld in the principality of Deux-Ponts (Germany), assistant of S. Dufour, master shoemaker, lived at his residence on rue Beaurepaire.

He is not given over to pederasty. /U/
C: W&R

Pierre Baillaux, 14, native of Paris, apprentice engraver on metal of S. Deletang in the enclosure of Saint-Jean de Latran, lived chez his brother-in-law Gravé, master shoemaker, on rue Saint-Jacques.

Two to three months ago a girl he did not know accosted him at Saint-Jean de Latran one Sunday about 10:00 am and asked him if he wanted to go with her. She led him to cul-de-sac des Quatre Vents, to the first door on the left, where there are three steps to climb. A man in a dressing gown or levite appeared, and this girl told him, speaking of him, the deponent, "Here is a young man as you desired." This man told him he could do nothing for

this, stroked his cheek with his hand, gave him three livres, and told him to come back during the week. As they left the girl grabbed the écu, kept it, handed him, the deponent, twelve sols, and said that was enough for what he had done. He went two more times to the residence of this man, who did nothing but stroke his face with his hand and gave him, one time, twenty-four sols and, the other time, eleven sols. He did not return there again. Ten days ago a mason he does not know led him to a demolished building behind the first barrier in Vaugirard[29] [15th arr.] and took his pleasure with him from behind, which hurt him so much he suffered from it for five days. /X/
C: P

98. Thursday, 30 June 1785, 8:30 pm–2:00 am
PP: exits of the Tuileries, place Louis XV, quays, OP

I: After 10:00. A man loitered in the Tuileries for a long time in the most suspect manner, picked up a man, took several turns and then sat down on a bench with him, made remarks about pederasty, and talked about going to sleep together in order to amuse themselves more comfortably. They appeared to stroke mutually. Another man, who frequented the garden in the evening and cruised "very openly," picked up several men.

Joseph Maille, 33, native of Paris, former journeyman cooper, domestic at the Hôtel-Dieu until two days ago, lodged chez a sword-furbisher on rue Saint-Honoré opposite the Commerce Café.

He used to be a stockman at the Pitié [hospital],[30] which he left around six years ago for saying silly things to a nun. He was indeed picked up in the Tuileries by a man with whom he sat down. They chatted together but did not do anything wrong at all. It is the first time this has happened to him. /U/
C: P

Pierre Chaudé, 18, native of Auxerre (Burgundy), tailor, unemployed for three weeks, without a residence, lodged with relatives.

It is out of need that he was cruising in the Tuileries today to earn something. A short young man who had been a jockey, whose name and address he does not know, with whom he amused himself several times, taught him he could earn something in the Tuileries. A gentleman picked him up there this evening. They sat down on chairs and fondled. This man suggested that he go have supper and sleep with him. /U/
C: P

JULY

99. Friday, 1 July 1785, 11:30 pm
I: A man loitered in the most suspect pathways and manner in the Tuileries, accosted a man, sat down with him, and made remarks about pederasty to him. They seemed to masturbate independently.

Denis de Suraune, 32, native of Saint-Germain-en-Laye (Ile-de-France), apprentice goldsmith of S. Duret in the Palais Royal, resided with Letort, journeyman cartwright, chez the grocer on rue de Richelieu opposite the small passage into the Palais.

He was debauched into pederasty three or four months ago by a wine vendor's assistant who is named Delbaut and is presently in the provinces. He ran the Gold Cross Café on rue des Moineaux in Butte Saint-Roch. He has surrendered himself to this debauchery with four other persons unknown to him in the Gold Cross Café. Having heard it said one goes to the Tuileries for this, he went there this evening and met a man unknown to him. They sat down on chairs and masturbated independently. This man suggested to him that he go sleep with him on rue Dauphine, where he told him he lives, but he, the deponent, refused. /de suraune/
C: P

100. Saturday, 2 July 1785, 9:45 pm
I: Foucault, called the Dragon, "intimately connected" with the late Ricard, a notorious pederast, given over to pederasty, cruised every day on the boulevards, the Half-Moon, in the Coal-Box, or the Tuileries. He loitered this evening in the most suspect pathways in the garden, accosted a man with whom he took several turns, and talked about pederasty.

Thomas Foucault, 31, native of Montereau-Fault-Yonne (Ile-de-France), secondhand dealer, lived on rue des Juifs at the corner of cul-de-sac Coquerel.

Coming back from Vaugirard with a wigmaker's assistant and secondhand dealer, whose name and address he does not know, but knows he had lived on rue Saint-Antoine, they met a man unknown to him, whom he has been with. They had supper together. He does not know where, in what street.

He did not enter the Tuileries, did nothing wrong, and is not given over to pederasty. He knew Ricard, who was given over to it, who was killed at his place. /U/
C: P

I: Two men accosted each other in the Champs-Elysées and took two or three turns. They loitered in the Tuileries, arm in arm, and took several turns there.

Charles Molumard, 23, native of Digne in Provence, unemployed wigmaker's assistant, lodged at the Grand Dauphin on place de Grève.

About 7:00 this evening he went to see his friend S. Emery, master wigmaker. They were boys together in Rouen. They went to walk together in the Champs[-Elysées], came back through the Tuileries, and were going to have supper chez Emery. /molumard/
C: W&R

Jean Marie Renezé, called Emery, 23, native of Belle-Ile-en-Mer (Brittany), master wigmaker, lived on rue de Richelieu at the corner of rue Neuve des Petits Champs.

He went to walk with his friend Molumard, wigmaker's assistant, whom he knew in Rouen, and then came through the Tuileries to go have supper with him at his place. They had no bad intention. /Renezé called Emery/
C: W&R

101. **Monday, 4 July 1785, 8:30 pm–2:00 am**
PP: northern boulevards, Coal-Box, marshy ground between rue Basse du Temple and La Courtille, small streets and cul-de-sacs off the boulevards, OP

I: 10:00. A man who surrendered himself to pederasty loitered for a long time on the boulevard and accosted another man. They went down to the Coal-Box, withdrew into remote corners, and seemed to stroke themselves. Two other men went down to the Coal-Box and loitered there for a long time. One of them escaped arrest.

10:30. A man known for cruising on the boulevard and in the Tuileries loitered around an observer on boulevard du Pont aux Choux and tried to shove his hand into his breeches.

Simon Le Lief, 23, native of Paris, gauze worker, lived at the Arts boardinghouse on rue du Faubourg Saint-Martin.

He indeed went down from the parapet of the boulevard to the Coal-Box with a man he does not know to amuse themselves together. They only touched themselves. They were disturbed two different times by the approach of others. It is the first time this has happened to him. /U/
C: P

Etienne Husson, 19, native of Paris, public coachman, lived chez Larue, wine vendor on rue de Charonne. He appeared to be drunk and in no state to account for his conduct. /U/
C: W&R

Jacques LeTellier, 62–63, native of Crevecoeur in the diocese of Beauvais (Ile-de-France), former wine vendor, lived off a small investment "without doing anything" and lodged chez Lefevre, who rented rooms on rue de la Tannerie. His outfit suggested indigence.

He is involved in a lawsuit with his wife, who is in the convent[1] in Saint-Mandé [partly in the 12th arr.]. He walked on the boulevard, was not with anyone, and did not do anything wrong. /U/
C: W&R

102. Wednesday, 6 July 1785, 10:00 pm
I: Two men loitered alone in the Tuileries, picked each other up, walked together under the thick trees, and left together.

Michel Alexandre Duperrier, 39, native of Dangu near Gisors (Normandy), domestic of S. Cabany, American, lived at his residence at the candle store on rue Platrière.

He went to serve dinner to his master at the hôtel d'Aligre on rue Saint-Honoré [no. 121–25]. He left about 8:00 pm and went to walk in the Tuileries. He indeed sat down on a chair there, and the man arrested with him came and sat next to him and spoke to him. He told him he was out of work, and it was most unfortunate for him. When he accosted him, they talked about the weather. He, the deponent, does not know his name, status, or address. He, the deponent, got up to leave, and the other man followed him. He is not given over to the vice of liking men. He does not know if the man

arrested with him is given over to it, but he did not speak to him about it. /Duperrier/
C: W&R

Pierre Roberval, 17, native of Saverne in Picardy, wallpaper worker, lodged chez Baillon, wallpaper printer, chez the wigmaker on rue de la Parcheminerie.[2]

He went to walk on the quays and in the Tuileries this evening. He saw a seated man and went to sit down near him. A moment later he got up to go away. The other asked him, "Are you leaving already?" It is true he told him he had no work, as, in fact, he has none. It is Baillon who feeds him and gives him money. He is not given over to liking men. He goes to the Tuileries very often in the evening and does nothing wrong there. /U/
C: W&R

103. Thursday, 7 July 1785, 11:30 pm
I: A man loitered in the most suspect manner in the Tuileries, took several turns, sat down several times, and walked in the most suspect places.

Nicolas Roche, 18, native of Rochefort in Beauce (Maine-et-Loire), nicknamed La Roche and Saint-Louis, unemployed domestic, lodged with his brother at 17, rue Quincampoix.

He went to the Tuileries to walk, spoke to no one there, took two turns, and walked. He is not inclined to like men. /U/
C: W&R

104. Saturday, 9 July 1785, 8:30 pm–2:30 am
PP: Champs-Elysées, Cours de la Reine, stone port, site of the Colosseum, place Louis XV, northern boulevards, small streets and cul-de-sacs off the boulevards, OP

I: 11:30. A confirmed pederast who frequented suspect places loitered on boulevard Montmartre, accosted a man, and withdrew with him into rue Saint-Fiacre, where they took several turns. The first man asked the second, "Do you have crystalline [syphilis]? You appear quite changed to me. Let's see, I'll fondle your ass. It's a long time since we've done this together." He made several other remarks about pederasty.

Midnight. A man known for cruising often on the boulevards loitered on rue de Richelieu, picked up an observer, with whom he tried to strike up a conversation, then a man with whom he took several turns, who fled at the sight of observers.

Pierre Charles Vangette, 50, native of Paris, mattress carder, lived chez the basketmaker on rue du Vertbois.

He encountered a man whose name he does not know, whom he used to know, who accosted him and took him by the arm. They walked on the boulevards and rue Saint-Fiacre. He did not wish to discuss the subject of their conversation. /U/
C: P

Louis Sébastien David, 37, shoemaker, lived on cul-de-sac Basfour off rue Saint-Denis.

He was waiting on the boulevard for his wife, who worked chez an upholsterer on rue Favart, where she had to remain until midnight. A man he does not know told him the weather was fine when he accosted him. He did not speak to him. /U/
C: W&R

105. Monday, 11 July 1785, 11:00 pm
I: A pederast who had amused himself on various occasions in the Tuileries picked up men and amused himself with one at the foot of a tree.

Jacques François Le Lièvre, 41, native of Saint-Eugène in the diocese of Lisieux (Normandy), who sold wine in taverns outside the city but had done nothing for six weeks. He lived chez Thevost, mason and tavernkeeper, in Little Poland.

He is not given over to liking men. He went to the Tuileries and sat down on a chair. Another man came to sit near him and said he knew him. They did nothing wrong. As he left he was arrested. He has gone to the Tuileries often in the evening for six weeks. /Le Lievre/
C: P

106. Tuesday, 12 July 1785, 11:00 pm
I: One man amused himself in the Tuileries "with three different men in succession." Another, given over to pederasty, who "had himself paid for his obligingness," loitered in the garden and asked "to play a john [*miché*]."

François Girard, 32, native of Saumur in Anjou, personal valet of Messire Perrinet de Thauvenay, receiver general of finances,[3] currently in Germany, lived at his residence on rue du Cherche Midi.

After having supper at the Image of Saint Peter on rue de Clichy,[4] he went to the Tuileries, where he met a man unknown to him, with whom he talked about rain and fine weather. He left by way of the Carousel gate instead of the Pont Royal gate because he was chattering with this man. He admits he is given over to the debauchery of men and was debauched into it by a master he had served, who is no longer in Paris, who is the comte du Roure, now deceased,[5] who debauched him around ten years ago. He lived at his residence for three years. He does not usually go to the Tuileries in the evening, but he went there this evening because he had had something to drink. Nothing but touching happened between him and the man. He does not amuse himself often at this vice and does not know any of the persons with whom he has amused himself. /Girard/
C: P

Pierre François Dorat, 19, native of Bergues near Dunkerque (Flanders), journeyman cooper "doing nothing" during his six months in Paris, lodged at the Artois boardinghouse on rue Tireboudin.

He surrendered himself to pederasty only six days ago. He has been in the Tuileries, where he has earned around six livres from several persons. One wanted to put it into him in the Tuileries a week ago, but he, the deponent, did not want it. That man gave him {twenty-four sols, although he had promised him} a small écu he had promised him in the Palais Royal garden, where he had met him. He has also amused himself in this way with another who gave him twenty-four sols and others who gave him eighteen sols or twelve sols. He does not know any of them. He did not meet anyone in the Tuileries this evening from whom he could have gotten money, although he went there for that purpose. /U/
C: P

107. Wednesday, 13 July 1785, 11:30 pm
I: Dittely, a known pederast, loitered in the Tuileries for several days, and picked up men, including one with whom he left the garden after making remarks about pederasty. Another man cruised there and picked up men, including one he agreed to dine and sleep with for six livres. A known

pederast, previously arrested and imprisoned, loitered in the Palais Royal and picked up a man there.

Samuel Antoine Dittely Petit, 31, native of Blois (Orléanais), former soldier in the Agenais regiment in Port-au-Prince (capital of Haiti), unemployed, lodged with LeClerc, silkworker, at the Arts boardinghouse on rue Saint-Denis in faubourg Saint-Martin. He "sleeps with" LeClerc, his "friend and boy," who had lodged him for nothing since he came to Paris three months ago and made his acquaintance.

Coming back from the Champs-Elysées, he entered the Tuileries and met a man unknown to him who placed his hand on his breeches, which he pushed away. This man tried again and suggested that they go drink a bottle of wine in his room. He, the deponent, consented, left with him, and was arrested. He is not given over to the vice of liking men. It is true he surrendered to the vice of pederasty with his sergeant, named Bertrand, when he was in the Béarn regiment and consummated this crime with him in the passive role. /Dittely/
C: P

Jean Baptiste Manoury, 27, native of Franconville in Beauce (Ile-de-France), tailor's assistant, did not work today and lived chez Simon, shoemaker, who rented rooms on rue de Seine in faubourg Saint-Germain.

Coming back from the Champs-Elysées this evening, he entered the Tuileries, where he met a man unknown to him, spoke to him about libertinage with men. He left with this man and was arrested in leaving, but he did nothing wrong and is not given over to the vice of liking men. /U/
C: W&R

Nicolas Mercier, 28, native of Reims (Champagne), domestic cook, unemployed for three weeks, lodged chez a baker on rue Mouffetard near Saint-Médard (no. 141). He had lived there for three weeks there "with and in the room of" Raimond, pawnshop worker, "with whom he sleeps," who lodged him without charge "out of friendship." He had "an extremely narrow waist" and was dressed in "the costume of pederasts" (wide cravat, rosettes on shoes, levite with two wide collars).

He is not given over to pederasty. He has been in the Tuileries and the Palais Royal in the evening sometimes and was in both gardens this evening. As he sat on a chair in the Palais Royal garden this evening, a man unknown

to him came to sit down near him and suggested to him that he go have supper with him, which he refused. They left together, and the man took him by the arm. He was arrested in leaving. /U/
C: P

108. Thursday, 14 July 1785, 10:00 pm–2:30 am
PP: exits of the Palais Royal, quays, OP

I: 11:30. A known pederast, who often loitered and cruised in the Tuileries and Palais Royal, loitered in the most suspect manner in the Palais Royal and picked up a man with whom he sat down and took a turn. He made remarks about pederasty, and they stroked mutually. Another known pederast often cruised in the same garden in the evening and "had himself paid for his obligingness." He picked up men on the 8th and 12th and left with them. On the 8th they amused themselves together under a porte-cochère in rue de l'Oratoire. This evening he loitered in the most suspect manner and picked up men, including one to whom he talked about going to sleep together.

Midnight. A man who cruised in all the suspect places and "made money from his obligingness" picked up several men.

André Joseph Foriat, 21, native of Paris, farrier, lived with his father-in-law, farrier of the duc de Chartres,[6] on rue Saint-Thomas-du-Louvre.

He was in the Palais Royal garden, and a man he does not know accosted him and asked him who he is. He told him he is from Fontainebleau, is a locksmith, and lives on rue de Richelieu. He walked with this man, but they did not make indecent remarks and did not stroke. /X/

Foriat's mother showed up, stated that "she finds it hard to believe he is guilty of what he is accused of," requested his release, and promised he would not go out after supper.
C: W&R

André Bourgot, 21, native of Nancy (Lorraine), day laborer, lived on rue de Grenelle opposite the fountain,[7] in faubourg Saint-Germain.

He came from doing errands in place des Victoires and returned through the Palais Royal. He did not speak to anyone. He did not wish to answer questions. /U/
C: P

Jean Baptiste Gavard, 19, native of Paris, former domestic, unemployed wigmaker's assistant, lodged on rue Soly.

He was debauched into pederasty a year ago by a man who picked him up in the Palais Royal garden, with whom he left and went into an alley where he masturbated the man, who gave him thirty livres in the alley off rue du Petit Reposoir. He did not wish to answer any questions. /U/
C: P

109. Friday, 15 July 1785, 10:30 pm
I: Two men loitered in the Tuileries, picked up men there, and made remarks about pederasty.

Jacques Bertre, 42, native of Lisieux (Normandy), flannel vendor, lived on rue Grande Couture in Lisieux. In Paris for a week, he lodged in a furnished room chez a wigmaker on rue de Richelieu.

Coming back from Chaillot, he entered the Tuileries garden and walked under the trees. He met a man whom he asked what time it was, who replied it was nearly 9:00. He then walked a bit with him, then met another whom, to tell the truth, he took by the arm, although he does not know him, and asked the way to go to rue de Richelieu. He replied he would take him there. They left together, with him, the deponent, holding the other by the arm, and he was arrested. This evening is the second time he went to the Tuileries on this trip. He is not given over to the vice of liking men. He accosted these two men without bad intentions. /Bertre/
C: P

Pierre Etienne Papelard, 46, native of Paris, clerk in the office of Messire Bonnaire de Forges, intendant of finances,[8] lived on passage de la Cage off rue Traînée at the central market.

He went to the Tuileries this evening to take the air and was accosted there by a man unknown to him with whom he conversed and walked. The man spoke to him about the debauchery of men, told him he lives on rue des Boucheries Saint-Honoré, and urged him to go to his room. He feigned to consent. They left, with the man holding him by the arm, and he was arrested. He suspected this man wanted to rob him because in 1775 or 1776, in the same garden, one of two men greeted him and made the same remarks to him. They first took his buckles and then conducted him to his place, made

him give them twelve livres, and gave him back his buckles. He assumed he was to be released to the inspector who made arrests in the garden, and it depended only on them. He spoke to one of them about having him arrested and ruined. It is true he has had the misfortune to be given over to gambling for five or six years. Having ruined himself, he is in no state to go after women. He has surrendered himself to the vice of pederasty in the Tuileries and masturbated independently with persons he met there. He has not gone further in this debauchery than he did this evening. He promises not to fall back into it anymore and to correct himself of it. /P E Parelart/
C: W&R

110. **Saturday, 16 July 1785 11:00 pm**
I: A man in a frock coat loitered in the most suspect manner in the Tuileries, picked up two others, and stroked them. Another loitered, picked up a man, and talked to him about pederasty.

Jean Noël César Taillardant, 36, native of Samer in the diocese of Boulogne-sur-Mer (Picardy), monk of the (Brothers of) Charity[9] and surgeon at the hospice[10] in Petit Montrouge (14th arr.), lived there. He wore a levite and breeches of brown nankeen (cotton cloth)and a wide cravat.

He had nothing in ecclesiastical garb and went out this evening in secular garb. He went first to take a turn in the Champs-Elysées, then in the Tuileries, where he was accosted first by a man who only stroked him through the breeches, then by another who did the same and suggested to him that he go to his place. As he left with him, he was arrested, but did nothing else wrong. He left the monastery and was in the Tuileries around 6:30 to go chez Rouby, shoemaker for women on rue du Petit Reposoir, to find out if his, the deponent's, sister, who was supposed to arrive in Paris, had arrived. On the way he changed his mind and expected to come home at 11:00. /Epiphane Taillardant/
C: R in the custody of Desurbois, who was instructed to conduct him to his monastery

Jacques Foloppe, 38, native of Allainville in pays de Caux (Normandy), doorman of a house on rue des Petits Champs, lived there.

He went to walk this evening in the Champs-Elysées and Tuileries garden. He heard 9:30 strike and left to go home. In the Tuileries he met a

man unknown to him with whom he talked about the debauchery of men with each other. He has had the weakness to surrender himself to this debauchery for around a month. He was picked up in the Tuileries garden and amused himself [with another man] at fondling themselves independently in the Tuileries garden, for the first time two months ago. The man he met this evening told him he lives at 20, rue des Boucheries Saint-Honoré, where he suggested that he go with him. He was arrested in leaving. He does not know this man or any of the others with whom he has amused himself in the Tuileries garden. /folope/
C: P

111. **Monday, 18 July 1785, 11:00 pm**
I: Three men loitered in the most suspect places and manner in the Tuileries and picked up men. Two of them made remarks about pederasty.

Charles Christophe Le Vise de Montigny, 18, native of Paris, engraver on metal, then apprentice jeweler, currently unemployed, lodged at the Artois boardinghouse on rue Ventadour.

He went to walk in the Tuileries this evening and was accosted there by a short man dressed in a silk jacket who urged him to walk with him, made remarks to him about the debauchery of men together, urged him to go with him to his room to amuse themselves, and promised to give him two écus of six livres. He, the deponent, consented to everything he said but, however, without having ever surrendered himself to this vice. He was arrested in leaving with this man. /levise de Montigny/
C: W&R

François Desmarteaux, 16½, native of Severans in Franche-Comté, domestic, unemployed for three months, lived on rue Montmartre.

Coming back this evening from bathing at the stone port, he entered the Tuileries with his cousin Desmarteaux, who left him in the garden. He was accosted by a bowed man who offered to give him six livres to go to his room, which he, the deponent, refused. He even told him it was frightful and did not wish to leave with him. He is not given over to the debauchery of men. Another time he met another man in the Palais Royal garden who also wanted to take him to his place, which he did not wish to do. /francois Damartaux/
C: W&R

Louis Jean Baptiste Guénin, 22, native of Troyes in Champagne, tailor's assistant, without work today, lodged chez widow Rousseau, who rented furnished rooms to tailor's assistants on place de Grève.[11]

He went to walk in the Tuileries garden at 9:15 and met a man unknown to him, urged him to walk with him, which he did until after 10:30. They did nothing wrong and did not talk at all about debauchery, except that this man asked him if he had a mistress. He was arrested in leaving with this man, without knowing why. /Guenin/
C: W&R

112. Tuesday, 19 July 1785, 11:30 pm
I: A man loitered in the Tuileries and picked up a man with whom he took several turns and to whom he made remarks about pederasty.

Philippe Berneron, 21, native of Saint-Benoît-du-Sault in Berry, unemployed tailor's assistant, lodged at the Mint boardinghouse on rue Béthisy.

He goes to the Tuileries sometimes but with his friends and has never been there in the evening except for today. He was drunk and went there at 8:30 pm, lay down on the grass, and just dozed. A man unknown to him accosted him and urged him to walk with him, which he did. This man asked him many questions, suggested that he go with him to the Palais Royal, and spoke to him about the debauchery of men. As he left with him, he was arrested and does not know why. He did nothing wrong, is not at all given over to the debauchery of men, and has never surrendered himself to it. /philippe Berneron/
C: W&R

113. Wednesday, 20 July 1785, 11:00 pm
I: One known pederast on record loitered in the Luxembourg and picked up another, with whom he came to the Tuileries at 9:45. They walked together and sought to pick up men. Another man loitered for a long time in the Tuileries, in the most suspect places and manner, picked up several men, and stroked them.

Henry Louis Dallançon, 33, native of Paris, limonadier's assistant, unemployed since 12 June, lived at the Holy Spirit boardinghouse on rue du Chevet Saint-Landry.

He was debauched into the vice of pederasty around nine months ago by a man unknown to him who said he is a hairdresser, whose address he

does not know. He amused himself with this man and, since then, with several others in the Tuileries as well as the Luxembourg, but he does not know any of them. He has never made a profit from it. This evening in the Luxembourg garden he met the man who debauched him into this vice, who urged him to go to the Tuileries. He suggested to him that he go sleep with him, but he replied that he preferred to go to his room. /D'allançon/
C: P

Jean Missy, 32, native of Saint-Avold in Lorraine, assistant of Stoffel, master shoemaker, lived at his residence chez the apothecary on rue de Gesvres.
    He went out after supper to go walk in the Tuileries. He spoke to two men there about the debauchery of men. The second even suggested to him that he go to his place this evening, which he refused. He then suggested to him that he go there tomorrow, and he replied he could not do so. He has often been to the garden to walk after he has finished his work and had supper. He goes there without bad intentions. /U/
C: P

114. Saturday, 23 July 1785, 11:00 pm
I: A man loitered in the Tuileries and picked up men, including one who was urinating, whom he stroked. He then left with another man and returned with him. This man had loitered, picked up men, stroked some of them, and had them stroke him.

Benoît Morel, 22, native of Mions in Dauphiné, stocking worker, worked chez S. DeVaux, hosiery vendor on rue Saint-Sauveur, and lived with his cousin Bouillon chez S. Gras, baker, on rue du Temple opposite rue de Montmorency.
    He entered the Tuileries garden with his cousin after leaving his tailor on cul-de-sac du Coq. He entered, was on the terrace on the side of the château, and a man unknown to him accosted him and asked him what time it was. He, the deponent, told him it was 9:00. This man asked him what he does. He said he makes stockings. This man urged him to go to his place to give him two pairs of stockings to re-foot [and said] he did not live far. He left with him, and they went almost to the Carousel, where this man told him it had not yet struck time to go home, and he wished to take another turn. They reentered the courtyard, and he, the deponent, said he wished to leave. This man re-left the courtyard with him, and he, the deponent, was arrested. He had no other conversation with this man and is not

given over to the debauchery of men, to which he has never surrendered himself. /Morel/
C: P

Pierre Agneaux, 25, native of Vernon (Normandy), gardener's assistant, lodged on rue de Monsieur in faubourg Saint-Germain.

He was debauched into pederasty two years ago by Frédéric, domestic of Messire de Montesquieu's son. Since then he has surrendered himself to this vice, for which he has already been arrested in the Champs-Elysées a year ago and imprisoned. He does not know any of those with whom he has amused himself, except for Frédéric. He went to the Tuileries this evening with the intention of amusing himself. He chatted there with a man who stroked him, the deponent, at the foot of a tree. He, the deponent, did not do likewise with him. /pierre hagneaux/
C: P

115. Sunday, 24 July 1785, 11:00 pm
I: Two men loitered and cruised in the Tuileries, stroked men they picked up, and discussed pederasty. One, in a blue jacket and white breeches, sat down on a bench with his breeches down.

Charles de Ligny, 38, native of Compiègne (Ile-de-France), former haberdasher and tavernkeeper in Gamaches in Picardy, currently doing nothing, in Paris since Wednesday, lodged at an inn on rue des Cinq Diamants.

He was debauched into pederasty when he was young by a royal guard in the Luxembourg company formerly in Compiègne. He does not amuse himself often with men. He does not know the names or addresses of those with whom he has amused himself. He went to the Tuileries this evening and met a man unknown to him. They stroked themselves, and he then pulled up his breeches. The man suggested to him that he go to his place to amuse themselves. He, the deponent, left with him and was arrested. When he, the deponent, met him in the Tuileries, this man was making water, and he, the deponent, also made water next to him. They both fondled themselves. /celigny/
C: P

Antoine Daverdin, 13, native of Le Plessis-Evêque near Meaux in Brie (Ile-de-France), copper smelter, lived chez S. Du Channoy, wigmaker, on rue Jean Pain Mollet.

He went to the Tuileries this evening to walk, and a man unknown to him asked him what time it was. He replied that it was 9:00. He did not walk with this man until the moment of leaving. He did not sit down in the garden. He is not given over to the debauchery of men. He did not converse with the man. He came from the Champs-Elysées and only crossed the Tuileries garden in the central pathway. He goes to walk sometimes in the garden. /U/
C: P

116. Friday, 25 July 1785, 11:30 pm
I: A man loitered in the most suspect manner in the Tuileries, accosted and abandoned one man, and picked up another. They stroked mutually and conversed about pederasty. Another man loitered in the Mousetrap and appeared to seek "good luck."

Louis Fayet, 20, native of Versailles (Ile-de-France), domestic, unemployed for five months, lodged in a furnished room chez the locksmith on rue Etienne.
   Coming back from Boulogne, he entered the Tuileries and fell asleep there. Two men asked him what time it was, and he did not talk about anything else with them. He was debauched four to five years ago in Versailles by one François, who is dead, with whom he consummated the crime in the passive role. Around two months ago he went to rue Montmartre with a domestic, whose name he does not know, to his place at a limonadier's house. He also consummated the crime in the passive role with this domestic and slept with him. He has amused himself with several others he does not know on the boulevard and in the Tuileries garden. He has earned around fifteen livres from this in the Tuileries. The last man who accosted him this evening stroked him through his breeches. He was arrested in leaving with this man. /FAIIT/
C: P

Henry Piffault, 35, native of Melun (Ile-de-France), saddler's assistant, lived at the White Beard on rue de la Vannerie.
   He went down to the spot where he was arrested to do his business and had no other intention. He is not given over to the debauchery of men. /piffault/
C: W&R

117. Tuesday, 26 July 1785, 8:00 pm–1:00 am
PP: northern boulevards, Coal-Box, small streets and cul-de-sacs off the boulevards, OP

I: 9:45. A man loitered alone in the Coal-Box and then accosted a man who was urinating or pretending to do so. They struck up a conversation together, crossed the area, went behind a wall, appeared to look for an appropriate spot, finally sat down on the edge of a small rise, and appeared to stroke mutually. The first man resisted arrest, which allowed the second to escape.

Jean François Baillet, 21, native of Reims (Champagne), independent journeyman sword-furbisher, lived on rue de Lappe in faubourg Saint-Antoine.

He was alone when he was arrested. He did not speak to or accost anyone. Then he said it is true he walked with a man he does not know. They spoke about his situation and nothing else. Then he said this man made vile speeches to him, to which he replied nothing wrong. This man indeed stroked him through his breeches, but he did not do likewise to him. He was going to leave him because of his vile remarks when he was arrested. /U/
C: P

118. Wednesday, 27 July, 11:15 pm
I: A man loitered in the Tuileries and picked up a man under the trees. They masturbated independently.

Jean Baptiste Seitivaux, 37, native of Verdun (Lorraine), domestic of S. Poitier, American, lived at his residence on rue du Doyenné.

He was debauched into pederasty only five or six days ago in the Tuileries garden by a man unknown to him. Until then he had resisted various solicitations made to him to surrender himself to this vice, especially by a young Englishman he served and left on this account. Today is the third time he has surrendered to this debauchery in the Tuileries garden, each time with men unknown to him. He did not receive any money from him. They masturbated independently. /seitivaux/
C: P

119. Thursday, 28 July 1785, 10:30 pm
I: One man loitered in the Tuileries for several days and picked up men. Another loitered and cruised there this evening. Both stroked independently with the men they picked up.

Jacques Antoine Mussard, 20, native and citizen of Geneva (Switzerland), clockmaker, lodged at the Richelieu boardinghouse on rue Traversière Saint-Honoré with S. Poitier des Rollands, also clockmaker, who invited him to Paris and lodged and fed him.

He arrived in Paris on 29 June. He went to the Tuileries garden several times in the evening and was accosted on Tuesday by a man he met again this evening, who spoke to him about the debauchery of men. He walked with him arm in arm there, and the man stroked him through his breeches. They left together, and he, the deponent, was arrested in leaving. This man told him he lives on rue d'Argenteuil. He listened to this man's speeches only out of curiosity. But he is not given over to the vice of liking men and, on the contrary, has a horror of it. /Jacques Antoine Mussard/
C: W&R

François Boudard, 19, native of Mainvilliers in Beauce (Orléanais), domestic, unemployed for two months, lodged chez a doorwoman at 5–6, rue des Bons Enfants.

He went this evening to the Tuileries garden, where a man accosted him and asked him if he had earned something this evening and if he was for men.[12] He replied no. They took several turns together, then left, and he was arrested. He is not given over to pederasty. He said it is a domestic who taught him that one earns money in the Tuileries, but he did not earn any. /francois boudard/
C: P

120. Friday, 29 July 1785, 11:00 pm
I: A man loitered in the Tuileries, accosted a man, and struck up a conversation with him. They stroked together and hugged behind a carriage. Two others loitered alone, picked up men, accosted each other, took each other by the arm, took several turns, and sat down next to each other in several places. They pulled their hats down when they left together and adjusted their hats at the moment they were arrested.

Nicolas Musbien, 50, native of Paris, concierge of the archives of the dukes and peers[13] in the Louvre, lived there, on the courtyard of the old Louvre.

Coming back from [Little] Poland, he entered the Tuileries this evening and met a man unknown to him in the garden, who spoke to him as they walked together and tried to stroke him, the deponent, which he did not wish to allow. He walked under the trees purely out of curiosity, but he has never

surrendered himself to the debauchery of men. The man suggested to him that they go to his room, but he did not want to. They left together, and he, the deponent, was arrested. +To tell the truth, the man undid his breeches and stroked him. It is the second time this has happened to him. The first time was seven or eight years ago, with [missing words].+ /musbien/
C: P

Joseph Rouyère, 24, native of Juvigny in Clermontais (Languedoc), coachman of S. Vangammerin, surgeon, lived at his residence on rue Montmartre opposite rue du Croissant.

He went to walk in the Tuileries this evening with Louis, arrested with him, who lives at the same house he does. They did not do anything wrong at all, and he is not given over to the debauchery of men. /J Rouyere/
C: P

Louis Mulochot, 26, native of Rochefort in Beauce (Ile-de-France), domestic of Mme [illegible], whose husband is the receiver of finances for Montivilliers, lived at her residence on rue Montmartre opposite rue du Croissant.

He has never been given over to pederasty. He and Joseph went to walk in the Tuileries this evening. He sat down, and Joseph left him to follow a prostitute who was walking with a man. /U/
C: W&R

121. Saturday, 30 July 1785, 8:00 pm–12:30 am
PP: environs of the Comédie Française, quays, Coal-Box, Sofa, OP

I: 10:00. A shoemaker given over to pederasty, who had cruised and amused himself in the stoneyard, cruised there again.

10:30. Another man who gave himself over to pederasty loitered and cruised in the stoneyard.

Quentin Chabrier, 23, native of Aigueperse in Auvergne, shoemaker's assistant, worked and lived chez S. Picard, master shoemaker, on rue Saint-Jacques opposite the new church of Sainte-Geneviève.[14]

After he had supper he went to walk in the environs of the Comédie Française to wait for Rodet, upholsterer's assistant, from his native region, who had made a rendezvous with him. He was accosted there by a man unknown to him who asked him for directions to the Saint-Germain fair. It

is the first time he has gone into the stones in the environs of the Comédie. He did nothing wrong, he has never amused himself with men, and no one has ever suggested it to him. /Chabrie/
C: W&R

Emilan Loiseau, 43, native of Beaune in Burgundy, kitchen assistant, unemployed since Pentecost (15 May), lived chez the turner on rue des Canettes in faubourg Saint-Germain.

He went to walk in the environs of the Comédie Française this evening. He entered the stones behind the boards because he needed to do his business, and he was arrested there. He has never amused himself with men. Then he said he was debauched into pederasty three years ago by Rousseau, domestic, who is dead. He also amused himself with several others unknown to him below quai des Orfèvres and sometimes in the stones in the environs of the Comédie Française and sometimes on the new boulevards. He added that he has sometimes amused himself with French Guards he does not know. /U/
C: P

AUGUST

122. Friday, 5 August 1785, 11:00 pm

I: A man loitered and cruised in the Tuileries and Palais Royal for several days. This afternoon he accosted a known pederast in the Tuileries and left with him. They went to the Bois de Boulogne (16th arr.) together. Another man loitered and cruised in the Tuileries this evening.

Jacques Antoine Berard, 24, native of Lignières-le-Châtelain in the diocese of Amiens (Picardy), former student, boarded chez S. de Brugnyon, disabled noncommissioned officer, on rue de la Sonnerie.

He is given over to pederasty and was debauched into it at the collège d'Harcourt[1] by Delcourt, cavalryman, seven to eight years ago. He continued to surrender himself to this debauchery in the places where he boarded. In the Palais Royal garden yesterday he met a man unknown to him, who made a rendezvous with him for this afternoon in the Tuileries. They met each other, left about 5:00, arm in arm, and went to walk in the Bois de Boulogne. He does not know any of the men with whom he has amused himself by name. /Berard/
C: P

René Pavie, 32, native of Antony in Touraine, unemployed cook, lodged at the Notre-Dame boardinghouse on rue du Colombier.

He has never surrendered himself to the debauchery of men and is not given over to it. He sat down this evening in the Tuileries, and a man unknown to him passed by, accosted him, sat down near him, and stroked him on his breeches. He, the deponent, pushed him away and left the garden. This man followed him and took him by the arm. He was arrested in leaving. It is true he also stroked the man on his breeches in the Tuileries garden. Then he said he has not amused himself for more than a month at pederasty, to which he has been inclined since his youth. /X/
C: P

123. Saturday, 6 August 1785, 8:00 pm
PP: northern boulevards, Coal-Box, small streets and cul-de-sacs off the boulevards, OP

I: After 10:00. A known pederast, known by the name of Samson, cruised in suspect places in the evening and amused himself in alleys. He was connected with many young folks he debauched and paid for their "obligingness." This evening he loitered on the boulevard. Another man loitered in the most suspect manner, picked up a man next to the incline down to rue Amelot, and struck up a conversation with him. They went down to the Coal-Box together and appeared to look for a suitable spot "to surrender themselves to their pleasures." They stroked on the breeches, then came back up on the boulevard together. One of them escaped arrest. Two other men loitered on the boulevard. One approached the parapet, accosted a man, and struck up a conversation with him. They sat next to each other on the parapet for a long time, appeared to touch themselves, agreed to go sleep together, and left for that purpose. One of them escaped arrest. The other had been arrested in the act with Dory in a public carriage on 11 July 1784.

François Barry, 42, former secondhand dealer, bourgeois de Paris,[2] lived on rue Saint-Paul.

He denied he is given over to pederasty. He was returning from Café Alexandre and going home. /X/
C: W&R

Nicolas Jacquet, 40, native of Villers-la-Montagne in the diocese of Trier (Lorraine), domestic of the comtesse de Saint-Maurice de Carignan, lived at her residence on place des Vosges.

At night at the incline down from the boulevard he encountered a man he does not know but believed he knew. They walked together and talked about his native region. It is true he was wrong to walk at night with a man he does not know, but they did not do anything wrong at all. /U/
C: W&R

Salomon Caune, 24, native of Zurich in Switzerland, journeyman sword-furbisher, lived on rue de Lappe in faubourg Saint-Antoine.

He walked alone on the boulevard. /U/
C: W&R

Augustin Rome, 36, native of Poligny in Franche-Comté, journeyman locksmith, lived on rue de la Cerisaie, at a house in which S. Louvet is the principal tenant.

A man he does not know indeed made propositions to him and shoved his hand into his breeches. He, the deponent, suggested to him that he buy him some brandy, but his design was to have him arrested. /X/
C: P

124. Sunday, 7 August 1785, 10:45 pm
I: Two men loitered in the Tuileries and picked up men.

Louis Brelon, 31, native of Paris, day laborer, lived chez Deran, joiner, who gave him a place to sleep out of charity, on rue Couture de Sainte-Catherine.

He went to take a child as far as place Louis XV. On the way back he entered the Tuileries, where he met a man unknown to him, asked him what time it was, made remarks to him about the debauchery of men, and even stroked him through his breeches. They left together, and he, the deponent, was arrested. He does not usually go to the Tuileries and is not given over to pederasty. /U/
C: W&R

Jean Louis Moutin Hurier, nicknamed Martin, more than 17, native of Hamelet in Picardy, lived at the Condé boardinghouse on rue Traversière Saint-Honoré. He had rosettes rather than buckles on his shoes.

He has been given over to pederasty for only two weeks and was debauched into it by a man unknown to him he met in the Tuileries, who took him to the Bois de Boulogne, where they amused themselves together, and gave him three livres. He has amused himself with others at the edge of the water near the Pont Royal. They each gave him twenty-four sols. He earned nothing yesterday or today. /hurier/
C: P

125. Wednesday, 10 August 1785, 12:30 am
I: A known pederast loitered on quai des Augustins, took several turns, pretended to urinate several times, and picked up passersby. He had loitered in the same way on quai des Orfèvres.

Jean Alexandre, 23, native of Paris, bookseller in passage des Jacobins, lived chez S. Bâtonnier on rue du Bon Puits.

He often goes to walk on the quays in the evening. He spoke to no one except for a man on quai des Augustins who asked him what time it was. He replied it was after 11:00. He is not at all given over to the debauchery of men and walks without any bad design. It is true he was already arrested, as suspected of pederasty, on quai des Augustins two or three years ago. He was forbidden to return there in the evening, and he has returned because he does nothing wrong. Eight or ten days ago on quai des Quatre Nations he met a man unknown to him, who asked him to sleep with him. He, the deponent, indeed took him to sleep with him, and this man masturbated him. The next morning he asked him for money, but he refused to give him any. He gave him a place to sleep only because he told him he had no place to sleep. /allexandre/
C: P

126. Thursday, 11 August 1785, 11:00 pm
I: One known pederast loitered in pathways in the Tuileries, accosted others, and appeared to amuse himself with one of them. Another also loitered in the garden and picked up men, including one with whom he amused himself there.

Pierre Tessier, 33, native of Loches in Touraine, baker's assistant, worked and lived chez widow Aubert, mistress baker, on rue de l'Arbre sec.

He was debauched into pederasty by Cassolet, doll vendor on the boulevards,[3] near the depot of the French Guards, who debauched him around two years ago. He amused himself several times with Cassolet in the Champs-Elysées on the side of Clichy. On 23 June he went to sleep with a man he had met in the Tuileries, chez and with another man on rue de Rohan. He does not know them but believes they were connected. This evening in the Tuileries he met one of these men, who made a rendezvous with him for Saturday at the Arms of France tavern on rue de l'Arbre sec. He had met one of the men he slept with on 23 June in the Tuileries before, but he did not wish to continue to speak with him. /U/
C: P

Jean Laboubée, 39, native of the parish of Belmont in Guyenne, lieutenant of the wolf hunters of France in the department of Albi in Languedoc, previously in trade in Saint-Domingue, in Paris for three years, lodged at the Four Provinces boardinghouse on rue des Frondeurs.

He went to the boulevards this evening with three Americans named Pajot, Deshayes, and Merande, whose addresses he does not know. He lost them, followed the boulevard, and went to the Tuileries, where he sat down on a chair near a tree and fell asleep. He did not speak to anyone there. He walked there and did not accost anyone. If someone touched him, he felt nothing because he was sleeping. He is not given over to pederasty and has never surrendered himself to it. +Then he said he surrendered himself to pederasty only a month ago or thereabouts, with men unknown to him he met in the Tuileries and with whom he amused himself twice.+ /La BouBée/
C: W&R

127. Friday, 12 August 1785, 10:45 pm
I: A man who appeared to be a clergyman loitered in the most suspect manner from 9:00 to 10:30 pm and picked up several men, including one with whom he appeared to stroke and to whom he made propositions about pederasty.

Alexandre Chair, 42, native of Hamel in the duchy of Luxembourg, tonsured cleric in the diocese of Cologne, in Paris for five or six days to find a friend named Halle, whom he believed is a philosophy professor, who turned out to be a parish priest in the diocese of Reims, lodged on rue des Prêtres Saint-Germain-l'Auxerrois, at an inn whose master's name he does not know.

At 9:00 pm he went to the Tuileries, where a locksmith he knew in Givet had made a rendezvous with him for today between 9:00 and 10:00. He did not come there this evening. He, the deponent, walked there and met a man who touched his parts, whom he, the deponent, stroked only through the breeches. It also happened to him to surrender himself to pederasty in Brussels, in a promenade with men unknown to him. He left the Tuileries with the man who touched him in order to go amuse themselves elsewhere. /A Scheer/
C: P

128. Saturday, 13 August 1785, 10:15 pm
I: A pederast loitered in the Tuileries, picked up several men, and appeared to masturbate with one of them.

Charles Antoine Du Fossé, 38, native of Beau near Abbeville [Picardy], fruit vendor, lived on rue Coquillière near Saint-Eustache.
  Coming back from rue Royale at place Louis XV, he entered the Tuileries and sat down on a bench. A man unknown to him also sat down, approached him, and tried to shove his hand into his breeches. He, the deponent, got up immediately, left, and was arrested. He did not touch the man, is not given over to the vice of liking men, and has never surrendered himself to it. To tell the truth, in pushing the man away, he placed his hand on his thigh on his breeches, but without stroking him, without design. Then he said it is true he has already surrendered himself to pederasty twice in the Tuileries, where he amused himself and paid a man with whom he amused himself six sols. He was debauched by a domestic named Lapierre, now dead, with whom he drank in a tavern, but this has not happened to him again. /du fossé/
C: P

129. Sunday, 14 August 1785, 8 pm–1:00 am
PP: Champs-Elysées, Cours de la Reine, place Louis XV, environs and exits of the Tuileries, quays, OP

I: Three men loitered and cruised in the Tuileries.

André Marie Loulié, 23, native of Paris, domestic, formerly in Saint-Mâlo, in Paris since May 1783, worked as a wine vendor's assistant and then, after some time unemployed, as a domestic for several days of a provincial shopkeeper on rue de l'Hirondelle[4] whose name he does not know, who must leave in a few days for Saintonge. He lodged in a furnished room on rue du Champ-fleuri.

He went to walk this evening in the Tuileries and was accosted there by a man who had him sit down on a chair next to him, then took him by the arm, spoke to him about the debauchery of men, suggested that they go together to the Palais Royal, and stroked him through his breeches. He does not know this man. It is true this man touched him with his penis exposed. It is the first time he, the deponent, has surrendered himself to this debauchery. He was arrested in leaving with this man to go to the Palais Royal. He did not receive money from this man, who told him they would find a gentleman there who would amuse himself with him, the deponent, and would give him three livres, which he told him because he, the deponent, told him he was in need. To tell the truth, he went to the Tuileries in order to attempt to earn something there by amusing a man. He had heard it said that one earns money there. /Loulie/
C: W&R

Antoine Petit, 30, native of Villefolle (?) near Villeneuve-le-Roy in Burgundy, journeyman turner, worked chez S. Gréat, master turner on rue Sainte-Marguerite in faubourg Saint-Germain, and lived chez S. Damas, master joiner, on rue des Saints-Pères.

Coming back from Passy, he entered the Tuileries and met a man there who spoke to him about the debauchery of men. He, the deponent, told him he did not like men. The man suggested to him that he go to his place. As they left, he was arrested. He added that he went with this man to his place to see what he wished to do. It is true he told him he does not like women, others put it into him, and he puts it into men, but he said it only as a joke. /Antoine petit/
C: P

Joseph {Guet} Diet, 31, native of Tours (Touraine), journeyman currier chez S. Lalée, master currier on rue Sainte-Foy, lived chez Mme Guérin, innkeeper, on rue de Bourbon Villeneuve.

He has been given over to amusing himself with men for around two months. He has amused himself several times behind Sainte-Opportune,[5] in a room on rue de Cléry with a joiner's assistant whose name he does not know, this evening in the Tuileries with a man unknown to him, whom he met there, and once on the boulevard. He has as his friend in this debauchery

Regnier, also journeyman currier, who resided with him and still comes to see him from time to time, with whom he amused himself several times. /U/
C: P

130. **Tuesday, 16 August 1785, 11:15 pm**
I: Two men loitered and cruised in the Tuileries. One, who identified himself as a domestic, picked up a man, and they agreed to go sleep together. The other picked up a man, and they appeared to stroke.

Joseph Bertrand, 33, native of Saint-Seine in Burgundy, domestic, unemployed for three weeks, expected to enter a household the next day. He lived at the townhouse of the duc d'Harcourt[6] on rue de l'Université. He had worked for the duke as a floor polisher and slept there between positions, for the last three weeks.

He was debauched into pederasty around two years ago by Jourdain, first lackey of the comtesse d'Harcourt[7] at the time, who left her household, whose current address he does not know, with whom he consummated the crime in the passive role. Today is the fourth time he has gone to the Tuileries in the evening {with persons unknown to him} and accosted men. The other three times he amused himself with men unknown to him. Today he accosted a man with whom he agreed to go sleep at his place, who told him he lives on rue Saint-Honoré, but they did nothing. He added that he amused himself for the third time Sunday in the Tuileries. He has never been given over to pederasty. He has never given or received anything because of debauchery and even refused three livres offered to him by a chevalier de Saint-Louis with whom he amused himself in the Tuileries.
C: P

Antoine Marie de la Fosse, 29, native of Versailles (Ile-de-France), unemployed, seeking a job, lived chez Doucet, limonadier, on rue Galande near rue Saint-Julien-le-Pauvre.

He had heard that men surrender themselves to pederasty in the Tuileries garden and went there this evening to see if he could meet someone of this type. He has not surrendered himself to it since he left the collège in Versailles. To tell the truth, in the Tuileries garden this evening he met a man unknown to him, approached him where he was seated, and they masturbated independently. /Dela fosse/
C: P

131. **Wednesday, 17 August 1785, 10:30 pm**
I: A man loitered in the Tuileries, took several turns, accosted a man, and sat down with him. They appeared to stroke mutually. Another loitered and picked up a man with whom he sat down. They appeared to masturbate.

Louis Houdin, 32, native of Saint-Arnoult in Beaune (Burgundy), cook of the marquis de Rostaing,[8] lived at his residence on rue Neuve des Petits Champs near rue de Gaillon.

He was debauched into pederasty around four years ago by Ancelin, also cook, with whom he resided at the time, who is currently in Burgundy and likewise chez a marquise on rue des Minimes. He has already been once this year to the Tuileries, where he amused himself with a man unknown to him whom he met there. This evening he went there with the design of amusing himself. He met another man unknown to him there. They stroked mutually, and they were going to amuse themselves at this man's place when he, the deponent, was arrested. /houdin/
C: P

Etienne Lorion, 26, native of Mer near Blois (Orléanais), former wine vendor's assistant, now unemployed domestic, lived chez S. Ducamp, upholsterer, on rue de la Montagne-Saint-Geneviève.

He went to the Tuileries this evening, took several turns, and met a man whose name he does not know and recognized only by sight as a former domestic in Chaussée d'Antin. He said to him, "Good evening, François," the name he used when he was a wine vendor's assistant. They walked and sat down on chairs next to each other but did nothing wrong at all. He is not given over to the vice of liking men. They did not talk about this debauchery in the Tuileries. He was married a year ago, at the end of the month of June, and has already had a child, who died. /lorion/
C: W&R

132. **Thursday, 18 August 1785, 9:00 pm**
I: A known pederast, who had sex with a man at his place today, loitered in the Tuileries and sought to pick up someone.

Jacques Terroux, 21, native of Québec in Canada, which he left in 1779 to come to Europe, spent six weeks in London, and five years in Geneva, where his father, former merchant, lived. In Paris for six to seven months to learn how to mount watchcases, he lived at the Rouen boardinghouse on rue de la Licorne on Ile de la Cité.

He did not wish to reply anything about his actions today and about the places he had been. [We] asked [him] to tell us who the man is who went to his place yesterday, with whom he shut himself in for a long time. During this time he had a woman who lodges with him leave the room and left her on the stairway. He had stated to his landlord that she is his wife. [He] replied it is Amiet, also native of Québec, journeyman goldsmith, who lives on rue de Gesvres opposite rue Saint-Jérôme. He did not shut himself in. The woman who lodges with him, who is a widow, whom he brought from Geneva, in truth went out several times and is not his wife. /Jacques Louis Terroux fils/

The contents of his pockets included "a letter containing a narrative of debauchery committed by the one who wrote about it to his friend, without a date, signed T h t, which letter he told us was written by him, without design and to amuse himself."
C: P

I: 10:30 pm. A man loitered in the Tuileries and picked up several others, including one with whom he masturbated. He had been arrested and released on 12 June (#89).

Jean Naudin, 28, native of Bellême in Perche (Maine), independent tailor's assistant, lodged chez Jambon, innkeeper, who rented rooms on rue Jean de Lépine.

He went to walk in the Tuileries. A man accosted him, touched him, the deponent, who had removed his breeches at his request, and hugged him. It is the first time this has happened to him in the two or three months he has been in Paris. He has had this inclination since his youth. /U/
C: P

133. Friday, 19 August 1785, 8:00 pm–1:30 am
PP: Champs-Elysées, Cours de la Reine, site of the Colosseum, place Louis XV, exits of the Tuileries and Palais Royal, quays, OP

I (Noël): 9:45 pm. Two men loitered separately in the Tuileries, picked up men, and stroked with them. Two other men loitered together in the most suspect manner in the garden.

Germain Bernard, 20, native of Lyon (Lyonnais), upholsterer's apprentice, worked chez S. Lépine, master upholsterer, in Chaussée d'Antin, and lived at the café at carrefour Saint-Benôit, near the Cour du Dragon, in faubourg Saint-Germain.

He went to the Tuileries with his cousin Nouvelet, also upholsterer's assistant, who resides and sleeps with him. They took some turns there but without any bad design. He is not given over to the debauchery of liking men. /bernard/
C: W&R

Jean Claude Nouvelet, 21, native of Lyon, near Saint-Nizier (Lyonnais), journeyman upholsterer, resided in a furnished room at carrefour Saint-Benôit with his first cousin Bernard, also arrested, and worked, like him, chez S. Lépine, master upholsterer, on rue de la Chaussée d'Antin.

They entered the Tuileries on their way back from their master's, walked there, and took several turns to see the horrors it is said take place there between men, without, however, being given over to that debauchery. /Nouvellet/
C: W&R

Jean Charles La Rivière, 29, native of Nurlu in Picardy, domestic, unemployed since yesterday, lodged chez S. Lheureux, wigmaker, who rented furnished rooms on rue Mazarine.

He went to the Champs-Elysées this afternoon to see men playing boules. He entered the Tuileries, where he accosted a man whom he at first took for Didier, domestic, whom he knows, but who did not turn out to be Didier. This man unknown to him took him by the arm and stroked him through his breeches. They left together and agreed to go amuse themselves in his, the deponent's, room. He has been given over to pederasty since his youth and has amused himself several times in the Champs-Elysées with men unknown to him. He has never consummated the crime and has been satisfied with masturbating independently with those with whom he amused himself. /X/
C: P

François Audier, 24, native of Nontron in the diocese of Limoges (Limousin), domestic and cook, unemployed since the 7th, lodged on rue Saint-Honoré at the corner of rue des Frondeurs.

He went to walk this evening in the Tuileries and met a man unknown to him there. They masturbated independently. He had also amused himself already in his room with a kitchen assistant. He was debauched into pederasty only a year ago by a schoolmaster who taught him to read and write, who lives near the Pont Neuf, whose name he does not recall. [Unless this man moved, he also had sex with a man] who lives on the sixth floor chez a wine vendor in the courtyard on rue Guénegaud. /f audier/
C: P

134. Monday, 22 August 1785, 6:00 pm
I (Noël): A young man masturbated independently with another man in the Mousetrap. The latter avoided arrest.

Jean Baptiste Duplessis, around 20, native of Paris, assistant of his father, fabric vendor, lived with him on rue des Bourdonnais.

He went down to the spot where he was arrested to do his business. He goes there sometimes. He met a man unknown to him there and masturbated independently with him. He, the deponent, gave him twelve sols. This man wanted to take him to his place, but he did not wish to go there. He was in this spot for the first time around a year ago and has often found similar opportunities there but has surrendered himself to it only two or three times. /Duplessis/
C: P

135. Monday, 22 August 1785, 10:45 pm
I (Noël): A short man loitered in the Tuileries and picked up men, including one with whom he masturbated. A tall man, a known pederast, who loitered in the Tuileries and other public promenades every evening, picked up men, including one with whom he stroked. They "plotted" to go sleep together.

Jean Bourachaux, 16, native of La Palisse in Bourbonnais, unemployed domestic without certificates, lodged chez Mme Drouet, innkeeper, on rue du Pélican.

He had heard domestics say one earns money in the Tuileries by amusing men. He has already gone there twice and for the third time this evening. He met a man unknown to him there, and they masturbated independently. This man had promised to give him money, which, however, he did not give him because he told him to go to his place and he, the deponent, would be satisfied.

As they went there, he, the deponent, was arrested. It is need that convinced him to do this. /U/
C: P

Gabriel Laubertin, 25, native of Breteuil in Normandy, shoemaker's assistant, lived chez S. Albert, master shoemaker, on rue du Four Saint-Honoré.

He went to the Tuileries this evening to walk. He sat down on a bench, and a man came and sat down near him and asked him what time it was. They chatted about their native regions and left together, and he was arrested. He also went there once last week, but he did nothing wrong at all and is not given over to pederasty. Then he said that, to tell the truth, he went to the Tuileries this evening with the design of amusing himself. They indeed stroked each other through their breeches. He amused himself at pederasty in his native region only with one of his comrades named Rosse, baker's assistant. He left the Tuileries this evening to go chez the man he had met there. /U/
C: {W&R} P

136. Monday, 26 August 1785, 8:00 pm–1:30 am
PP: Champs-Elysées, Cours de la Reine, stone port, environs and exits of the Tuileries, quays, OP

I (Noël): 10:30 pm. A man loitered in the Tuileries and picked up a man he sat down next to. He conversed about pederasty, agreed to go have supper and sleep with the man, and told him he had not eaten for two days and needed money this evening.

François Pousset, 33, native of Beaugency (Orléanais), former grocer's assistant, unemployed and seeking a job, lodged in a furnished room chez Sabatier, fruit vendor, on rue Pagevin.

He went to the Tuileries to walk and met a man there to whom he indeed said he had not eaten all day and wanted to get some money this evening. This man suggested to him that he give him some for amusing himself with a man he would take him to. They left together for that purpose and to go have supper with this man. He has never surrendered himself to this debauchery until now, and it is need that made him acquiesce to the propositions of this man, whom he does not know, and go have supper with him. /f Pousset/
C: P

137. Monday, 29 August 1785, 10:45 pm

I (Noël): Two men loitered and cruised in the Tuileries. One picked up others, including a man with whom he talked about pederasty and agreed to go sleep with.

Claude Paul Wafflard, 31, native of Villers Cotterêts (Ile-de-France), journeyman inlay worker, lived and worked chez S. Beaucire, master fanmaker, at The Gold Shell on rue Saint-Martin.

He went to the Tuileries this evening to walk and fell asleep on a bench there. He was accosted by a man unknown to him, who talked to him about the weather, took him by the arm, and left with him, but they did nothing wrong. It is false that they conversed about the debauchery of men. He, the deponent, is not given over to it. /Wafflard/
C: W&R

Henry Ratz, 24, native of Aix-la-Chapelle (Germany), journeyman harpsichord maker, worked chez S. Dubois, harpsichord maker, on rue Saint-Honoré and lodged chez Guillez, journeyman clockmaker from his native region, on rue du Chantre.

He went to the Tuileries this evening to walk and was accosted there by a man who spoke to him about the debauchery of men, but he, the deponent, is not given over to it. To tell the truth, he told this man, to amuse himself, that he had received four louis from a chevalier de Saint-Louis to amuse him in the Tuileries, but it is false. He did not receive anything. On the contrary, a chevalier de Saint-Louis suggested it to him two weeks ago, and he, the deponent, slapped him.[9] He did not accept anything from the man this evening and left with him only to go home. /henry Ratz/
C: W&R

138. Tuesday, 30 August 1785, 5:00 pm

I: Three men loitered in the Tuileries and picked up men.

Jean François Bongran, 35, native of Paris, shoemaker's assistant, lived chez S. Maillet, master shoemaker, on rue de Richelieu.

Coming back from faubourg Saint-Germain, he entered the Tuileries and walked there. He was accosted there by a man unknown to him. He has been given over to pederasty for no longer than a year. He does not know the persons with whom he has amused himself. He was debauched into this vice

by one of his friends named Nardeau, also shoemaker's assistant, who lived in Saint-Cloud, who taught him that one goes to the Tuileries to amuse oneself. He has been there three or four times. This evening he did not do anything but stroke with the man he met there. They left to go amuse themselves at this man's place, and he was arrested. /Bongrand/
C: P

Louis de Forget, 19, native of Châteauneuf in Angoumois (Saintonge), unemployed, in Paris for five or six days to seek a job in some office, lodged chez a man who rented rooms on rue Saint-Jacques.

He went to the Tuileries this evening to walk. At 10:00 he sat down on a bench. A hunchbacked man sat down on a chair near him, talked to him about the fine weather, told him he lives on rue de Richelieu, and asked him his address. He, the deponent, left alone and did not do anything wrong. He is not given over to the debauchery of men and did not talk about it with this man. /L Deforget/

The contents of his pockets included cards from a gambling establishment where he played and what money he had and a half-year's leave from the French Guards, dated 20 August, for him to go to Angoulême until 15 March.
C: R in the custody of Desurbois, who was instructed to conduct him to the sergeant of the French Guards

Jean Louis Bernard, 22, native of Ile de Ré (Aunis), tailor's assistant, lived in a room chez a joiner on rue Saint-Honoré opposite rue du Four.

He goes to the Tuileries often. This evening he met a man who asked him if he likes to put it in or to have it put into him and stroked him, the deponent, as he made water. As he stroked him, people went by near them, and this man said to him, "Let's leave here." /bernard/
C: P

139. Wednesday, 31 August 1785, 8:00 pm–2:00 am
PP: Champs-Elysées, stone port, Cours de la Reine, environs and exits of the Tuileries, quays, OP

I: 9:30 pm. Three men loitered in the Tuileries, picked up others, and stroked with them, with their penises exposed.

Nearly 11:00 pm. A man picked up men on quai des Orfèvres, including one with whom he went down to the Mousetrap, where they stroked.

Jean Nicolas Larpenteur, 32, native of Fontainebleau (Ile-de-France), grocer, lived on rue de Gesvres at the corner of the Pont au Change.

He entered the Tuileries to cross the garden and walked there. He was accosted by a man unknown to him, who made remarks to him about pederasty and wished to stroke him, which he prevented, and refused to go to his place. He intended to part from him at the Carousel. To tell the truth, this man held him by the arm and wanted them to amuse themselves together in the garden, but he, the deponent, refused to. He has surrendered himself to pederasty for only three months, at his place with men who are no longer in Paris, among others Desjardins, who lives with one of his aunts in the Marais. He was given over to this debauchery in his youth with [one or some?] of his comrades. He does not know the one who spoke to him in the Tuileries this evening. /Larpenteur/
C: S&R

Noël Henry LeComte, 26, native of Beaumont-sur-Vingeanne in Burgundy, wine vendor's assistant chez Mme LeComte, his sister-in-law, wine vendor, in the Palais Royal, no. 99, and lived there.

Coming back from the residence of the archbishop of Narbonne,[10] he crossed the Tuileries and was accosted by a man unknown to him, who asked him if he wanted him to put it into him and touched him through his breeches. He, the deponent, touched him. He was debauched into pederasty about six weeks ago by Picard, who slept with him with his penis exposed. /Le Comte/
C: P

Louis Groux, 32, native of Dunkerque (Flanders), former soldier in the Aquitaine regiment, deserter from service in Holland, former pastrymaker's assistant, lived chez a man who rented rooms on rue du Pont aux Choux.

He entered the Tuileries this evening and met a man there who spoke to him, with whom he walked, but they did nothing wrong. He is not given over to pederasty. /U/
C: P

Claude Antoine Suchot, 46, native of Dufresne in Champagne, parasol worker with a royal pension, lived chez S. Poupart, joiner, on rue de la Tacherie.

He went to walk on quai des Orfèvres. A man accosted him there and walked with him. They went down below and came back up, and he was

arrested. He often goes to walk on the quays in the evening but does nothing wrong there and is not given over to the debauchery of men. /souchot/
C: W&R

SEPTEMBER

140. Thursday, 1 September 1785, 10:00 pm
I: A man had his breeches down on the Half-Moon, with a man who escaped. Another man cruised there, picked up men, and went to the Coal-Box.

Jean Baptiste Manny, 45, native of Vincennes (12th arr.), domestic of S. de Voulget de Chanteclaire, lived at his residence on rue Saint-Paul.

As he made water, a man approached him and touched him. He, the deponent, likewise touched him. He was debauched into pederasty around a year ago by choirboys in Vincennes, where he {lived} went then. He does not know any of the men with whom he has amused himself. He has only ever masturbated with the men with whom he amused himself. He knows well that one amuses oneself in the spot where he was this evening. /Manny/

The contents of his pockets included a coin worth twenty-four sols, in case "those with whom he might amuse himself obliged him to pay them."
C: P

Thomas Feron, 57, native of Vernon-sur-Seine (Normandy), master building painter, lived on Vieille rue du Temple near the hatter.

As he went to the residence of S. Dalby on rue des Amandières, he was accosted by a man with whom he indeed took several turns. This man talked to him about the debauchery of men and suggested that he take him to his place. To get rid of him, he, the deponent, agreed to go there to amuse himself, but this man wished to oblige him to give him three livres and twelve sols in advance, which he did not wish to do. Around a year ago another man, a priest who lodged near Saint-Gervais,[1] took him to his place for the same debauchery, but he has not surrendered himself to this debauchery much. This man only fondled him. He returned there one other time. He does not even know the name of this priest, who lived chez a wholesale fabric vendor on the fourth floor. He has often been accosted on the boulevards when he sat there. /feran/
C: W&R

141. Friday, 2 September 1785, 9:45 pm

I: Three men loitered in the Tuileries and picked up men. One said he was an unemployed tailor's assistant and agreed to go sleep with a man and put it into him, for six livres, but he did not want to have it put into him.

Charles Dangois, 42, native of Paris, independent tailor's assistant, lived on rue du Cygne.

Crossing the Tuileries garden, he spoke to a man who asked him what time it was, to whom he said it was 7:00, but they did not say or do anything wrong. He is not given over to the debauchery of pederasty. He entered by the gate on the side of the Pont Royal and went toward rue de la Madeleine in faubourg Saint-Honoré. He met the man with whom he conversed, came back, and left through the Carousel because he would have taken rue Saint-Honoré. /X/
C: P

Nicolas Robert, 17, native of Andelot near Chaumont-en-Bassigny (Champagne), unemployed tailor's assistant, lodged chez a man who rented rooms on rue de la Vannerie.

He went to the Tuileries to walk, as he does sometimes in the evening when he has no work. He was accosted there by a man unknown to him, who told him he is Italian, who suggested to him things that he, the deponent, does not understand. He suggested to him that he go have supper and sleep with him and offered to give him six livres. He refused it all and went away. This man followed him, and in leaving, he, the deponent, was arrested. He has never been given over to the debauchery of men and does not know what it is. /U/
C: W&R

Etienne Bougere, nicknamed Dulis, 25, native of Angers (Normandy), wigmaker's assistant, arrived in Paris from Spa on Sunday. He acted in provincial theater companies.

He went to walk on the quays, entered the Tuileries, and left at once. As he was ready to leave, a man unknown to him accosted him and asked him what time it was. He replied it was 9:00, and 9:00 indeed struck an instant later. This man walked near him, and he said to him, "You see, sir, that I did not deceive you. It's striking 9:00 now." He said nothing more. He does not

know why he was arrested. He has never been given over to the debauchery of men. /Bougere/
C: W&R

142. Saturday, 3 September 1785, 8:00 pm–2:00 am
PP: northern boulevards, Coal-Box, small streets and cul-de-sacs off the boulevards, place des Vosges, quays and below, OP

I: A man loitered on boulevard Saint-Antoine and picked up a man with whom he walked and then went down to the Coal-Box. He stroked with him and "polluted himself" before him, then came back up on the boulevard.

Eustache Le Cerf, 33, native of Paris, glazier, had not worked for two weeks because of drinking and lived on rue de Reuilly in faubourg Saint-Antoine. He refused to take the oath to tell the truth.

He did not go down to the Coal-Box and did not speak to anyone. /U/
C: P

I: An old man "entirely given over to pederasty in all the suspect places" amused himself, fondled, and masturbated with a young man, with his breeches down, near the parapet on boulevard Saint-Antoine.

Jacques Daniel Chauveau, 15, native of Saint-Germain-en-Laye (Ile-de-France), journeyman cabinetmaker chez Caguélerd, cabinetmaker, on rue Saint-Nicolas, lived on rue de Clignancourt.

He was sitting on the parapet on boulevard Saint-Antoine, and the man arrested with him approached him. After making several idle remarks to him, he shoved his hand into his breeches, in spite of him, unbuttoned them, and was masturbating him when they were both arrested. But he neither touched nor wished to touch this man, whom he does not know. He came to the boulevard to take the air and walk. /chauvoux/
C: P

Jean François Quentin, 55 or thereabouts, native of Maubeuge (Flanders), retired merchant, lived chez a grocer on rue Saint-Louis in the Marais across from the Daughters of the Holy Sacrament.[2] His shirt was largely out of his breeches.

He went to walk for his rheumatism on the boulevard. A young man he approached said to him that the days are getting shorter. Nothing wrong happened between them. /X/
C: P

The commissaire recalled Chauveau, who reaffirmed his statement. Quentin acknowledged "that what Chauveau had said is true, but it is the first time this has happened to him." The younger man signed again, but the older man declined again, "saying this is pointless and why crush a man."

I: A man stroked and masturbated in the Coal-Box with another man, who escaped.

Antoine Proff, 23, native of Strasbourg (Alsace), tailor, lived on rue de la Vannerie at the Grève.
    A man approached him in the Coal-Box and shoved his hand into his breeches. They fondled, and this man masturbated him. It is a weakness he has had, but this is the first time. /proff/
C: P

143. Monday, 5 September 1785, 9:45
I: Two men loitered in the Tuileries, picked up men, accosted each other, took each other by the arm, and left the garden.

François Gérard, 24, native of Semide in the diocese of Reims (Champagne), surgery day-student at the Hôtel-Dieu, lived on rue de l'Archevêché.
    He went to the Tuileries with a gentleman and lady of his acquaintance. In leaving he encountered S. Aubry, also arrested, whom he knows from dissecting in the same amphitheater but had no other relations with. /Gerard/
C: W&R

Alexis Aubrée, 30, native of Dives in Normandy, surgery student, lived chez the baker on rue de Bourbon Villeneuve opposite the Daughters of God.[3]
    Coming back from faubourg Saint-Germain, he crossed the Tuileries garden and, in leaving the garden, encountered and accosted the man arrested with him, whose name he does not know, with whom he dissected last winter in S. Pelletan's[4] amphitheater. He accosted him only to say good evening to

him. He has worn rosettes for two weeks because he hurt one leg with a buckle. /aubrée/
C: W&R

I: A known pederast amused himself with a man on chairs in the Tuileries last week. This evening he amused himself with a man while standing.

César Auguste Frédéric du Rieux, 48, native of Dunkerque (Flanders), former musketeer in the first company, lived at 87, rue du Four Saint-Honoré, on the mezzanine.

He went to walk in the Tuileries garden this evening and was accosted there by a man unknown to him, who asked him for money to buy a mug. He, the deponent, gave him a coin worth twelve two {twenty-four} sols. When they were in the courtyard of the garden, this man asked him if he would like to go amuse himself among the stones, which he, the deponent, refused. He is not given over to this vice and has never surrendered himself to it. /Caesar du Rieux/
C: W&R

144. **Wednesday 7 September 1785, 8:00 pm–2:00 am**
PP: environs and exits of the Tuileries, quays, OP

I: A man loitered in the Tuileries and picked up others. He stroked with one on the breeches and agreed to go amuse themselves in his room. When they left, the second man escaped arrest.

Jean Renault, 24, native of Augerville in the diocese of Sens (Champagne), former corporal in the Royal Marine (infantry) Corps, from which he has leave for abdominal blockages as of 20 May, currently unemployed, seeking a position as a domestic, lived chez his cousin, master baker, on rue Montmartre.

He walked in the Tuileries garden from 7:00 pm on and was arrested as he left it at 9:00 pm. It is true a man he does not know asked him where he was going, and he replied that he was going to bed. This man followed him out of the Tuileries to the Louvre, where he was arrested. /jean Renault/
C: W&R

I: 11:00. A man loitered on the parapet of quai des Orfèvres, picked up a man, stroked with him, and walked with him on the parapet.

11:15. A man loitered on the quays, picked up others, and went down to the edge of the river with one of them. They masturbated independently, and the second man escaped arrest.

Michel Tonnere, 45, native of Vienna in Austria, mathematical instruments worker, lived chez widow Marteau, jeweler, on the Pont au Change.

Passing on quai des Orfèvres for relaxation, he met a young man unknown to him there, who came near as he made water, tried to fondle him, and suggested that he go down under the archways, which he refused. He followed him until the moment he was arrested and tried to take him by the arm. He acquired the taste for pederasty in his youth without knowing what it was. It rarely happens to him to surrender himself to it, and he does not know any of those with whom he has amused himself. He had already been arrested on rue Saint-Antoine.[5] /Tonner/
C: P

Charles Balthazar Berthellier, 25, native of Paris, unemployed hosier's assistant,[6] lived with his aunt chez S. Doinet, dyer, on rue de Gesvres.

He has been given over to pederasty for around four years and was debauched into it by Franque, journeyman goldsmith, who lived at the time chez S. Boucher in the new courtyard of the Palais, who is no longer in Paris. He does not know those with whom he amused himself except for two persons, Lacroix, jeweler, who lives chez S. Manon, who makes eyeglasses, on quai des Morfondus, and S. Charvais, secondhand dealer, who lives chez a smelter on rue de la Licorne and sells at the Holy Spirit [hospital], with whom he consummated the crime in the passive role. This evening he was on quai des Orfèvres and met a man unknown to him with whom he went down below to amuse himself. After this man undid his breeches, he, the deponent, was arrested. He was already arrested on 24 November 1784. /Berthelier/
C: P

I: Midnight. A pederast on record, known by the name of Michel Albert, known for cruising, prostituting himself, and making money from his obligingness, loitered on quai des Augustins and picked up a domestic. They went to the watering spot on quai de Conti[7] to amuse themselves.

Michel Albert, 16, native of Saumur in Anjou, shoemaker's assistant, lived chez his uncle, master shoemaker, on rue Saint-Jacques.

He was debauched into pederasty in his native region around two years ago by Chauveau. Since he has been in Paris he has surrendered himself to it and consummated the crime in the passive role with a man unknown to him, who put it into him in an alley. Passing along quai des Augustins this evening, he met a man, a domestic, unknown to him, who took him to the watering spot on quai de Conti and fondled him. He has never received anything [for sex] but twelve sols from a man who lives on quai des Orfèvres. He also went to amuse himself chez a limonadier on rue Galande at the corner of rue du Fouarre, on the second floor, with a young man who lodges there. He consummated the crime with him in the active as well as passive role, last month. /michel albert/
C: P

145. Saturday, 10 September 1785, 10:00 pm
I: A man picked up a man on the boulevard. They went down to the Coal-Box and stroked independently together. The second man escaped arrest.

Jean Philippe Marie Denis Desenneville, 41, native of Paris, commissioner of war for the gendarmes of the royal guard, lived on rue de Thorigny in the parish of Saint-Gervais.

He went down to the spot where he was arrested to do his business, which he did. A man in a white jacket passed before him and seemed to want to stroke him. At that moment he was arrested by others. He did not do anything wrong. /Denis desenneville/
C: S&R

146. Sunday, 11 September 1785, 11:00 pm
I: A man loitered on quai des Orfèvres and picked up a man. They went down to the watering spot, came back up, and walked off arm in arm by way of rue Saint-Louis, Pont Saint-Michel, rue Saint-André-des-Arts, rue de l'Eperon, and other streets. They ended up among the stones in place de l'Estrapade, where they appeared to masturbate.

Nicolas Hyacinthe Juillien de Dugny, 23, native of Verdun (Lorraine), journeyman printer, worked for Mme Herissant on rue de la Parcheminerie and lodged in a furnished room at the Burgundy boardinghouse on rue des Deux Portes Saint-Severin.[8]

He was not on any quay today. He went to The Icehouse this afternoon and drank there with a German printer whose name and address he does not know. He came back with him this evening, as far as Montagne

Sainte-Geneviève, and was arrested there as he came back. He has not been elsewhere and has not spoken to or accosted anyone. He did not pass through rue Saint-André-des-Arts, rue de l'Eperon, or rue Hautefeuille. Then he said he is given over to pederasty because he does not like women. He was debauched into it around six years ago by a verger [caretaker] in the parish of Saint-Pierre Langelé in Verdun. He has consummated the crime twice in the passive role with a naval captain whose name he does not know, in the house where he, the deponent, lived at the time. He amused himself with another man whose name and address he does not know. This evening he met a man on quai des Orfèvres with whom he indeed went to drink on rue Saint-Jacques. Then they went to l'Estrapade, where they stroked independently. He does not know who this man is. He promised him, the deponent, to come to his room. He stated that he was arrested on 2 January.[9] /juillien de Dugny/
C: P

147. Wednesday, 14 September 1785, 11:00 pm

I: A man loitered on quai des Augustins and picked up the same man twice, with whom he appeared to amuse himself. He led him to the Sofa, where he told him it would not be long before he discharged.

Jean Baptiste Frade, 40, journeyman joiner, native of Paris, lived on rue Saint-Lazare in the Porcherons (9th arr.).

He passed along quai des Augustins and met a man unknown to him there who asked him what time it was, stroked him through his breeches, and followed him to quai du Louvre, but he, the deponent, did not do anything. He is not given over to pederasty. /frade/
C: P

148. Friday, 16 September 1785, 8:45 pm

I: A known pederast named David loitered on quai des Orfèvres.

Joseph David, 30, native of Paris, hairdresser for women, lived chez Mme Cousin, dairywoman, on rue aux Ours, in a room of his own on the fourth floor.

Coming back from rue de Sèvres to go to rue du Temple, near the Temple, he passed along quai des Orfèvres without stopping there or speaking to anyone. He has never surrendered himself to the debauchery of men. /U/
C: W&R

149. Saturday, 17 September 1785, 7:30 pm–2:00 am
PP: quays, place Louis XV, northern boulevards

I: 8:45 pm. A baker's assistant, a known pederast, staged parties, loitered, and cruised in suspect places in the evening. The day before yesterday he was almost caught while masturbating with another man at the New Market. This evening he loitered on quai des Orfèvres.

9:00 pm. Another man loitered there, picked up men, went down to the Mousetrap, pretended several times to do his business, and exposed himself in front of people.

10:30 pm. One known pederast loitered on the boulevard and masturbated with a man in the Coal-Box. Another, known for cruising often in suspect places, had been arrested with another man in the Coal-Box on 1 September and released.[10] This evening he loitered and cruised on the boulevard for a long time and made remarks about pederasty.

Pierre La Place, 29, native of Mâcon (Burgundy), baker's assistant, lived chez S. Mire, master baker, on rue de la Vieille Draperie.

He was debauched into pederasty two years ago in Mâcon by Vondière, wine vendor there, who came to sell wine in Paris, now deceased. He has amused himself in Paris with several men whose names he does not know, among others at one's place on rue des Poulies, where he went. The day before yesterday, yesterday, and today he went on the quays with the design of amusing himself. He consummated the crime in the active role with the one whose residence he was at on rue des Poulies. /laplace/
C: P

Jean Jacques Hildebrand, 34, native of Hanault in Hesse-Kassel (Germany), stocking worker, lived chez S. Charoy, ragpicker, on rue Neuve Saint-Martin.

He went down to the watering spot at quai des Orfèvres to do his business, which he did. He has never been given over to the debauchery of men. /Jean Jacques hildebrand/
C: W&R

René Jean Baptiste Le Sueur, 51, native of Paris, journeyman joiner, lived on rue du Faubourg Saint-Denis.

He passed through the Coal-Box and met there the man with whom he was arrested because he had had something to drink, but they did nothing wrong. He came back from working on rue de Charenton and had fallen asleep

in the Coal-Box when this man accosted him. He was accused of stealing a watch and put in the Châtelet prison for a month around two years ago. /Lesueur/
C: P

Claude Jolly, 46, native of Paris, journeyman clockmaker, lived chez Masset on rue Sainte-Marguerite in faubourg Saint-Antoine.

He is in the habit of going on the boulevards on Mondays and Saturdays. He is not given over to pederasty. Several days ago he met a man unknown to him on boulevard de la Porte Saint-Antoine, who suggested to him that they amuse themselves. The guard came at that moment and tried to arrest them. This evening he met the same man on the boulevard, who made the same propositions to him, but they did nothing wrong. /U/
C: W&R

150. Monday, 19 September 1785, 9:30 pm
I: Two men loitered and cruised in the Coal-Box. One of them amused himself with another man. The other, a known pederast, made propositions to observers last Monday and Tuesday.

Jacques Louis Vincent, 44, native of Paris, locksmith, lived on rue Saint-Nicolas in faubourg Saint-Antoine.

It is true that passing along boulevard Saint-Antoine he met a man unknown to him, with whom he went down to the Coal-Box. They touched mutually. He was drawn into the vice of liking men by one of the men with whom he drank, specifically with a limonadier's assistant who lived on rue de la Comédie Française, who was the first with whom he amused himself, around two years ago. He knows LeJeune, bourgeois, owner of a house where he lives on rue Saint-Nicolas, to be given over to this vice. /vincent/
C: P

Alexis Trouillet, 46, native of Paris, master shoemaker, lived chez the swordfurbisher on rue des Gravilliers.

Going to faubourg Saint-Antoine, passing along the boulevard, he encountered a man who had lived in a furnished room at his place for a month eighteen months ago. He accosted him and suggested that they sit on the parapet, which they did. They went down below together. He is not given over to pederasty. /U/
C: P

151. Wednesday, 21 September 1785, 9:00 pm
I: A man loitered on boulevard du Pont aux Choux, sat down on the parapet, accosted a man, and made remarks to him about pederasty. They hugged several times and went away together.

Nicolas Paular, 61, native of Paris, former charcoal vendor, now bourgeois de Paris, lived in a house that belonged to him, in which a seed vendor occupied the shop, on rue de Boffrant.

After having supper at Deep in the Valley, he came to take the air on the boulevards. He met a domestic unknown to him there, who asked him what time it was. He told him it was nearly 9:00. This domestic said he had to get back at 9:30 and went by way of rue du Temple. He, the deponent, said he was going to go the same way to return home. To tell the truth, this man took him by the arm, but it is false that they hugged each other. They did nothing wrong. He is not given over to pederasty and has never given himself over to it. /U/
C: W&R

152. Thursday, 22 September 1785, 9:00 pm
I: A known pederast, who loitered daily on the boulevard in the evening, loitered there yesterday and went down to the Coal-Box. This evening he accosted a man with whom he went down to the Coal-Box, where they masturbated independently.

Jean Pellé, 27, native of Sainte-Croix near Cherbourg (Normandy), domestic of Mlle Dossin, lived in the courtyard of the convent of the Daughters of Saint Thomas[11] on rue des Filles Saint-Thomas.

He did not feel well this evening after drinking in La Courtille and went to walk on the boulevard. He did not speak to anyone and is not given over to pederasty. He did not go down to the Coal-Box and never goes on the boulevard. /X/
C: W&R

153. Friday, 23 September 1785, 11:00 pm
I: A man loitered and cruised on quai des Orfèvres, picked up a man, went down to the Mousetrap with him, and appeared to amuse himself with him under the first archway of the Pont Neuf. Another man loitered and cruised and went down to the watering spot with a man. They went under the same archway, where he undid his breeches.

Noël Pierre Foullon, 58, native of Paris, master beltmaker, lived chez Despreneur, gunsmith, on rue de Grenelle Saint-Honoré.

    He has been given over to pederasty for three years. It is true that this evening on quai des Orfèvres he met a man unknown to him, with whom he went down to the Mousetrap. They masturbated and stroked, and this man put it into his mouth. He does not know any of the men with whom he has ever amused himself. He has always amused himself in the Mousetrap. /foulon/
C: P

Georges Eléonor Boutait, 44, native of Paris, doorman of abbé Bardonnet, lived at his residence on rue des Vieilles Tuileries.

    He went down to the watering spot on quai des Orfèvres to do his business, which he did. He was alone and did not speak to anyone on the quay or below. He is not given over to pederasty and has never surrendered himself to it. This evening he came back from the residence of S. Remond, master gilder on rue Guérin Boisseau, on rue Saint-Denis. As he came back, after drinking with Remond at the corner of rue Thévenot, he passed along quai des Orfèvres again. /X/
C: P

154. Saturday, 24 September 1785, 9:00 pm
I: A man loitered on quai des Orfèvres and picked up men, including one in colonial costume, to whom he made remarks about pederasty. He appeared to want to go down to the Mousetrap with him. Two known pederasts were on quai des Augustins.

Jean Louis Broquin, 46, native of Paris, journeyman goldsmith, rented rooms and lived on rue de la Savonnerie.

    He went to quai des Orfèvres to keep an eye on the conduct of his son, 14½, apprentice chez S. Baillet on rue de la Pelleterie, whom he had heard engaged in dissipation in the evening.[12] He spoke to only one man, who asked him what time it was, to whom he replied it was 8:00 and had no other conversation with him. He has not done anything wrong and is not given over to pederasty. /U/
C: W&R

Michel François Nollet, 26, native of Dreux (Orléanais), where he lives, seeking a job in Paris since Tuesday, lodged with his mother on rue Dauphin.

As he passed along rue des Fossés Saint-Germain-des-Prés, the man arrested with him accosted him, said he knew him, walked with him, wanted to lead him to the quay des Augustins, and suggested that he go with him to a friend's place on rue de la Vannerie, near the Grève, to amuse themselves. As they talked, they were arrested. /Nollet/
C: W&R

Etienne Legivre de La Fayette, 22, native of Saint-Ciergues in Lorraine, in the diocese of Trier, former notary's clerk, doing nothing, lodged with his aunt chez S. Laurandeau on rue de la Parcheminerie.

He was debauched into pederasty around two and a half months ago by a Knight of Malta[13] who lives on cul-de-sac des Quatre Vents. He amused himself with him in the courtyard of the Saint-Germain fair. He has also amused himself with several other men unknown to him in various promenades and on rue de la Vannerie, chez a man whose name he does not know, with whom he amused himself and masturbated. Several suggested putting it into him, but he did not want to do it. He saw the man arrested with him twice, two years ago. He, the deponent, encountered and accosted him this evening on rue des Fossés Saint-Germain-des-Prés and suggested that he go with him to the man's place on rue de la Vannerie. They were arrested. /le Givre De Lafayette/
C: P

155. Sunday, 25 September 1785, 7:00 pm–1:00 am
PP: Pont Neuf, quays, northern boulevards, taverns on the boulevard and adjacent streets

I: 9:30 pm. A man known for suspect conduct for a long time accosted a man in the Coal-Box, seemed to stroke with him, suggested that he go to his place, and made a rendezvous with him in the same place on Wednesday.

Claude Philibert Monneret, 44, native of Saint-Claude in Franche-Comté, personal valet of the comte d'Orfeuille,[14] at whose residence he lived in the Temple.

He does not have a confirmed taste for pederasty. Around fifteen months ago, when he was a bit drunk on wine, he encountered a man on the boulevard who made propositions to him, with whom he amused himself. Since then he has amused himself several times with men he does not know, but

this does not happen to him anymore. He senses the full horror of it all the more from being summoned. As he went to do his business in the Coal-Box this evening, he encountered a man with whom he stroked and masturbated. As he came up onto the boulevard, he was arrested. /Monneret/
C: W&R in the custody of his master, who claimed him and promised to keep an eye on his conduct

156. Monday, 26 September 1785, 10:30 pm
I: A man loitered on boulevard Montmartre and picked up a man with whom he entered rue Saint-Fiacre, where they chatted and masturbated independently, after which he returned to cruising on the boulevard.

François Maujean, 24, native of Bar-le-Duc (Lorraine), shoemaker's assistant, worked chez S. Deslandes, master shoemaker, on rue Montorgeuil and lived chez S. Fradieline, joiner, on rue du Sentier.

He did not speak to or accost anyone on the boulevard and was not in rue Saint-Fiacre. He is not given over to the debauchery of men. /Maujean/
C: P

157. Tuesday, 27 September 1785, 10:30 pm
I: A known pederast loitered in the most suspect manner on quai des Orfèvres, took several turns, went down to the Mousetrap, and picked up a man with whom he went under an archway, where they appeared to stroke.

Jean Paul Roussel, 30, native of Paris, tailor's assistant, worked and lived with his brother, also tailor's assistant, chez the wigmaker on rue Pavée Saint-Sauveur.

He does not know which streets he passed through, did not go down to the edge of the river, did not speak to anyone, and is not given over to the vice of liking men. He walked this evening. /rousselle/
C: P

158. Friday, 30 September 1785, 7:00 pm–1:00 am
PP: northern boulevards, small streets and cul-de-sacs off the boulevards, OP

I: 9:00. A known pederast, arrested on 7 September 1784,[15] loitered on rue Saint-Antoine, picked up several others, struck up conversations with them, and went down to the Coal-Box with one of them, where they appeared to stroke. He came back up alone and cruised again.

Charles Pancelot, 46, native of Javerdat in Anjou, day laborer, lived on rue Saint-Pierre at the Pont aux Choux.

He was making his way along the boulevard, where he was walking. He is not given over to pederasty and was already arrested once on the boulevard. /U/
C: P

I: 9:30 pm. Two known pederasts who lived together cruised on the boulevards every evening.

Guillaume Bornan, 31, native of Rumilly in Savoy (Italy), former gingerbread vendor, then involved in smuggling brandy, lodged chez a cobbler who rented rooms on rue du Faubourg Saint-Denis, beyond Saint-Lazare.[16]

He was debauched into pederasty around twelve years ago by an old man whose name he does not recall. He does not know the other man arrested with him and was on the boulevard with another. To tell the truth, he spoke to the man arrested with him and does not remember if he spoke to him yesterday. /U/
C: P

François Nicolas Mignot, 21, native of Paris, glaziery worker, lived at the Desire boardinghouse on rue du Faubourg Saint-Denis.

He has known the man arrested with him for four years, whom he knows by the name of Mauny, who has slept under the same tester [in the same bed] as him for a month. To tell the truth, he goes to the boulevards in the evening sometimes. He is not given over to the vice of liking men. He was arrested and imprisoned in the month of September 1782[17] and enlisted in the Paris regiment, in which he is still a soldier. /U/
C: P

OCTOBER

159. Monday, 3 October 1785, 8:00 pm
I: Two men appeared to masturbate mutually in the Coal-Box. The taller one, who had his breeches down, fled when observers approached but came back later.

Nicolas Joseph Simon, 17, native of Paris, parish of Sainte-Marguerite (11th arr.), cabinetmaker, worked and lived chez his father, cabinetmaker, on rue de Charenton opposite the Convent of the English Women.[1]

After leaving work he encountered Antoine +Pringal,+ journeyman sculptor, arrested with him, whom he has known for a long time. They had been to The Little Charonne[2] and came back to the boulevard and then to the Coal-Box. He went there at the solicitation of Antoine Pringal, who debauched him into pederasty around a year and a half ago. They amused themselves together several times in the Coal-Box, where they consummated the crime several times in the active and passive roles, alternatively, in the Coal-Box as well as alleys and the lane called ruelle de Terre-forte. This evening they put it into each other in the Coal-Box. /Simon/
C: P

Antoine Romegout, called Pringal, 17, native of Paris, parish of Sainte-Marguerite, journeyman sculptor, lived with his father, sweeper at the Quinze-Vingts hospital,[3] chez S. Claveris, upholsterer, on rue de Charenton.

Since 6:00 he has been with Simon, also arrested with him, with whom he was in school, whom he had stopped seeing and met again only a month ago. They went to walk on the boulevard and did not do anything wrong. He is not given over to pederasty and has never surrendered himself to it. /romegout/
C: P

The commissaire recalled Simon, who reaffirmed his statement, which Romegout denied. Simon signed again, but Romegout refused to do so.

160. Wednesday, 5 October 1785, 8:00 pm
I: A man loitered in the Luxembourg and picked up a man, with whom he sat down on a bench in the darkest pathway. They appeared to stroke. The first man persuaded the second to leave with him. He took him by the arm and gave him money in rue de Tournon.

Jean Louis Daniel, 32, native of Paris, domestic, formerly at the Collège des Trente-Trois,[4] currently unemployed, lived with his father, limonadier, on rue du Faubourg Saint-Jacques.

He went to walk this evening in the Luxembourg garden, where he often goes. As he was sitting on a bench, a young man who seemed drunk came

and sat near him, asked him what time it was, unbuttoned his breeches, and tried to take his hand and place it on him. He, the deponent, withdrew his hand and told him he was a rascal [*polisson*]. This man placed his hand on his thigh, on his breeches, and he pulled back. This man, with whom he conversed for a while, told him he had been in Paris for two weeks, is from Provence and a jeweler, and lives chez S. Du Bertrand, jeweler, on rue Saint-Honoré. Seeing that another man accosted this one, fearing for him that he would be arrested, he, the deponent, took him by the arm and obliged him to leave with him. He intended to walk him back to his place and alert S. Du Bertrand about his imprudence. Before leaving the garden the man gave him a piece of paper, which he said was his address. He held it in his hand as far as rue de Tournon, where, by some light from a shop, he tried to read it but could not and put it in his fob pocket. He did not take money out and did not give any to this man, who, on the contrary, offered to give him an écu worth three livres, which he, the deponent, refused. He is not given over to pederasty. /Daniel/
C: W&R

I: A man masturbated on the Sofa with a man who escaped arrest.

Marc Antoine Hervieux, 36, native of Orbec in Normandy, unemployed domestic, lived on rue Jean Saint-Denis.

    For three or four years he has had the misfortune, at times when he has been drinking, to give himself over to pederasty. He was debauched into it when he was a wigmaker's assistant, by another wigmaker's assistant, whose name he does not know. On quai du Louvre this evening he met another man, unknown to him, and they masturbated independently. He was already arrested for this reason around three years ago and conducted to the hôtel de La Force.[5] /hervieu/
C: P

161. Thursday, 6 October 1785, 10:00 pm
I: A known pederast, already arrested on 23 August 1784,[6] loitered in the Coal-Box and picked up men.

Olivier Chatenet, called Laurent, 53,[7] native of Paris, journeyman smelter, worked at his place and lived at the Châlons boardinghouse on rue du Figuier near Saint-Paul.

For around two years he has been given over again to pederasty, which he had abandoned for several years, after being given over to it twelve years ago. This evening he went to the Coal-Box and met a man, but they did not amuse themselves because they did not have time. To tell the truth, he went there with the intention of amusing himself. /U/
C: P

162. Friday, 7 October 1785, 11:00 pm
I: A known pederast staged parties, brought the men he picked up to sleep with him at his place on rue Montmartre, and paid them. He cruised on that boulevard and in rue Saint-Fiacre.

Joseph Brunet, 30, native of Paris, journeyman mason, lived chez S. Brière on rue du Faubourg Montmartre opposite the Saint-Jean chapel.

 He was debauched into pederasty on the boulevards three years ago by a young man. He has consummated the crime several times in the active and passive roles with men unknown to him, on the boulevards and once in his room with a man he does not know, who told him he is a hairdresser, with whom he likewise consummated the crime. He went to the boulevard this evening to find someone with whom to amuse himself. He went into rue Saint-Fiacre and lowered his breeches when he saw a man coming, whom he expected to stop with him. /U/
C: P

163. Friday, 7 October 1785, 8:00 pm
I: A man who stroked with a man in the stoneyard yesterday stroked mutually this evening with a man who escaped arrest.

Pierre François Le Grault, 28, native of Paris, cook of Messire Desprez, clerk in the Châtelet, lived at his residence on rue Neuve Saint-Merri.

 He was debauched into pederasty only around two months ago by Morin, fruit vendor, who lives on rue de la Savonnerie, with whom he has masturbated several times. He had abandoned this vice, which he had been previously debauched into seven to eight years ago by Petit Jean, wine vendor's assistant, who left Paris around six years ago. He went into the stones that are near the Comédie Française yesterday to do his business. He was accosted there by a man unknown to him, who stroked him. He, the deponent, suggested that he take him to his place, but this man did not want to and made

a rendezvous with him this evening at the billiard parlor on rue des Fossés de Monsieur le Prince. He, the deponent, was there this evening and did not find him in the billiard parlor but met him again among the stones. They did nothing but hug each other. This man told him he lives on rue Saint-Germain-l'Auxerrois, and they agreed to go there to amuse themselves. As they went there with this design, he, the deponent, was arrested. /legroult/
C: P

164. Saturday, 8 October 1785, 6:30 pm–12:00 am
PP: northern boulevards, Coal-Box, small streets and cul-de-sacs off the boulevards, quays, OP

I: 8:15. A man picked up a man on the boulevard. They went down to the Coal-Box and masturbated. The first man had his breeches down, and the second man escaped arrest.

Nicolas Hilaire {Jolly} Gelé, 36, native of Meaux (Ile-de-France), mattress carder, lived chez S. Monnier, perfumer, on rue aux Ours.

He is not given over to pederasty. He was accosted on the boulevard this evening by a man unknown to him, who persuaded him to go down to the Coal-Box. He went there with him and had the weakness to amuse himself with this man. It is true he had his breeches down when he was arrested. /Gele/
C: P

165. Monday, 10 October 1785, 8:00 pm
I: Two men close to each other in the darkest spot in the Coal-Box separated when observers approached.

Mathieu Lenoir, 22, native of Metzerwisse in Lorraine, domestic of M. Villiot, officer in the royal guards, lived at his residence on rue de la Boucherie in Gros Caillou.

He was a bit overheated with drink and went to walk on boulevard de la Porte Saint-Antoine. He went down to the Coal-Box to do his business. While he was there the man arrested with him accosted him, stood near him, and pissed. He, the deponent, told him there were no prostitutes in this spot this evening. The other told him, "No, but one can jerk off," and at that moment placed his hand on his parts. He, the deponent, also stroked him and then

said, "This does not go well when one does not see any prostitutes." They then separated, and he was arrested. This is the first time this has happened to him, and it will not happen to him again. /matts chvartz [Schwartz]/
C: P

Jacques Ternisien, 41, native of Herly in Boulonnais [Picardy], majordomo of M. de Villedeuil, intendant of Rouen,[8] lived at his residence on place des Vosges.[9]

He is not given over to pederasty. He was alone in the Coal-Box, did not accost anyone, and did not speak to the other man. Neither one of them stroked. /ternisien/
C: P

The commissaire recalled Lenoir, who reaffirmed his statement, which Ternisien denied. He had been arrested on 20 December 1782,[10] "improperly."

I: 9:00 pm. A known pederast loitered and cruised on the boulevard.

Denis Schpiler, 21, native of Montmartre, floor polisher, lived at the Princes boardinghouse on rue de Bondy.

He is not at all given over to pederasty. It is true that on the second of this month he met a man unknown to him on the boulevard, a hairdresser, and slept at his place on rue de l'Arbre sec. He is the only one with whom he has had relations. /denis spieller/
C: P

166. Tuesday, 11 October 1785, 7:30 pm
I: A known pederast amused himself with another man in the Mousetrap on Saturday and loitered on quai de Conti yesterday. Today he loitered there and then on the Sofa. He accosted a man, apparently the same man as on Saturday, and struck up a conversation with him. This man escaped arrest.

Jean Charles Michel, 21, native of Paris, unemployed journeyman jeweler, lived chez the perfumer on rue des Marmousets on Ile de la Cité.

He has surrendered himself to pederasty only since Saturday. He amused himself below quai des Orfèvres with a man unknown to him, whom he met on the quay. This man persuaded him to go down and made him many fine promises, among others to procure him to someone proper who would give

him money, which made him yield. They masturbated independently. They met again yesterday evening on the same quay but did nothing and made a rendezvous on quai de Conti in front of the Mint. He, the deponent, went there but did not find him. As he, the deponent, went away, he met this man at the end of the Pont Neuf. They went off together on quai du Louvre, and as soon as they arrived there, he, the deponent, was arrested. He has never amused himself at this vice with other persons and only on Saturday with this man. /Michel/
C: P

167. Wednesday, 12 October 1785, 7:30 pm
I: A man observed several times in the Mousetrap loitered for a long time there, went back up on quai des Orfèvres, picked up a man, and went back down with him under the archways, where they were next to each other for a long time. One resisted, which allowed the other to escape arrest.

Louis Ribot, 22, native of Sceaux in Maine, journeyman mason and soldier in the Vivarais regiment, on leave in Paris, lived with his father, stonecutter, chez S. Lefevre, employee of the Chambre des Comptes,[11] on rue de la Calandre.

He went down to the watering spot below quai des Orfèvres to do his business. After that he walked along the edge of the river and went back up. He met a man on the quay who said to him, "The weather is fine. Would you like to come and walk?" He, the deponent, said nothing to him but followed him and went back down after him under the houses [on rue Saint-Louis], where they rejoined each other. This man asked him if he amuses himself often, to which he replied no, and it is very rarely. He asked him if he had a [missing word] at his place, and he, the deponent, said yes. He is not given over to pederasty and has never surrendered himself to it. /Ribot/
C: P

I: 11:45 pm. A man loitered on boulevard Montmartre for more than an hour and picked up men with whom amused himself.

Antoine Besson, 24, native of Rouillat in Auvergne, domestic of M. Augeard, private secretary of the queen,[12] lived at his residence on boulevard Montmartre.

While he was on the boulevard, he amused himself by looking at a man who masturbated himself before him, the deponent, and tried to touch him. Then another man came and shoved his hand into his breeches. To tell the

truth, he, the deponent, allowed it, but he is not given over to pederasty and has never surrendered himself to it. /antoine besson/
C: W&R

168. Thursday, 13 October 1785, 6:30 pm–12:30 am
PP: quays, northern boulevards, Mousetrap, Coal-Box, small streets and cul-de-sacs off the boulevards, OP

I: 7:45. A man loitered in the Mousetrap and picked up a man, remained with him for a long time, and appeared to stroke and give him money.

8:45. A known pederast had lived with Albert, previously arrested and exiled, and had been arrested on 5 July 1781.[13] Since then he loitered and cruised "openly" on the boulevard and this evening in the Coal-Box for more than an hour.

Jean Baptiste Thirion, 44, native of Versailles (Ile-de-France), former officer of the goblet of Monsieur, supplied the royal household with cream and butter and lived on rue des Recollets in Versailles, parish of Saint-Louis.

He is not given over to pederasty. Feeling pressed by a need to go, he went down below the quay to satisfy it and set about it. A man unknown to him passed and repassed before him several times and asked him what time it was. After doing his business, he wished to know, out of curiosity, who this man was, whom he saw go under an archway near the spot where he was. He went there, and this man came to him, asked him if he wanted to amuse himself and go further, and stroked him through his breeches. Having then understood this man's intentions, he told him that he was not of that condition[14] and that he practiced a vile trade. This man replied that he did it because he had no bread. He, the deponent, gave him three or four sols in change he had and said to him, "Here, my child, here is enough to buy some, and don't do this vile business anymore." He withdrew and was arrested after leaving this man, who told him he is a glazier. /thirion/
C: P because he had no papers on him to verify his identity

André Forch, 37,[15] native of Riga in Livonia,[16] lived on his own resources after leaving commerce, lived at the house where the sign of The Doe's Foot used to hang on rue du Faubourg Saint-Denis. He had rosettes on his shoes.

He walked on the boulevards this evening, went down below, did not see anyone there, and did not speak to anyone on the boulevards. He said he

is not given over to pederasty and admitted he had been arrested on the boulevard four years ago. /forch/
C: W&R again

169. 15 October 1785, 8:45 pm
I: A man loitered and cruised on the quays for several days and amused himself with a man in the Mousetrap yesterday. Today he loitered on quai des Orfèvres, picked up a man, and struck up conversation and entered several alleys with him.

Louis Isidore Charpentier, 18, native of Mesnil near Epernay in Champagne, journeyman casemaker and soldier in the Paris regiment, lived at the Saint-Martin market.[17]

He went to walk on the quay this evening and met a man on quai des Augustins who made propositions about pederasty to him and led him into an alley, but he did not wish to go all the way into it or to go further with this man. It is true he amused himself yesterday, below the quay, with another man he does not know. It was the first time he amused himself at this debauchery. /U/
C: P

170. Monday 17 October 1785, 6:00 pm–1:00 am
PP: quays, exits of the Tuileries, place Louis XV, OP

I: 8:30 pm. Three men loitered in the Tuileries, picked up men, and stroked with them.

Jean Libéral, 18, native of Paris, shoemaker's assistant, lived chez Ferdinand, master shoemaker, in Roule (8th arr.), and did not work today.

He had the misfortune to be debauched into pederasty around a year ago by Bourguignon [Burgundian], also shoemaker's assistant, with whom he slept chez S. Meny, master shoemaker, on rue Bergère. They consummated the crime together several times in the active and passive roles. Bourguignon also took him to the Tuileries, where he informed him that one amuses oneself at this debauchery. He has also surrendered himself to this debauchery with some other persons, specifically in a room on the fifth floor in the first alley on the Pont au Change,[18] near rue de Gesvres, with a man who took him to his place, with whom he also consummated the crime in the passive role, who

gave him three livres. This evening he went to the Tuileries and met a man there who promised to pay for his supper and give him three livres. /U/
C: P

Pierre François Pecquet, 18, native of Paris, assistant of his father, grocer and apothecary, lived at his residence on rue du Faubourg Saint-Jacques opposite the Val-de-Grâce.[19]

Led on by Marion, sacristan of the Val-de-Grâce, Bigonnet, minor clerk of a notary on rue de Condé, +Santigny, apprentice upholsterer of S. Letoffe in faubourg Saint-Jacques,+ his comrades, and one Lanois, he went yesterday evening and this evening in order to see the men who amuse themselves and in order to get money from them. One gave Lanois eighteen sols yesterday. This evening he, the deponent, met a man in the garden who promised him six livres for going with him to his place and amusing themselves. As he went with him to a tavern near the Louvre gate, where they were going to fondle, he, the deponent, was arrested. Before he saw this man he had already spoken to another in the Tuileries, who wished to lead him chez the Swiss [Guard], but he was not there. It is his comrades who advised him to lend himself to these sorts of men to get money. /P. f. Pecquet/
C: R in the custody of his mother, who promised to keep an eye on his conduct

Charles Joseph Hoffmann, 24, native of Bounettz (?) near Aix-la-Chapelle (Germany), tailor's assistant, lodged in a room for tailor's assistants on rue des Boucheries in faubourg Saint-Germain.

He has never surrendered himself to the debauchery of men. Today he had only twenty-four sols and, after spending them, went to the Tuileries and sat down there. A well-dressed gentleman came and accosted him. They fondled independently. This gentleman promised him three livres to go amuse himself with him. As he left he was arrested. /Hoffmann/
C: P

171. Tuesday, 18 October 1785, 7:30 pm
I: A known pederast who prostituted himself for money left Paris and returned five or six days ago. He loitered and cruised, even in broad daylight, in the Tuileries and Palais Royal. He picked up a young man in the Tuileries yesterday at 1:00 pm. They agreed to go amuse themselves and left together. He

picked up an old man in the Tuileries today between 3:00 and 4:00 pm. He then returned to the Palais Royal, where he picked up, across from the Comic Medley, the same man with whom he left the Tuileries yesterday.

Jean Baptiste Senemaud, 18, native of Limoges (Limousin), unemployed journeyman jeweler, back in Paris for four or five days, after ten months away, lived chez Deschamps, bachelor from his native region, also jeweler's assistant, on rue des Arcis.

He was debauched into pederasty three or four years ago by a friend of his whose name he does not recall, who is no longer in Paris. Since his return to Paris he has been to the Tuileries and the Palais Royal. Yesterday he was accosted in the Tuileries by a man unknown to him, who took him to his room on a street he does not know, where they amused themselves together and this man paid for his drink and food. He, the deponent, returned there at 10:00 pm yesterday and slept with the man. He left there about 8:00 am. They made a rendezvous for this evening in the Palais Royal. Before going there, he, the deponent, went to the Tuileries and spoke to no one there. He came back to the Palais Royal, where he met the man with whom he had slept. As they left together, he, the deponent, was arrested, and the other escaped. /Sénémaud/
C: P

172. **Wednesday, 19 October 1785, 8:00 pm**
I: A known pederast, arrested in the Mousetrap on 13 November 1784 and imprisoned, picked up men on quai des Orfèvres, entered an alley with one of them for a few minutes, then walked along quai de la Vallée and through the Palais de Justice to place Dauphine. He picked up a man and urged him, on rue de Nevers, to take him to his place, "inasmuch as there was too much risk in the Mousetrap and elsewhere."

Philippe Rousseau, 33, native of Nouans (Maine), domestic of his aunt, fruit vendor, lived at her residence on rue aux Fers.

On the parapet of quai des Orfèvres he met a man he does not know, who offered to go to his place to amuse themselves, or another day. He was on rue de Nevers, retraced his steps, and returned to the Pont Neuf, then place Dauphine, where he was arrested. He had indeed just spoken to the same person for the second time but did not wish to go to his place. He offered

to go down to the Mousetrap with him, but he did not want to and told him there was too much danger, but there is no danger. He will not expose himself to it any longer. He has been in Paris for fifteen years and has never seen a woman for fear of catching a disease. /rousseau/
C: P (La Force)[20]

173. Thursday, 20 October 1785, 8:00 pm
I: Two men masturbated in the Mousetrap with a third who loitered in the same spot. He picked up a man with whom he appeared to masturbate under the archways under quai de Gesvres.

Jean Jacques Mainot, 36, native of Rouen (Normandy), tree vendor in Rouen, where he lives on the boulevard in the parish of Saint-Patrice, in Paris as of today to go to Vitry to buy trees, lodged chez a seed vendor on rue de la Huchette, on the side of Pont Saint-Michel.

It has never happened to him to amuse himself with men in Paris. He went down to a spot to do his business, and a man unknown to him came to him. They masturbated independently. /Jacques Maimot/
C: P

Louis Hadet, 48, native of Montreuil-sur-Mer (Picardy), rents rooms on rue Jean Robert near Saint-Nicolas-des-Champs.[21]

He had never amused himself with men. He did it today for the first time below quai des Orfèvres, where he went down to do his business. He met a man unknown to him there. They masturbated independently. /hadet/
C: P

174. Saturday, 22 October 1785, 7:30 pm
I: A man loitered on the Sofa and picked up a wigmaker's assistant, whom he appeared to wish to stroke, which the latter appeared to refuse. He went down to the edge of the river, picked up someone else, and struck up a conversation with him. The wigmaker came back up and asked him, "Which of these two rascals is it?" The first man and the second man he picked up went to quai des Orfèvres and down to the Mousetrap, appeared to stroke, came back up, went to drink in a tavern on rue Saint-Louis, then went to place Dauphine. They hugged several times, stroked, and appeared to look for a spot to amuse themselves. One escaped arrest.

Pierre Patelle, called The Stone, 65, native of Billy in the diocese of Verdun (Lorraine), domestic, unemployed for nine months, without certificates, lodged chez Mme Andrieu, vegetable vendor, on rue Mazarine.

    He is not given over to pederasty. On quai de l'Ecole, near the Pont Neuf, he met a man, a wigmaker's assistant, who spoke to him and told him there was a man lying on the steps that go down to the river. Then another man unknown to him suggested to him that they go walk by the edge of the water. They went down to the watering spot at quai des Orfèvres, where they did their business. The man suggested to him that they go under the archways, to do he does not know what, which he, the deponent, refused. Then they came back up and went to drink a mug of wine in a tavern on rue Saint-Louis. When they left, he, the deponent, made water in the street near the gate of the First President [of the Parlement]'s residence.[22] While he was there, the man stroked him. They went on by way of rue du Harlay, where the man hugged him several times. He told him to go away, and he, the deponent, was arrested. He is not given over to pederasty. /U/
C: P

175. Monday, 24 October 1785, 8:30 pm
I: Two men loitered in the Tuileries, picked up men, with whom they appeared to stroke, and talked about pederasty.

Hugues Louis Huby, 20, native of Paris, water carrier, lived with his mother, laundrywoman, on rue de Beaujolais, at the former Quatre-Vingts hospital.

    As he was in the Tuileries and pissed near a tree, a gentleman came near him and fondled him. He goes to the Tuileries often in the evening and was fondled another time by another man. He left with him to go to his room. +Another time in the summer he pulled his breeches down one time before another gentleman, but he has never received money.+ /U/
C: P

Antoine Pierre Turet, 16, native of Paris, apprentice wigmaker in the Palais Royal.

    As he entered the Tuileries this evening, a man urged him to go to his place with him and told him they would amuse themselves together. He suggested that he give him six livres and said that if he was pleased with him, he would buy him an outfit and find him a position. He, the deponent, hoped

that he could place him as a domestic and consented to go with him. When they left, he was arrested. /Thuret/
C: W&R

176. Tuesday, 25 October 1785, 7:00 pm
I: Four known pederasts who committed extortion, "through finesse or violence," cruised around the Comédie Française every evening.

Jean Dumas, 18, native of Clermont in Auvergne, errand boy, lived chez Mme Tonette, coal-woman who rented rooms on rue de Buci.

At the beginning of the summer, Poignon, errand boy at the Comédie Française, who had no home, debauched him into pederasty and took him {among the stones at the Comédie Française} to look for the chevalier de Béarn,[23] on cul-de-sac des Quatre Vents, who touched them both, masturbated Poignon, and gave them eighteen livres, which they divided. Yesterday evening a gentleman he does not know picked him up, took him to a stairway in the Luxembourg where he, the deponent, masturbated him, and gave him forty-eight sols. He knows André, arrested with him, has also been to the chevalier de Béarn's place, amused him, received from him he does not know how much. This evening near the Comédie Française a man also picked him up with André and promised each of them six livres to go party with another man. They were going there when they were arrested. /U/
C: P

André Carié, 17, native of Sougy in Bourbonnais, errand boy, resided on rue de Buci with his comrade Clément.

On Sunday a gentleman {he does not know}, vigorous, around 40 to 45, dressed in a gray jacket, left the Comédie Française about 8:00 pm and took him, on the pretext of an errand, to the residence of some prostitutes on a small street off rue Saint-Martin. He sent one of the women to get a birch broom, made a large fistful from it, which he tied with cord, and wet it. He undid his breeches and told him to whip him with all his strength and he would give him three livres. He did it until he had enough. He received three livres from him and fled. Around six months ago, Poignon, errand boy, took him to the chevalier de Béarn's place on cul-de-sac des Quatre Vents, where they amused, fondled, and masturbated him, and he gave him twelve francs. This evening a man he does not know picked them up in the courtyard of fountains in the Luxembourg, suggested a party, and told them they would

each have six francs for it. They were going there when they were arrested on the Pont Neuf. Poignon, who is the one who debauched him, unfortunately, into pederasty, in recent days stole three louis from a young man and a frockcoat of good grayish white ratteen from him, the deponent. He has not reappeared at the Comédie Française since. /U/
C: P

Jean Baptiste Brondel, called Baptiste, 15 to 16, native of Aurillac in Auvergne, errand boy, lived chez a fruit vendor who rented rooms {on rue Saint-Jacques} at the entrance to faubourg Saint-Jacques.

He is not given over to pederasty. He ran an errand with a letter a woman had him take to the chevalier de Béarn on cul-de-sac des Quatre Vents, whom he knows to be given over to pederasty. The chevalier de Béarn gave him six sols and jingled many écus of six livres but did not make any propositions to him. It is false that he amuses men among the stones. There are several of them who made propositions to him, which he refused. +He amused a hunchback he does not know, whom he believes to be English, on rue des Cordeliers, around three weeks ago. He gave him six sols. This evening he indeed went off with his comrade to amuse another who had taken three livres from him.+ /U/
C: P

Michel Blanchard, 14, native of Brouains in the bishopric of Avranches (Normandy), bootblack and errand boy, lived chez Picard, secondhand dealer, on rue des Postes.

He is not at all given over to pederasty and has never amused himself with any man. Several he does not know made propositions to him, which he never accepted. A man picked him up this evening, along with his comrade Baptiste, and promised each of them three livres to amuse a man. His comrade went there, and he went there only because he was forced by this man. Then he said that around a month ago a man who lives on an alley across from an eating house, near the collège d'Harcourt, debauched him. He masturbated him and let himself be fondled by him. He gave him twenty-four sols and urged him to return, but he has not been there again. As for his comrade Baptiste, he has fondled and amused several men, among others one near the Cour du Commerce [Saint-André] and told him he would find hardly any others to amuse because he is too badly fitted out. /U/
C: P

177. Wednesday, 26 October 1785, 1:00 am

I: André Bourgot, called Poignon, a known pederast, arrested and imprisoned on 14 July (#108), released on 4 August, promised to leave Paris but did not. He "continued to surrender himself to pederasty to make money from it and to subject persons who yield to him to extortion." He was also suspected of theft, specifically of three louis from a young man and of a frock coat loaned to him by André Carié.

André Bourgot, called Poignon, 17, native of Paris,[24] day laborer, lived chez Mme Dupré, who rented rooms on rue Barre du Bec.

Since he left prison in the month of August, he has remained in Paris but has earned nothing from pederasty. He does not return to the doors of the Comédie Française because one of his comrades, named André David, whose mother lives in Vaugirard, entrusted a silver watch to him, and a secondhand dealer, to whom he sold it, withheld it from him, without paying for it, unless he explains where it came from. He went to find David's mother, who went with him and waited for him. She went away, and he did not find her again.
/bourgot/
C: P

NOVEMBER

178. Tuesday, 1 November 1785, 1:30 am

I: Two men loitered arm in arm on boulevard du Temple, from the Temple gate to the Pont aux Choux, then went to ruelle de l'Ane Rayé, where they stopped several times.

Jean Baptiste Chilliatre, nicknamed de Courval, 31, native of Châlons in Champagne, journeyman marble mason chez S. Levrot at the Pont au Choux and grenadier in the Paris regiment, lived on rue Neuve Saint-Martin.

This evening he went to drink in La Courtille with Monnier, arrested with him, as well as Monnier's father, mother, and brother. Then he, the deponent, and Monnier went to the boulevard, believing they would find a café open there in which to drink brandy. They found them all closed, and he walked back with Monnier, who lives on rue des Maures in faubourg Saint-Laurent. He was arrested as they passed through rue de Lancrey, and

he does not know why. He did nothing wrong, had no bad intentions, and is not at all given over to pederasty. /U/
C: W&R

Pierre Monnier, 21, native of Rouen, gauze worker, lived with his parents on rue Saint-Maur in faubourg Saint-Laurent.

He was drinking in La Courtille with his father, mother, brother, and Chilliatre, called de Courval, also arrested. After they left the tavern, Chilliatre and he went to the boulevard to drink brandy, believing they would find the Chinese Café still open, but they found it closed. They returned, and Chilliatre walked him back. They passed through rue Lancray to return and were arrested. He does not know why. He did nothing wrong and is not at all given over to pederasty. /monnier/
C: W&R

179. Wednesday, 2 November 1785, 10:15 pm
I: A man unbuttoned his breeches, stroked, and talked about pederasty with a man in the Coal-Box.

Louis Mathieu Collin, 25, native of Basel in Switzerland, engraver on wood, lived at S. Ponce's house, on the fifth floor, on rue de Saintonge in the Marais.

In passing along quai des Orfèvres, he encountered a man unknown to him, who struck up a conversation with him, in the course of which this man asked him if he likes women. He, the deponent, had heard there are men on this quay who like men. He suspected this man is of this stripe [*trempe*][1] and wished, out of curiosity, to hear him reason and see how far he would take things. He replied no, he does not like women. The man caressed his chin, told him he is nice, and urged him to go down to the edge of the river with him. He went down there, and the man led him under an archway between the watering spot and the Pont Neuf. He drew three or four écus of six livres [from his pocket] and offered them to him. He, the deponent, refused them. He told him that if he were a good boy, he could come see him at his place but, however, did not give him his address. To see how far this man would go,[2] he, the deponent, told him that if he found a man who pleased him well, he would lend himself to this debauchery. At that moment he, the deponent, was arrested. He did not do anything else. Everything he did and said was only out of curiosity. He has never surrendered himself to the debauchery of

men, married four years ago, lives with his wife, has one child living, and had another who is dead. His wife is pregnant with a third. /Louis Matthieu Collin/
C: P

180. Friday, 4 November 1785, 8:00 pm
I: A young man who surrendered himself to pederasty to earn money loitered in the stoneyard yesterday and followed a man. Today he loitered and picked up a man with whom he appeared to masturbate and stroke.

Nicolas Camus, 13, native of Dijon (Burgundy), son of a deceased day laborer named Bourguignon, errand boy at the Comédie Française, lodged chez widow Girardet, who rented rooms on rue Copeau.

He was debauched into liking men by Poignon and Baptiste around a year ago. He does it now only from time to time. He was already arrested and imprisoned for this in the month of April [#61]. This evening in the stones at the Comédie Française he met a man unknown to him, who fondled him and had himself fondled by him, the deponent. He, the deponent, asked him for something to buy bread, but he gave him nothing. Another time he amused a doorman who lives on rue Feron, who gave him twelve sols. That is all since he left prison. Yesterday he tried to find someone in the stones but found nothing there. /U/
C: P

I: 9:00 pm. Two known pederasts picked up men in the Tuileries. One cruised there often. He made remarks about pederasty and agreed to go to a man's place. The other accosted a man who was urinating, then two others with whom he took several turns and made remarks about pederasty. These two escaped arrest.

Gaetan Lehardelay, 16, native of Orléans (Orléanais), building painter, lived with his father, master painter, chez a ropemaker on rue Pastourelle in the Marais.

It is the chevalier de Béarn, who lives on cul-de-sac des Quatre Vents, at whose residence he worked with his father, who urged him, five months ago, to go to the Tuileries in the evening. He told him he would find men there who would give him money for amusing himself with them, which would pull him

out of the indigence he was in. His father does not allow him to go out, so he could not profit from this advice. But this evening his father sent him with his little brother, aged 9 and a half, chez M. Michelon, physician, who lives in the Tuileries palace. He left his brother at the end of the Pont Royal and went to the residence of S. Michelon, whom he did not find at home, then went to walk under the trees in the garden with the intention of finding someone who would give him money, as the chevalier de Béarn had told him. He indeed met a gentleman in a jacket with silver braid who told him he would give him three livres if he wished to go with him to his place to amuse themselves. He, the deponent, consented, and when he left, he was arrested. He, the deponent, believed the amusement this gentleman spoke to him about was both of them masturbating. He has never done it, however, with any man. /lehardelay/
C: P

Pierre Bruno Lefuelle, 20, native of La Roche Guyon (Ile-de-France), assistant of S. de Grandmaison, fabric vendor,[3] lived at his residence at the Providence boardinghouse on quai Pelletier.

He was in the Tuileries with S. de Grandmaison, and they walked there. S. de Grandmaison spoke to a man in a jacket with gold braid. He had heard it said that S. de Grandmaison is given over to pederasty, but he, the deponent, is not given over to it. His parents boarded him chez S. de Grandmaison nearly six months ago. It is S. de Grandmaison who persuaded him to go to the Tuileries with him. /Lefuel/
C: W&R

181. Saturday, 5 November 1785, 7:00 pm
I: A man picked up a man on quai des Orfèvres. They walked, stroked through their breeches, chatted about pederasty, and walked away to the New Market to find a convenient alley in which to amuse themselves.

André Lebel, 40, native of Paris, day laborer, lived on rue des Nonaindières.

As he passed along quai des Orfèvres, a man unknown to him asked him, "Where are you going?" He replied he was going to the New Market to buy herring and, as we went there, he was arrested. He has never amused himself with men, and he did not stroke at all with the man. They did not chat about men or amusement at all. /U/
C: W&R

182. Sunday, 6 November 1785, 8:30 pm
I: A known pederast sat on a bench with another man in one of the darkest pathways in the Tuileries. The first one had his breeches unbuttoned. They stroked and agreed to go elsewhere.

Louis Langlois, 20, native of Amboise (Touraine), former wigmaker's assistant in Orléans, domestic of S. de Villemary, commissioner of war,[4] lived at his residence, for the last ten days, at the Béarn boardinghouse on rue Feydeau.

He was in the Tuileries and sat down on a bench. A gentleman unknown to him came and sat near him, unbuttoned his breeches, touched him two times, and suggested that he go have supper at his place. He, the deponent, told him he could not do so because he was obliged to get back by 9:00 at the latest. This gentleman suggested to him that they go drink in a tavern where they could amuse themselves. He, the deponent, consented to it in hopes of getting a drink and going away. It is the first time he has surrendered himself to this debauchery. /U/
C: P

183. Monday, 7 November 1785, 6:00 pm–12:00 am
PP: quays, exits of the Tuileries and Palais Royal, OP
I: A known pederast cruised on quai des Orfèvres and picked up two young men, with whom he talked about pederasty. They disappeared. He reappeared with one of them, who escaped arrest. Two other men loitered in the Tuileries, separately and then together, in the most suspect manner and pathways.

Jacques Des Vignes, 61, native of Aubergenville (Ile-de-France), notary in Pontoise, lodged at The Image of Saint Claude on rue Montorgueil.

He passed along quai des Orfèvres about 5:00 and met a young man there whom he had seen a year ago in Paris, who asked him if he would like to buy him a bottle of wine. He went with him to a room on rue de l'Arbre sec, with another young man whom the first one encountered on the Pont Neuf. They drank some bottles of wine that he, the deponent, paid for. He, the deponent, and the first man masturbated independently. He gave them six livres to pay them for what they spent on wine, cheese, and wood. He took up this taste while boarded when he was young. He surrendered himself to it in Paris about a year ago with {a man unknown to him} +the man from

today, who sold powder to him then+. He knows no one in Pontoise given over to this debauchery and has never surrendered himself to it there. /Des Vignes/
C: S⁵ & R

Jean {Louis} Baptiste Teytaud, 21, native of Bellac in Basse Marche (Marche), former Benedictine novice at the abbey of Saint-Denis, which he left after a month on 28 July, medical student for around two months, lodged on rue des Astorg in faubourg Saint-Honoré with Auneveu, surgeon of the vicomte de Mérinville,[6] and ate with him chez Marchadier, arrested with him, hairdresser at carrefour de Buci.

    He has never surrendered himself to the debauchery of men and does not know about it. He passed through the Tuileries garden with Marchadier in returning from rue des Astorg to rue de Buci. /Taytaud/
C: W&R

Jean Baptiste Marchadier, 22, native of Le Dorat-en-Marche[7] (Marche), hairdresser for women, lived at carrefour de Buci.

    He passed through the Tuileries with Teytaud, arrested with him, in coming back together from the residence of the vicomte de Mérinville to his, the deponent's, place on rue de Buci. He is not given over to the debauchery of men. /Marchadei/
C: W&R

184. Tuesday, 8 November 1785, 11:15 pm
I: A known pederast picked up an observer, who refused to listen to him, on boulevard Montmartre and then a man with whom he entered rue Saint-Fiacre, where they masturbated independently. He resisted arrest and tried to rouse "the public."

Louis Bennezé, 31, native of Paris, gauze worker, lived chez S. Deslin, gauze maker, on rue du Pont au Choux near the boulevard.

    Coming back from La Nouvelle France, he passed along the boulevard. He did not speak to anyone there, was not in rue Saint-Fiacre, did not amuse himself with anyone, and is not given over to pederasty. /Louis Bénézet/
C: P

185. Thursday, 10 November 1785, 7:30 pm

I: A man loitered on the boulevard and picked up a man near the parapet with whom he appeared to stroke. They went down to the Coal-Box, where they masturbated independently. The second man escaped arrest.

Louis Antoine Peigné, 32, native of Fresnay l'Evêque in the diocese of Chartres (Orléanais), grocer and apothecary, associate of S. Claye, grocer and apothecary, with whom he resided on rue Saint-Antoine at place Baudoyer.

He walked on the boulevard to take the air. As he repaired his garter, a man accosted him and chatted with him. They told each other they were both going to faubourg Saint-Antoine, and they went down to go there. When they were down below this man asked him for money and told him he was not rich and needed some. He, the deponent, refused to give him any. The man said he would go with him, and he, the deponent, told him he was going to the guard post, and he was arrested. He did not do anything else with this man, whom he does not know, and is not given over to the debauchery of men. /Peigni Claye[8]/

C: W&R

186. Sunday, 13 November 1785, 7:30 pm

I: Two men loitered in the most suspect manner and picked up several men, including a known pederast. Both went down to the Coal-Box with men they had picked up and appeared to stroke reciprocally and masturbate. One had his breeches down. The other took several turns and masturbated with a man who escaped.

Charles Quentin, 26, native of Bernot in Picardy, domestic of commissaire Dassonville, lived at his residence on rue du Temple,[9] parish of Saint-Nicolas-des-Champs.

He went to the spot called the Coal-Box alone to make water there and then walked. He was accosted there by another man he does not know, who asked him if he had an erection and how much he wanted to give him. He replied he did not have an erection at all and did not have any money to give him. He then touched him, as he had his breeches down. He was debauched into pederasty on the boulevard two weeks ago by a man who made a rendezvous with him for today. He promises this will not happen to him again. /quentin/

C: W&R

Jean Jacques Edme Bérault, 48, native of Fontainebleau (Ile-de-France), clockmaker, lived on rue Saint-Denis in the parish of Saint-Eustache.

He went to walk this evening in the spot called the Coal-Box and took several turns there, out of curiosity, to see what happens there. He was accosted there by a man he does not know, who suggested to him that he amuse himself with him. He stopped with this man only to listen to his propositions, which he refused. He knows very well that men amuse themselves there, but he did not have the intention to do so. He told this man he did not wish to amuse himself at all because there were exempts [police agents]. +He has never known a woman.+ /Besnault/
C: W&R

187. Wednesday, 16 November 1785, 9:00 pm
I: A man loitered in the stoneyard, picked up a man with whom he conversed, pretended to urinate, and went away with him.

Silvain Petit, 25, native of Arpajon (Ile-de-France), domestic of widow Le Gras, lived at her residence on rue de la Montagne Sainte-Geneviève.

He went to walk this evening under the arcades of the Comédie Française and then among the stones. He met a man unknown to him there, with whom he conversed. He does not know what they said to each other. As this man told him he lived on rue de l'Arbre sec and he, the deponent, intended to go visit his brother, journeyman maker of edge-tools on rue Thibault aux Dés, he went with the man, who took him by the arm. He does not recall if this man spoke to him about the debauchery of men or not and does not remember the subjects they conversed about. He, the deponent, is not given over to the debauchery of men. /U/
C: W&R

188. Thursday, 17 November 1785, 7:15 pm
I: A man loitered on quai des Orfèvres and accosted a man with whom he struck up a conversation. They entered an alley, where they appeared to masturbate independently, then entered the Palais, where they took some turns among the stones and seemed to seek a suitable spot for "surrendering themselves to their pleasures," then returned to the quay.

Edme Venet, 41, native of Sens (Champagne), upholsterer's assistant, who lived in Lyon, on rue du Vieux Colombier, and worked in the neighboring countryside, was in Paris[10] for around a week and lodged with his sister Mme Gagniard, linen vendor, on rue de Buci at the corner of rue des Boucheries.

He has been given over to pederasty for around a year. He was recruited [*engagé*][11] into it in Lyon by a man unknown to him. This evening he passed along quai des Orfèvres and met a man unknown to him, who made propositions to him. They entered an alley where he, the deponent, stroked the man, with his penis exposed. He did not wish to let himself be touched by the man. Before this, he, the deponent, went down below the quay, where he did not find anyone but some laundrywomen who were working. He was already recruited into this debauchery in Paris twenty years ago, during his apprenticeship, but he left Paris at that time to give up [*se retirer de*] this penchant. /Venet/
C: P

189. Saturday, 19 November 1785, 7:00 pm
I: A known pederast loitered in the most suspect manner on quai des Orfèvres, went down to the Mousetrap, tried to pick up an observer who refused to listen to him, then came back up on the quay and picked up another man, a known pederast, with whom he appeared to stroke through the breeches. They went away together and entered a house on rue de l'Arbre sec and remained there for quite a while.

Etienne Boisseau, 36, native of Vanves (Ile-de-France), laundryman there, lived formerly on rue de la Brieche (?).

He was not on quai des Orfèvres. While looking for ash he encountered a floor polisher whom he asked for some. They went to drink a mug of wine together in a cellar. He did not enter any house in the last street and has never been given over to the debauchery of men. /etienne Boisseau/
C: P

I: Two men loitered in the stoneyard and picked up others, whom they stroked through the breeches.

Jean Baptiste Thevenet, nearly 18, native of Paris, domestic of M. de Neuville, maître des comptes,[12] lived at his residence in the Saint-Honoré cloister.

He was debauched around a year ago into pederasty, to which he surrendered himself with a little comrade. Then he said it was not with a comrade. It was with a stranger among the stones at the Comédie Française. It has happened

to him several times to amuse himself with strangers among the stones, with whom he masturbated. This evening he met a man among the stones who stroked him through his breeches, with whom he went into an alley with the design of amusing himself when he was arrested. He said he was debauched into the vice by +Prudhomme, gauze worker. He went twice to his room chez the pork-butcher in faubourg Saint-Laurent, on the third floor.+ /thevenet/
C: P

Guillaume Mougin, 18, native of Paris, journeyman jeweler, worked at his place chez the pork-butcher on rue Neuve Saint-Laurent in the parish of Saint-Nicolas-des-Champs.

He went to the Palais Royal about 4:00 and found there a man whose acquaintance he made in the hôtel de la Force prison, whose name he does not know. They went together to go to the Comédie Française. He indeed gave this man an écu of six livres to get tickets. This man told him he is given over to the debauchery of men and earns money [from men] and tried to persuade him to do the same, but he refused. He is not given over to it. He remained among the stones only while waiting for the man who entered there to do his business. He, the deponent, has never surrendered himself to this debauchery. +He was sent to the hôtel de la Force in May for taking to the municipal pawnshop a gold watch that belonged to S. Dessalles, jewelry vendor, for whom he worked. He spent a week there.+ /mougin/
C: P

190. Sunday, 20 November 1785, 7:15 pm
I: A young man loitered on quai des Orfèvres and accosted a man, with whom he went down to the Mousetrap, almost under the third archway, where they appeared to masturbate.

François Michel Hurier, 18, journeyman brushmaker, native of Ham in Picardy, lodged chez Perichon, who rented rooms on rue Maubuée.

He went to walk on quai des Orfèvres this evening. While he was leaning on the parapet, he was accosted by a man unknown to him, dressed in a gray frock coat, who said to him, "The weather's fine." He, the deponent, replied yes. The man told him if he wished to amuse him, he would give him some money. He suggested to him that he go down to the edge of the river with him and took him under an archway. The man unbuttoned his breeches, fondled him, and suggested that he put it into him, which he, the deponent,

did not want. He rebuttoned his breeches, came back up, and in going away he was arrested, but he did nothing else wrong. It is the first time these propositions have been made to him. The man gave him nothing. He has never received anything from anyone. /hurier/
C: P

191. Monday, 21 November 1785, 6:00 pm–1:00 am
PP: quays, exits of the Tuileries, place Louis XV, OP

I: A man loitered in the most suspect pathways in the Tuileries and picked up men. He stroked with one of them and told him he liked to have himself masturbated.

François Joseph Gouy, 31, native of Douai (Flanders), cook, unemployed for three months, lodged with his brother, journeyman upholsterer, chez M. Chandor on rue Neuve Guillemin.

    He went to the Tuileries this evening and was accosted there by a well-dressed man, with whom he walked. This gentleman urged him to go to his place with him to drink a bottle of wine and amuse themselves. He consented to it. This gentleman touched him through his breeches. He, the deponent, did the same to this man, who had a jacket with braid. It is the first time he has surrendered himself to this debauchery. He refused several times when other persons suggested it to him on the quays. The gentleman this evening asked him if he liked to have it put into him. He, the deponent, told him yes, and he had already had it put into him, but this is not true, and he does not know why he said it to this gentleman. He added that it is need that persuaded him to do what this gentleman wanted, believing he would be given some money. /gouy/
C: P

192. Tuesday, 22 November 1785, 6:30 pm
I: A young man cruised in the stoneyard yesterday and told a man he picked up that he would return this evening with one of his comrades who would amuse him. These two loitered in the stoneyard this evening, spoke to the same man, and promised to go to his place.

Pierre Girard, 14½, native of Paris, parish of Saint-Severin (5th arr.), apprentice printer, unemployed for two months, lived with his father, porter at the Beauvais butchery,[13] and mother, fruit and vegetable vendor, on rue Sainte-Marguerite.

He went among the stones at the Comédie this evening with Cadet Des Courty, arrested with him. He, the deponent, went there to do his business and met a man unknown to him, who talked to them about depravity [*polissonerie*] and urged them to go to his place on rue du Roule, without saying why or offering or promising them money. As they went there, they were arrested. He did no harm and was not there yesterday. He has never received anything. Several times during the conversation he said he was in the stones yesterday and then said he was mistaken. /Girard/
C: P

Charles François Descourty, nearly 18, native of Paris, tile-layer, lived with his parents chez a laundryman on rue du Bouquet.

This evening he met Girard, arrested with him, who persuaded him to go walk toward the Comédie Française. In going there, he told him that he had met a gentleman yesterday who was supposed to be in the stones near the Comédie this evening and that this gentleman would give them money to amuse him. As they passed, Girard indeed recognized this gentleman, spoke to him, and told him it was he, the deponent, he brought to him. This gentleman told them to go to his place at the end of the Pont Neuf. As they went there, they were arrested. He, the deponent, has never been in this spot or with Girard and does not know what Girard meant in telling him they would have to amuse this gentleman. /U/
C: W&R

The commissaire recalled Girard, who admitted he had already met the same man, who fondled him yesterday and "told him to bring him another this evening." He received nothing from this man.

193. Wednesday, 23 November 1785, 7:00 pm
I: A known pederast loitered in the most suspect pathway in the Tuileries and picked up a man. They stroked independently.

François Rullier, 63, native of Crocy in Lower Normandy, caretaker of the apartment of S. de La Tour, royal painter,[14] lived chez S. Longuemarre, haberdasher, on rue Saint-Honoré opposite rue du Champ-fleuri.

After leaving S. de La Tour's place, he went to the quay to buy some apples for his supper and was immediately arrested. He does not know why. He has not entered the Tuileries garden for a long time. Then he admitted he went to the Tuileries garden this evening, under the trees, and spoke to a man unknown to him who, to tell the truth, tried twice to stroke him, took him by the arm, and talked to him about debauchery with men. To tell the truth, he, the deponent, told him he has not seen women in fifteen years. He did nothing else wrong and has never surrendered to pederasty. /Rullie/
C: W&R

194. Saturday, 24 November 1785, 7:30 pm
I: A man loitered in the Tuileries and picked up a man, with whom he appeared to stroke. They left, returned, and walked in the most suspect pathways. Two other men loitered together, then separated. One of them picked up a man, struck up a conversation with him, and rejoined the other man, who was seated on a bench.

Louis Devaux, 13½, native of Sézanne in Brie (Ile-de-France), jockey of Mme de Briolle, lived at her residence on rue Royale, at the White barrier.[15]

He was debauched into pederasty four months ago by a man who lived at the time at the Jabat boardinghouse on rue de Rohan, on the mezzanine. He took him to his place after they met in the Palais Royal and consummated the crime with him, the deponent, in the passive role. He passed through the Tuileries this evening and met another man, in a blue jacket with small gold braid, who talked to him about this debauchery and urged him to go to his place to amuse themselves. He, the deponent, consented to it, in return for three livres, which he asked from this gentleman, who promised to give them to him. He left the first time with this gentleman and got as far as the grille, then returned to the garden, where this gentleman said he had made a rendezvous with someone. He stroked him, the deponent, through his breeches, but gave him nothing. The one who debauched him gave him three livres. /louis Devaux/
C: P

Jean Baptiste Louis Petit, 32, native of Paris, furniture vendor's assistant, worked and lived chez Sieurs de la Roue at the Royal Toilette on rue de la Verrerie.

He went with Laurent, domestic of the de la Roues, to take some furniture chez Mme Fontaine at the Feuillants. They passed through the Tuileries several times and could not speak to the lady the first time. They did not part or separate and did not speak to anyone. He, the deponent, is not at all given over to the vice of pederasty and has never surrendered himself to it. /Petit/
C: W&R

Joseph Michel Jérôme Laurent, 25, native of Méry-sur-Seine (Champagne), domestic of Sieurs de la Roue, furniture vendors, lived at their residence on rue de la Verrerie.

He went with Petit, assistant chez Sieurs de la Roue, chez Mme Fontaine at the Feuillants, then to rue de Buci, then returned chez Mme Fontaine. Each time they passed through the Tuileries without separating or speaking to other persons. They did not do anything wrong. He, the deponent, is not given over to the debauchery of men. He married a year ago, and his wife is cook chez Sieurs de la Roue. /Laurent/
C: W&R

195. Friday, 25 November 1785, 7:00 pm
I: A man loitered in the Tuileries, picked up a man, struck up a conversation with him, and stroked him. Another man loitered in the stoneyard and picked up a man, with whom he went to the quays, courtyard of the Palais de Justice, and New Market. They entered an alley, where one had his breeches unbuttoned, and the other escaped arrest.

Hubert Bonnet, 22, native of Cavaillon in Comtat d'Avignon (Provence), stonecutter, unemployed for two weeks, lodged chez Cotinot, who rented rooms on rue de la Parcheminerie. He received four louis for conditional enlistment in the dragoons several days ago and had to return it at the end of the month if he did not serve.

He went to walk in the Tuileries garden and was accosted there by a man unknown to him, spoke to him about sodomy[16] and tried to stroke him through his breeches, which he refused. This man urged him to go to his place to warm up and told him he lived on the quays. He did not want to go there but left with this man to go home. He, the deponent, has a horror of this vice, far from being given over to it. +The day before yesterday, however, he had the weakness to let himself by touched by a man unknown to him, a

wigmaker he also met in the Tuileries, who paid for his supper. To tell the truth, he, the deponent, returned to the Tuileries this evening believing he would meet him again.+ /imbert bonnet/
C: P

Louis Claude Lapointe, 21, native of Nantes (Brittany), limonadier's assistant, unemployed for a week, lodged chez a fruit vendor who rented rooms on rue Mazarine, whose name he does not know.

After leaving the post of the Swiss Guards in the Luxembourg, he met a man unknown to him in rue Neuve de la Comédie, and they conversed in walking. +This man told him it is dangerous to see women because one caught disease and it is much better to amuse oneself with men.+ They finally entered an alley that the man told him was a passageway to go to his place. In this alley the man suggested that they amuse themselves and offered to give him six livres. He, the deponent, told this man he did not understand what he meant, and at that moment he was arrested. His breeches were not unbuttoned, and he has never amused himself with men. /Lapointe/
C: W&R

196. Saturday, 26 November 1785, 7:00 pm
I: A known pederast cruised in all the suspect places, including the stoneyard and the Mousetrap. He picked up a man in the stoneyard, struck up a conversation with him, and appeared to stroke. Another man loitered and cruised in the Tuileries.

Charles Antoine Duval, more than 60, native of Airaines in Picardy, domestic of Messire Bourdois, magistrate (since 1768) in the tribunal with jurisdiction over waterways and forests within the Parlement, lived at his residence on rue d'Enfer near the Carthusians.[17]

He was debauched into pederasty more than thirty years ago, when he was a wigmaker's assistant, by men, also wigmaker's assistants, whose names he has forgotten. The last man with whom he amused himself, around six months ago, is a man unknown to him he met one evening in the Luxembourg, where they masturbated independently. Coming back from an errand on rue des Cordeliers this evening, he passed along rue Neuve de la Comédie, where he was accosted and followed by a man unknown to him, said he knew him. As he went away he was arrested. He did nothing wrong and did not even talk about this debauchery with the man. They did not stroke each other.

It is true that around two weeks ago, at 5:30 pm, in the courtyard of the Palais, he met a man unknown to him except for having seen him sometimes chez S. Palais, horsehair broom vendor near the Palais. They went to drink a mug of wine together on rue de l'Arbre sec, at the corner of rue des Prêtres, on the second floor. This man walked him back as far as the courtyard on rue Dauphine, where he, the deponent, gave him twenty-four sols because he had told him he had no job or money, but they did not amuse themselves. /duval/
C: P

Jean Henriet, 22, native of Courtisols in Champagne, unemployed domestic, arrived in Paris from Spain twelve days ago, lodged chez LeBrun, shoemaker, who rented rooms on rue des Grands Augustins.

He went to walk in the Tuileries garden this evening and was accosted there by a gentleman who persuaded him to go to his place by telling him he could oblige him by finding him a household. He left with him and was arrested. He does not know why. He did not do anything wrong and is not given over to the debauchery of men. The gentleman did not talk to him about it at all. /jean henriet/
C: W&R

197. Sunday, 27 November 1785, 6:15 pm
I: A man loitered in the stoneyard and picked up a man with whom he appeared to stroke.

François De Villecavoisin, 21, from near Chambéry in Savoy (Italy), day laborer, lived on quai des Augustins, next to the coaches office.

He was debauched into pederasty around three weeks ago by a man whose name he does not know, around 40, whom he met in a billiard parlor at the Grève. He took him to his place on rue des Arcis, on the third floor, where they consummated the crime with him, the deponent, in the passive role. This man was dressed in a gray vest, red breeches, and white stockings and gave him, the deponent, six sols. This evening, among the stones near the Comédie Française, he met another man unknown to him. They masturbated independently. This man promised to give him six livres to go to his place to consummate the crime but gave him nothing. He, the deponent, was arrested as he tried to go chez the man, who told him he lived on rue Saint-Thomas-du-Louvre. It was the first man with whom he had relations who taught him that one could find men, among the stones near the Comédie,

who would give money. He urged him to return to his place, but he, the deponent, did not return. /U/
C: P

198. Monday, 28 November 1785, 8:00 pm
I: A man loitered in the most suspect pathways in the Tuileries and picked up a man there with whom he struck up a conversation and stroked, with their penises exposed. Then they went to an alley off rue Saint-Honoré, near rue des Poulies, where they masturbated independently.

Laurent Cotentin, 28, native of Genets near Bayeux (Normandy), domestic of abbé Bossuet, canon of Bayeux, in Paris with his master for around three weeks, lodged at the Artois boardinghouse on rue Montmartre.

Coming back from Roule, he entered the Tuileries garden, where he met a man unknown to him, with whom he talked about the bad weather. As they were going the same way, they went together. As he, the deponent, was going home, he was arrested. He did not enter any alley or spot with this man, did not do anything wrong, and is not given over to pederasty. /Cotentin/
C: W&R

199. Tuesday, 29 November 1785, 5:30 pm–12:00 am
PP: quays, environs of the Tuileries, place Louis XV, northern boulevards, OP

I: 7:00 pm. A known pederast on record picked up men in the Tuileries. He stroked with one and left with him. They masturbated in a corner at the Louvre and then took two or three turns on quai des Orfèvres.

Pierre Henry Prudhomme, 26, native of Reims (Champagne), former jeweler's assistant, apprentice jeweler, and grocer's assistant, made boxes and hatboxes for the last six months and lived on rue des Vertus.

He went to the Tuileries garden this evening with the intention of getting picked up by a man. He was under the trees, and a man unknown to him accosted him and asked him what time it was. He shoved his hand into his breeches and then suggested to him that they drink a mug. He, the deponent, accepted, and they went through various passageways, in one of which the man masturbated him and offered him six livres for him, the deponent, to put it into his mouth or to let him, the man, put it into him from behind, which

he, the deponent, did not want to do. This man told him he is a domestic and is named Antoine and showed him the place where his master lives, where he told him to go see him because he would secure him a job as domestic. He has known for a long time that the pathway in the Tuileries where he met the man is the spot where men who amuse themselves together are, but this is the first time he has surrendered himself to this debauchery. /Prudhomme/
C: P

200. **Wednesday, 30 November 1785, 7:30 pm**
I: A taller man loitered in the Tuileries garden and picked up a man with whom he stroked, with their penises exposed. They left and went to port Saint-Nicolas,[18] where they again stroked mutually. The second man escaped arrest. A shorter man picked up a man in the garden. They pulled their breeches down all the way, smacked their buttocks, and masturbated.

Philibert Sacqueney, 29, native of Dijon (Burgundy), secondhand dealer, lived chez S. Regnier, master locksmith, on rue Neuve Saint-Eustache.
    Coming back from faubourg Saint-Germain, he passed along quai du Louvre and made water there. A gentleman going by said to him, "There's a broken-down boat," and he was immediately arrested. He did not enter the Tuileries, did not speak to anyone, and did not amuse himself with anyone. Then he admitted he entered the Tuileries by way of the courtyard of the riding school and, near the great basin in the garden, along the ironwork, met a man who asked him what time it was. He replied he knew nothing about it and does not have a watch. The man asked him if he had someone there to amuse him. He, the deponent, told him he did not know what he meant. They left together and went to the quay, where he, the deponent, made water. The man also made water near him and said to him, "There is a boat that sank today." It is true that they stopped three times along the parapet, but they did not stroke. It is true that the man tried to stroke him in the Tuileries, but he, the deponent, refused, and he is not given over to the debauchery of men. +Then he told us he was debauched into pederasty two weeks ago by one Comtois, domestic of a painter on rue Beaubourg near rue Grenier Saint-Lazare, but he is no longer there, with whom he masturbated independently, who taught him to go to the Tuileries to amuse himself. He went there this evening with the intention of amusing himself but did nothing more than he told us with the man he met there, with whom he was going to his place to

amuse themselves. He amused himself around ten times with Comtois, at his place, and with others unknown to him, in the Tuileries.+ /Jacquenet/
C: P

Germain Claude Cochois, 36, native of Paris, unemployed, survived on what his family gave him and lived at 14, rue de la Sourdière, on the fifth floor.

He is not fit for men or women. He was in the Tuileries to walk and met a man unknown to him there. They stroked independently. He goes to the Tuileries habitually because of his weak health and speaks to men as well as women there. It has not happened to him often to amuse himself with men because his health is too delicate. He acquired this taste from boarding and retained it. /G. C. Cochoit/
C: P

DECEMBER

201. Thursday, 1 December 1785, 7:30 pm
I: Two men masturbated independently in the stoneyard, and one of them escaped arrest.

Louis Candre, 43, native of Chartres in Beauce (Orléanais), unemployed wine vendor's assistant, lived chez the Brothers of Christian Schools on rue Neuve Notre-Dame-des-Champs.[1]

This evening he went chez a wine vendor where he used to live and passed near the Comédie Française. He was accosted by a man unknown to him, talked to him about the weather and the cold and then about the debauchery of men and first touched him. Then they went into the stones, where they masturbated independently. It is the first time he has surrendered himself to this debauchery. He does not know how he let himself go to it and has never been inclined to it. /candre/
C: P

202. Friday, 2 December 1785, 7: 15 pm
I: A man known for often picking up men in the Tuileries was there Sunday and Monday. This evening he picked up a man and masturbated with him. Another man picked up men yesterday and today, including one with whom he walked and stroked, then stopped and masturbated.

Jean Léon Grosmenil, called Martin, 23, native of Paris, worked at the tobacco office[2] and lived chez widow Rechaume on rue Jean Saint-Denis.

In passing through the Tuileries he encountered a man unknown to him. They did nothing. He was also in the Tuileries on Sunday and did not speak to anyone there. He was already arrested for pederasty in the Champs-Elysées, more than two years ago, spent a year in Bicêtre, and left with a letter of exile, at least a year ago August. +It is indigence that leads him to go to the Tuileries in the evening.+ /U/
C: P

Victor Daniel Housel, 25, native of Villers-le-Bel (Ile-de-France), soldier in the Auvergne regiment, on leave for half a year, lodged with his grandmother, chez S. Paquiot, wine vendor, at The Gold Bell on rue Saint-Martin.[3]

Today is the third time he has let himself go to the debauchery of men,[4] each time in the evening in the Tuileries with men unknown to him, accosted him. Before this he never surrendered himself to it. This evening he stroked with a man he met. He has been in Paris only since 16 November. /housel/
C: P

203. Saturday, 3 December 1785, 8:00 pm
I: A known pederast on record, known by the name of Adam, called Lallemand, picked up men and took them to his place to consummate the crime with them in the active and passive roles. This evening he loitered in the Tuileries and picked up a man with whom he caressed and masturbated. Two other known pederasts, known by the names of Antoine and Lelancé, cruised daily in the royal gardens and lived "only from the fruit of their prostitution." This evening in the Palais Royal, with another known pederast who escaped arrest, they picked up an officer with whom they chatted for a few minutes, who did not wish to listen to them. They reproached each other for their libertinage, which caused a scene in the garden. After making up, they planned to go earn a louis at a man's place.

Anzalen Bour, nicknamed Adam and Lallemand, 42, native of Sarailh (?) in Germany, coachman for three months of the marquis de Choiseul,[5] lived at his residence on rue des Capucins Chaussée d'Antin.

He crossed the Tuileries and met a boy there who told him he is a wigmaker, who shoved his hand into his, the deponent's, breeches. They left together. This person spoke to him about amusing themselves and wanted to

take him to his room, which he, the deponent, refused. He also tried to touch him on the quay, but he, the deponent, did not wish to allow it. He has never amused himself with men. [illegible signature]
C: W&R

Antoine Perrot, 17, native of Meung-sur-Loire (Orléanais), domestic for nearly three months of abbé Tistan, lodged in a furnished room chez an upholsterer at 141, rue du Four Saint-Germain.

Since his master is in the country, he goes to walk in the Palais Royal in the evening, like everyone. He is not given over to pederasty and has never surrendered himself to it. +He did not quarrel with Lelancé, arrested with him, in the Palais Royal, and they did not reproach each other for anything. He was going home and does not know where the others were going.+ /U/
C: P

François Mercier, 18½, nicknamed Lelancé, native of Asnières in Burgundy, domestic, unemployed for a month, learning how to dress men's hair chez S. Petit, wigmaker in the Palais Royal, lived at the little Normandy boarding-house on rue Tiquetonne.

He went to the Palais Royal to walk and, what is more, he is not made to say fuck or no fuck.[6] He is not given over to pederasty and has never surrendered himself to it. It is true that he had a little quarrel in the Palais Royal with Antoine, arrested with him, about nothing. He does not know about what or what reproaches they made to each other. It is one Bailly, personal valet of the abbé de Perochel on rue Basse du Rempart, with whom he amused and fondled himself, and it is only with him he amused himself. In leaving the Palais Royal, he went with Antoine, who told him to go to a place. He does not know where or why. /Mercier/
C: P

204. Monday, 5 December 1785, 7:30 pm
I: Two men loitered in the stoneyard, picked up men with whom they stroked, then went with them to alleys off rue de Vaugirard, where they appeared to masturbate.

François Bucher, 31, native of Neuvy-le-Barrois near Nevers (Nivernais), surgeon at the Carthusian monastery, lived there, on rue d'Enfer.

He passed near the Comédie Française and was accosted by a young man unknown to him. He had the weakness to stop with him and go into an alley, where this young man indeed stroked him. He does not know how he had this weakness. He is not given over to the vice of liking men and has never surrendered himself to it. He even refused propositions made to him several days ago by another man, also near the Comédie Française. /Bucher Deniverois/
C: S&R

Pierre Montreuil, 48, native of Bernay in the diocese of Evreux (Normandy), innkeeper, operated the Grenada boardinghouse on rue des Maçons and lived there.
 He has always had the misfortune to like men. For acquaintances in this debauchery he had one Loiseau, kitchen assistant like himself, who lived at the same house, with whom he amused himself from time to time for around ten years. This Loiseau returned to Rouen, in his native region, where he died two years ago. He, the deponent, married in hopes of correcting himself of this vice, which he has not been able to do. His wife has been ill since the month of March. Around three months ago he amused himself with a man unknown to him in an alley near the Comédie Française. Today, in more or less the same spot, he met another, with whom he went into an alley, where they stroked independently. This man suggested to him that they ago to his place on rue Saint-Hyacinthe to amuse themselves, and he accepted. As he went there he was arrested. He has never taken things farther in this debauchery than masturbation. /montreuil/
C: P

205. Tuesday, 6 December 1785, 9:00 pm
I: A man loitered in the Tuileries, picked up a man, and struck up a conversation with him.

Pierre Nicolas Palliée, 17, native of Paris, apprentice upholsterer chez S. Fontaine, personal valet and upholsterer of the duchesse de Bourbon,[7] lived chez S. Fontaine at the townhouse on rue Neuve des Petits Champs at the corner or rue de Gallion.
 He walked in the Tuileries this evening and met a man unknown to him there who spoke to him, walked with him, and tried to persuade him to go

have supper with him, which he refused. He then urged him to go take him [missing words]. He was there, they left by the gate on the side of the Pont Royal, and he was arrested. He does not know why. He did nothing wrong, is not given over to the debauchery of men, and has never surrendered himself to it. /U/
C: W&R

206. Wednesday, 7 December 1785, 7:00 pm
I: A man loitered in the Tuileries and accosted a man. They stroked through their breeches, left together, walked by the Louvre, went behind wood piled on the parapet of the quay, and appeared to stroke again.

Laurent Guay, 26, native of Gatin in the diocese of Sens (Champagne), priest, curé of Courpalay in that diocese, arrived in Paris today and lodged at the Imperial boardinghouse on rue des Poulies.

He went to walk this evening in the Tuileries, where he was accosted by a young man who seemed respectable to him, who talked to him about the fine weather and the time, then about women. His conversation displeased him, the deponent. He left the garden to go away to his inn, and the man followed him. He, the deponent, was arrested but does not know why. It had nothing to do with the debauchery of men between him and this man. He, the deponent, is not given over to it. /Guay/
C: W&R

I: A known pederast loitered in the Tuileries and accosted a man with whom he took several turns in the most suspect places. They sat down on a bench, stroked, and left.

Antoine Voutancia, 22, native of Lyon (Lionnais), unemployed domestic, lived chez Mme Tourelle, who rented rooms on rue des Lavandières Sainte-Opportune and lodged him until he found a job.

This evening he passed through the Tuileries, where he met a gentleman unknown to him, with whom he sat down on a bench, where this gentleman touched him and tried to touch him a second time, but he did not want [to allow it]. He, the deponent, did not touch him. It is the first time he has surrendered himself to this debauchery. /U/
C: P

207. Thursday, 8 December 1785, 8:00 pm
I: A known pederast, arrested, warned, and released on 4 March (#35), loitered in the Tuileries and picked up men, including one with whom he took several turns in the pathways and on the terrace along the water. They stroked independently, with their penises exposed, left together, and fled at the sight of observers. One of them returned to the garden, and the other escaped arrest.

Alexandre Charles Gabriel Brochet, 33, native of Paris, upholsterer's assistant chez S. Favier, at the central market, lived chez S. Boudin, painter, at 40, rue Jacob.

He only passed through the Tuileries and did not speak to or stop with anyone. He is not given over to pederasty. /brochet/
C: P

208. Friday, 9 December 1785, 5:30 pm–12:00 am
PP: quays, exits of the Tuileries, place Louis XV, northern boulevards, OP

I: Two men loitered in the most suspect alleys and sat down on a bench on quai du Louvre with another man. They stroked independently, with their penises exposed, and said they were going to amuse themselves chez one of them.

Louis Guillaume Ligneux, 18, native of Clichy-la-Garenne (Ile-de-France), domestic of S. Mousset, bourgeois de Paris, lived at his residence on rue Thévenot.

Coming back from Gros Caillou, he entered a skiff[8] and met a man whose name, status, and address he does not know, whom he had seen at the Saint-Cloud ball.[9] They entered the Tuileries together and met the other arrested man, who seemed to an acquaintance of the first man, but whom he, the deponent, does not know. They took several turns and sat down, all three, on a bench, where they chatted about libertinage with women. They did not do anything else and did not stroke. What is more, if he was in bad company, it is not his fault. He was debauched into pederasty around four years ago by a domestic named Lafitte who slept, at the time, chez the deponent's father. He has amused himself only with Lafitte. They did nothing this evening. /Ligneux/
C: P (La Force)

Louis Claude Beaugrand, 28, native of Saint-Denis (Ile-de-France), groom turned writer, arrived from Holland on Saturday and lived chez a wigmaker on rue Saint-Honoré near rue Tirechappe.

He does not know the other arrested man or the one he was with, who came to accost him, the deponent, in the garden. These two persuaded him to go sit on a bench with them, He went there, and all three of them stroked the other two, with their penises exposed. It is the first time he has surrendered himself to this debauchery. To tell the truth, he went to the Tuileries out of curiosity about this debauchery, knowing there are men there. The one of the three who was not arrested told them they were going to his place to refresh themselves. He and the other arrested man accepted. All three left together with the intention of going to the other man's place. He did not say where he lives. /Beaugrand/
C: P (La Force)

209. Monday, 12 December 1785, 6:45 pm
I: A known pederast on record, who staged "pederasty parties," loitered in the Palais Royal with another known pederast. They talked about "this debauchery."

Louis Pouteau, 20, native of Choisy-le-Roi (Ile-de-France), independent feather vendor, lived on rue du Faubourg du Temple.

He went to S. Tissot's shop in the Palais Royal, where he had business. He met a young man named Le Beau there, whom he has known for four months, with whom he walked. He had already met him on Saturday, and they ate waffles together. He is not given over to the debauchery of pederasty and has never surrendered himself to it. It is true that he has an acquaintance named Des Hayes, who sells paintings, who was with him, the deponent, at the Two Mills tavern when he was reproached for being given over to this vice, as a result of which he, the deponent, has not seen him since. /pouteau/
C: W&R

I: A man who loitered in the Tuileries every evening loitered in the most suspect pathways this evening and picked up a man with whom he left. They parted at the Carousel, where the first man immediately picked up another man, with whom he planned to have supper and sleep at his place. The first man resisted arrest, which allowed the other to escape.

Maxi Mitraff, 20, native of Saint Petersburg in Russia, domestic of S. Seminien, secretary of the Russian ambassador,[10] lived at the townhouse on the boulevard opposite the Comédie Italienne.

He passed through the Tuileries on the way back from seeing his compatriots chez prince Galitzin.[11] He did not speak to anyone. After he left he met another man on rue Saint-Honoré, who asked him about a street he does not know and told him to go with him to drink a bottle of wine. He thanked him [but declined since he did] not know [him]. /U/
C: W&R

210. Tuesday, 13 December 1785, 8:30 pm

I: Two men accosted each other in the Tuileries, conversed, and loitered together. The older one picked up a man with whom he loitered, sat down on a bench, and stroked. The younger one accosted two known pederasts, took several turns with them, and stroked with them near the trellises near the central basin. Another man loitered in the garden, picked up several men, and left with one of them, and appeared to masturbate behind a cider vendor's hut on the quay. When he was arrested, he had his breeches down and shirt untucked.

Pierre Nicolas Hoart, 66, native of Paris, retired jewelry vendor, lived at The Golden Fleece on Pont Saint-Michel.

He rarely goes to the Tuileries and went there this evening on the way back from the Champs-Elysées. He was accosted there by a man with whom he conversed about pederasty, who suggested to him that they go drink a bottle of wine. He told this man he does not consummate the crime but amuses himself only at masturbation. To tell the truth, he has surrendered himself to it sometimes but does not recall with whom. He did nothing this evening but stroking independently through the breeches. /Hoart/
C: P

Louis Duhamel, 40, native of Beaugency, between Orléans and Blois (Orléanais), domestic for three months of M. Lambert, royal councilor, lived at his residence on rue Christine.

He is given over to pederasty only through passion. He has consummated the crime three or four times purely from obligingness, because he does not like it and surrenders himself only to masturbation. He surrendered himself to this debauchery with Cosse, Fragmere, and several others unknown to

him. He went to the Tuileries this evening to see if he would meet someone of his acquaintance. He met a young man there he does not know, who was with another man. He took two turns with them and talked with them about their tastes in this debauchery. He and the younger one stroked reciprocally through their breeches. /X/
C: P

Jean Baptiste Gabriel Melard, 20, native of Paris, assistant of S. Bourgarel, wigmaker, lived at his residence on rue Saint-Dominique in Gros Caillou. He had part of shirt untucked from his breeches.

   He did not go to the Tuileries. Then, after we pointed out to him that he is not telling the truth, he admitted he went to the Tuileries and was accosted there by a man unknown to him, who told him he is named Bertrand and lives at the Brittany boardinghouse on rue Dauphine. They left and went behind a hut on the port, where this man undid his [Melard's] breeches. As they were fondling, he, the deponent, was arrested, and the other man escaped. It is the first time he has surrendered to this debauchery. /Méllard/
C: P

211. Wednesday, 14 December 1785, 6:00 pm
I: A man loitered in the Tuileries and picked up a man with whom he took two turns. They left together and went behind a cider vendor's hut at port Saint-Nicolas, where they stroked. The first man had his breeches undone and shirt untucked when he was arrested. The other man escaped arrest. Another man loitered in the stoneyard and picked up a man. They went to cul-de-sac des Quatre Vents, withdrew when they saw observers, and went to an alley off rue du Coeur Volant, where they masturbated. One of them escaped arrest. The other, who had his breeches unbuttoned, offered to give the observers his watch and money to let him go.

Jean Charles Michel Chaumette, 24, native of Meaux in Brie (Ile-de-France), domestic of commander[12] Geoffroy, had lived at his residence on rue Saint-Dominique, near place Saint-Michel, for eight months.

   He went to walk in the Tuileries this evening and met a man unknown to him, with whom he walked and left. Outside the garden this man made propositions to him that excited him. They went first behind one hut, where this man stroked him, then behind another hut, where this man masturbated

him. His breeches were still unbuttoned, and his shirt was still untucked when he was caught and arrested. The other man escaped. It is the first time he has surrendered himself to this debauchery. He had heard it said that men given over to this debauchery go to the Tuileries. When the other man accosted him, he suspected he was a man inclined to this vice, and he remained in his company to see what was what. This man told him he is retired from trade, is well off, and lives on rue Saint-Thomas-du-Louvre and suggested to him that they go there to amuse themselves, but he, the deponent, refused. /chaumette/
C: P

Isidore Le Plat, 28, native of Longperrier near Dammartin-en-Goëlle (Ile-de-France), domestic of widow Dumont, lived at her residence in the Notre-Dame cloister.

He was debauched into pederasty in his tender youth by young folks in Dammartin. He has surrendered himself to this debauchery, since adulthood, with, among others, François Tuquel, vineyardist in Dammartin, and Pierre Poupée, mason in the same place, specifically in the month of November. He has also amused himself several times in Paris, in various places where he found himself, among others in the Tuileries, among the stones at the Comédie Française, and in other places, all with men unknown to him. This evening he went to amuse himself in an alley with a man he knows only by sight from seeing him often in places where men given over to this debauchery go. He takes it only as far as masturbation. It is true he offered the observers his watch and money to let him go. /isidore leplat/
C: P

212. Thursday, 15 December 1785, 8:00 pm
I: Two men masturbated with others, who escaped arrest, behind a cider vendor's hut on port Saint-Nicolas. Both had their breeches unbuttoned and shirts untucked. One of them had loitered in the Tuileries, accosted a man, sat down with him on a bench, and left with him.

Jean Clautaux, 17, native of Longwy (Lorraine), wigmaker's assistant, lived chez S. Devorre, wigmaker, in Roule.

He left his master's place to visit his mother, who lives in faubourg Montmartre and passed through the Tuileries to buy a comb. He was accosted there by a man unknown to him, who suggested to him that they go to his

room to divert themselves, which he refused. The man sat him down and tried to touch him. He got up and left with the man, who led him to the edge of the water, against some barrels, where the man undid his breeches, touched him, and suggested putting it into him, which he did not wish to allow. It is the first time this has happened to him. He admits that he had the weakness to give in to the man's solicitations. About two years ago, [while he was] living chez M. Mohimont, wigmaker, near the White barrier, a wigmaker's assistant who was also there, whose name he does not know, tried to take him by force. Having gone up to the latrine after him, on the very day when Paschal was broken on the wheel,[13] he took his head, which he placed on the seat, pulled down his breeches, removed his own, and tried to put it into him. He could not yell because he pressed his neck. A female neighbor who noticed what was going on yelled, which made him let up and prevented the wigmaker's assistant from consummating his crime. At the time he was innocent and had no idea of this debauchery. /X/
C: P

Gapella Auguste Perretton, 14, native of Paris, student of M. Brunet, professor at the Royal Academy of Painting,[14] lived with his mother, maid of the duchesse de Luxembourg,[15] at her residence on place Vendôme.[16]

He was debauched into pederasty about two months ago in the Champs-Elysées by a man with whom he masturbated independently. The man gave him six sols. This evening, as he was passing along the galleries of the Louvre, he met another man there, unknown to him, who promised him six livres, which he did not give him. As they began to masturbate, he was arrested, and the other escaped. He had his breeches undone when he was caught. /Perretton/
C: P

213. Saturday, 17 December 1785, 7:00 pm
I: Two young known pederasts had cruised in the stoneyard for some time. The taller one masturbated with a man there yesterday. This evening they both loitered and cruised.

Jean Michel Marie Brincman, 15½, native of Paris, tailor, lived with his father, master tailor, chez S. Marie, who rented carriages, on rue du Four in faubourg Saint-Germain, at the corner of rue de l'Egout.

He has gone near the Comédie Française in the evening for around three weeks. Yesterday he met a man unknown to him there, who led him into

the stones, where they masturbated independently, which he, the deponent, did only by force. The man bought him a mug of wine and told him to return this evening, He came there and found the man he met two weeks ago today in the courtyard of the Saint-Germain market, the chevalier de Béarn. He wanted to take him to his place on cul-de-sac des Quatre Vents to amuse themelves +and promised to give him eighteen livres.+ He went as far as the passage and did not wish to go farther. He has never surrendered himself to this debauchery except for yesterday. He knows the other man arrested with him by sight and knows he goes under the arcades of Comédie and in the stones in the evening. He has seen him several times with well-dressed gentlemen. /Brincman/
C: P

Jean François Ratier, 13, native of Paris, did nothing and lived with his father, master tailor, chez the wigmaker on rue de Savoie near rue des Grands Augustins.

He was debauched into pederasty by a chevalier who lives on cul-de-sac des Quatre Vents whom he met in the street, who took him to his place, undid his breeches, fondled him, masturbated before him, the deponent, gave him six livres, and told him to return two weeks later, which he did only around a month later. He encountered the chevalier, who gave him twenty-four sols. He met another old gentleman, with a muff and sword, in the stones at the Comédie. He paid a prostitute to go with him, the deponent, and fondle him, the deponent, in front and in back. The old gentleman watched them, then sent him, the deponent, away and was with the prostitute. Another day he, the deponent, and three comrades of his, one of whom is a jockey, received ten francs from a gentleman with whom two of them went down into the ditch in the stones. He, the deponent, and another remained above to watch for the guard. They went to spend these ten francs at the White Cross tavern near rue des Quatre Vents, a cider vendor's place, another café, and a grocer's shop. He, the deponent, was drunk and fell three times on the way home. He knows Brincman, arrested with him, amused himself yesterday in the stones with a gentleman. This evening this same gentleman met him, the deponent, near the Comédie and suggested to him that he go to the entrance to rue Saint-Hyacinthe, where there is a gentleman who would give six livres. As he went there he was arrested. /Rattier/
C: W&R because of his youth

214. Friday, 17 December 1785, 10:00 pm
I: A known pederast, who took men he picked up to sleep with him, loitered for around an hour in the most suspect manner in the Palais Royal.

Antoine Rémy Trelon, 27, native of Dormans in Champagne, tutor in boardinghouses, unemployed for three weeks, lived on rue du Dauphin opposite Saint-Roch.[17] He had applied to enter the Jacobins on rue du Bac as a novice.[18]
 To tell the truth, he walked alone for around an hour this evening in the Palais Royal garden, where he often goes with no other design than walking. He is not given over to the crime he is suspected of and has never surrendered himself to it. If he has rosettes on his shoes, it is because they are old shoes he put on this evening when he took off his boots, which shoes his sister Mlle Trelon, housekeeper of S. Châtelet, royal painter,[19] on quai des Théatins, gave him three days ago. /Trelon/
C: W&R

215. Monday 19 December 1785, 7:15 pm
I: A known pederast on record, known by the name of Clermont, called Countess of Seven Points,[20] domestic, cruised in all the suspect places, recently in the stoneyard, and was connected with several notorious pederasts, most of them arrested and imprisoned. He did time in Bicêtre for theft. He was with another man for a very long time in the stones, and they appeared to stroke.

Pierre Pallardel, 40, native of Montzéville in Clermontais near Verdun (Lorraine), domestic of the marquise de la Maisonfort[21] for two months, lived at her residence on rue Saint-Hyacinthe Porte Michel.
 Going to do errands in rue Saint-André-des-Arts, he passed near the Comédie Française. He did not stop there and did not speak to anyone. He has never been given over to pederasty. It is true he amused himself by disguising himself like a woman several times and took great pleasure in seeing men given over to this vice play cancan. To that end he was with them several times in a room on rue Verte where he lived, which Pontchartrain, domestic of a bishop, had given him. It is also true these men nicknamed him, the deponent, The Countess of Seven Points, but he never amused himself with any of them at pederasty. To tell the truth, he remained around the Comédie Française this evening for half an hour, but he did not speak to anyone. He passes that way often but does not recall if he has spoken to anyone recently there. /palardelle/
C: P

216. Wednesday, 21 December, 8:30 pm
I: A man loitered in the Tuileries and picked up men, including one with whom he masturbated independently along the wall below the terrace along the water.

Jean Hurel, 35, native of Conteville in Normandy, domestic for two months of widow Burrett, lived at her residence at 12, place des Vosges.

He went to walk this evening in the Tuileries and met a man unknown to him there who told him he is a shopkeeper and lives on rue Saint-Thomas-du-Louvre, who accosted him and said to him it was quite cold. They chatted together. This man made water next to him, the deponent, and suggested that they go warm up in his room. He, the deponent, refused at first, then consented, and left with him to go there. This man did not make any indecent propositions to him, and he, the deponent, is not given over to the debauchery of men. Before meeting this man, he, the deponent, asked what time it was but did nothing wrong. He gladly jokes about everything. /hurel, called Constan/
C: W&R

217. Friday, 23 December 1785, 5:30–11:00 pm
PP: quays, exits of the Tuileries and Palais Royal, place XV, northern boulevards

I: A known pederast, German, loitered every evening in suspect places and prostituted himself for money. This evening he picked up men in the Tuileries and stroked with one of them. Another known pederast, who loitered in suspect places, picked up men in the garden and stroked with one of them.

François Guilbert, 20, native of Brussels (Belgium), domestic, unemployed for nine days after leaving the service of S. Du Tranoy, who operated the Artois boardinghouse on rue Beauregard, lodged chez a man who rented rooms chez S. Rousseau, wigmaker, on rue Saint-Guillaume.

He left the Tuileries with a man who made a rendezvous with him there, who had promised to secure a job for him. He, the deponent, took him to his room, but they did nothing wrong. He the deponent, is not given over to the debauchery of men. On the contrary, he left Du Tranoy because he had suggested to him that he surrender himself to this debauchery. He left the same day and suddenly. /U/
C: P

Paul Bourgeois, 24, native of Combles in the diocese of Noyon (Picardy), wigmaker's assistant, unemployed before All Saint's Day (1 November), lived chez the pork-butcher on rue Saint-Antoine opposite rue Royale, on the fifth floor in the rear.

He was debauched into pederasty around eighteen months ago by a button vendor who lives at the abbey of Saint-Germain, whom he lodged and with whom he amused himself. Since that time he has amused himself with several others, all unknown to him, in various places on various occasions, specifically in the Tuileries garden, where he went this evening but did nothing. /paul bourgeois/
C: P

218. Monday, 26 December 1785, 7:15 pm
I: A man loitered, cruised, and stroked with another man in the Tuileries.

François Vauflard, 18, shoemaker's assistant and lantern lighter, native of Paris, lived chez Picard, master shoemaker, on rue Mouffetard.

He was debauched into pederasty fourteen months ago by a man named Baudi and de Marville, who lived chez a laundrywoman on rue du Bon Puits, with whom he amused himself around fifteen times at masturbating independently, chez Baudin or de Marville. Then he likewise amused himself around six months ago with a young man named Drouin who currently lives with S. de Marville, who amuses himself with him. Yesterday evening he met a gentleman in the Tuileries who give him twenty-four sols, but they did not do anything together. Today he met another man in the Tuileries, and they touched themselves, with their penises exposed. He was going to amuse himself at this man's place when he was arrested. /vauflard/
C: P

219. Tuesday, 27 December 1785, 7:15 pm
I: A man masturbated on the Sofa, behind some carriages, with another man who escaped because the first man resisted arrest.

Hubert Jacques Gabriel Finot, 21, native of Paris, clerk of his uncle, attorney in the Parlement (since 1764), lived with him on cul-de-sac Sainte-Croix off rue des Billettes.

He was debauched into pederasty no more than three years ago by a young man named Gérard, law student, who lodged at the time in a

furnished room on rue Béthisy and has now returned to Lille in Flanders, his birthplace. He amused himself in Gérard's room two or three times at masturbating independently. In addition, he amused himself with another man unknown to him and does not recall where or where he met him. In addition he went three or four times to the Tuileries but never amused himself there. He went to the Tuileries this evening and met a man unknown to him, who appeared to him to be given over to pederasty. They walked together, left, and went to the quay, behind a cart. This man tried to stroke him, which he, the deponent, did not wish to allow, and he was arrested. /finot fils/
C: S&R

220. Wednesday, 28 December 1785, 6:30 pm
I: A man loitered in the Luxembourg and picked up a man in the pathway of the Carthusians.

They walked, stroked near a tree, left together, and entered the stoneyard, where they stroked independently.

Pierre Danjou, 29, native of Abbecourt near Beauvais (Ile-de-France), unemployed cook, resided on rue Saint-Honoré next to Saint-Roch, in the room of and with Le Gendre, also unemployed cook.

He dined with Le Gendre on rue des Boucheries chez a wine vendor who served meals. They parted, and he, the deponent, went to rue Hillerin Bertin, from which he came back by way of rue de Grenelle, rue du Four, rue de Buci, and rue Dauphine. He was arrested at the Pont Neuf and does not know why. He went to rue Hillerin Bertin to see Surville, cook, who lives there, who was not home. He was not in the Luxembourg or in the stones near the Comédie and did not speak to anyone. He is not given over to pederasty. /U/

The contents of his pockets included two suspect letters "related to the debauchery of pederasty," signed Clément and Fargis, and a note for sixty-six livres, dated 22 August, payable to Danjou and signed Clément Brochet.
C: P

221. Thursday, 29 December 1785, 8:30 pm
I: A man loitered in the Tuileries in the most suspect manner and picked up a man with whom he walked and stroked.

Emmanuel, chevalier de la Villelouays, 28, native of Pontivy in Brittany, first underlieutenant in the Quercy cavalry regiment, lodged at the France boardinghouse on rue de Bourbon in La Villeneuve.

He went to walk in the Tuileries garden for the first time this evening and met a man unknown to him, who said to him it was quite cold and urged him to go to his place to warm up. He, the deponent, refused at first but, at his insistence, consented after this man said to him, "It's not good weather for getting an erection." At the same time, he placed his hand on his breeches, which he pushed away. He left with this man, who made water and urged him to come close to him and do likewise, which he, the deponent, refused, and he was arrested. He knows it was imprudent on his part to go with this man, but he is not given over to the debauchery of liking men and has never surrendered himself to it. /Le chevalier de La Villelouays/
C: W&R

APPENDIX

Convers Desormeaux's papers include multiple references to some individuals. These sample documents from 1784 and 1786 provide more information about the Du Chenu mentioned in #19.

1. Y 11724, 29 OCTOBER 1784, 7:30 PM

I: A known pederast cruised in the Palais Royal.

Charles Simon Thuillier, 19, native of Soissons, domestic, unemployed for two weeks after leaving the service of S. Rousseau, major-domo of the comtesse d'Artois, lodged on rue Saint-Nicolas in Chaussée d'Antin.
 He has been given over to pederasty since Easter and is nicknamed the baroness of Popincourt [11th arr.] in this debauchery. He was debauched into this vice by Iroux, obliging domestic of Du Chenu, garde du corps. Iroux, with S. Du Chenu and the chevalier de Fage, in the guards of the comte de Provence, went to find him on rue de Popincourt, persuaded him to climb into a carriage, and took him first to a tavern on rue Saint-Antoine, where nothing happened, and then chez S. Lalouette, medical doctor, on rue Saint-Benoît in faubourg Saint-Germain, where they all set upon him, threw him on a damask bed, and drew him into this vice. Since then he has consummated [the crime] five times, with Lefort, Lajeunesse, postilion, Saint-Germain, and two others whose names he does not recall. In addition he amused himself with Leclerc, wine vendor in Versailles, at whose residence orgies took place, and with Bayard, called the duchess of Angoulême, and Saint-Louis, called The Big Female Cousin, Savary, self-styled cook chez the prince de Lambesc, André, called the Female Baker, currently domestic of S. Lalouette, The Rose Girl, and others in Versailles as well as Paris, and twice in orgies chez Leclerc, whose names he does not recall. He has been to the marquis de Créquy's place and received twenty-four livres from him, without, however, amusing himself with him, but he told him to procure men for him. He, the deponent, went away from Versailles for fear of being arrested. Leclerc and others given over to this vice who went to his place were arrested about two weeks ago. One day in Paris he went to the residence of Bouquel, who sold English merchandise in the courtyard of the Saint-Germain fair. He was taken there by Bayard as an assembly house for this debauchery. He indeed saw many of this type there, but nothing was done there in his presence. +Abbé de la Poterie, whom he had never seen, picked him up in Paris around six weeks ago, opposite Saint-Roch, and persuaded him to go eat soup with him. The five times he consummated the crime he did so in the passive role. He has never done it in the active role.+
/thuillier/
C: P

2. Y 11724, 9 NOVEMBER 1784, 9:00 PM

I: A known pederast, closely linked to three men already arrested, picked up men in the Tuileries and Palais Royal.

Clauder Bertier, 16, called Cadet, native of Clermont in Auvergne, unemployed domestic, former jockey in the service of Rampon, single woman, living on rue des Boucherons in faubourg Saint-Germain, lived chez Mme Rouget, fruit vendor, on rue Mercière.

He has been given over to pederasty since the beginning of summer and was debauched into it by a postilion named Laboullaye, who lived chez the papal nuncio, friend of Vichery, whom he, the deponent, also knows. He has consummated this crime twice in the passive role with S. Du Chenu, garde du corps, in his lodgings on rue du Cimetière Saint-Andre-des-Arts. He paid him three livres each time. He has also surrendered himself to several other persons in hackney carriages. He picked these persons up in the Palais Royal but does not know their names. Some paid him six livres, others less. He was in the Tuileries and the Palais Royal this evening and accosted several persons who did not wish to amuse themselves. They said it was too cold. He knows La Chapelle to be given over to this vice. It is need that caused him to surrender himself to this vice. /bertier/
C: P

3. Y 11728, 16 SEPTEMBER 1786, 7:00 PM–1:00 AM

PP: quays, place Louis XV, Champs-Elysées, stone port, exits of the Palais Royal, OP

I: 9:45. Three men given over to pederasty, who supported themselves through debauchery and extortion, drank and hugged in a tavern.

Alexandre Cartery, 15, native of Paris, unemployed postilion, lodged on petite rue Saint-Roch.

It is true that he was in the Palais Royal garden yesterday and picked up a man unknown to him in the salesroom. He does not know his name or address. He is around 45 years old, was dressed in a grayish white jacket, and seemed to him to be a cook. He went to have supper with him in a tavern on rue Saint-Nicaise, where they ate pigeons and a quarter of a turkey. They touched themselves independently in the tavern. When they left they went into a small street where there is an archway and entered an alley where they consummated the crime of pederasty, with him, the deponent, in the passive role and the man in the active role. This man did not have any money and gave him, the deponent, his silver watch and his cane, a nettle tree one with an ivory pommel with a gilded copper circle on the back. He, the deponent, then went to find Persan, arrested with him, who was in the Palais Royal, with whom he had supper again. They ate a turkey thigh left over from his first supper, which he had taken away. His, the deponent's, brother was also at this supper. Today he, the deponent, was with Persan and sold the watch, for thirty-six livres, to a Jew who passed through the courtyard of the old Louvre. He gave six of these thirty-six livres to Persan and bought himself some hide breeches for ten livres. He has sixteen livres and six sols left. In fooling around with the cane today he broke it. He has been given over to pederasty for two months and was debauched into it by Du Chenu, who also took his pleasure with him, the deponent, and gave him several shirts, a vest, a white cravat, an écu worth three livres, and one worth six livres.

Asked if he stole the silver watch and cane from a man he picked up in the Palais Royal yesterday.

Said no, and the man gave them to him for taking his pleasure with him.

Asked if he has had relations with several other men, how much he has earned from surrendering himself to this crime, and what he lives on.

Said he has had relations, in addition, with a gentleman on rue Dauphine in Versailles for three or four days. He gave him twenty-seven livres. He might have earned in all three and a half louis. He usually drinks and eats with his parents. /ALexandre Cartery/
C: P

The other two men, unemployed limonadier's assistants, 18 and 17, did not mention Du Chenu.

NOTES

ADDITIONAL ABBREVIATIONS

AB Bibliothèque de l'Arsenal, Archives de la Bastille
FR Merrick and Ragan, *Policing Homosexuality in Pre-Revolutionary Paris* (Foucault's Reports, 1780–83)
Y Archives Nationales, series Y (Châtelet)

INTRODUCTION

1. Dover, *Greek Homosexuality*; C. Williams, *Roman Homosexuality*.
2. For outdated syntheses of a scholarly rather than popular nature, see Crompton, *Homosexuality and Civilization*; Aldrich, *Gay Life and Culture*.
3. Rocke, *Forbidden Friendships*.
4. Gerard and Hekma, *Pursuit of Sodomy*; Higgs, *Queer Sites*; Betteridge, *Sodomy*; O'Donnell and O'Rourke, *Queer Masculinities*.
5. Trumbach, "London's Sodomites," and many other articles, as well as the forthcoming second volume of his *Sex and the Gender Revolution*. For more on gender issues, see Merrick, *Sodomy*, chap. 2.
6. Foucault, *Volonté de savoir*, 59; Foucault, *Introduction*, 43.
7. Foucault, *Volonté de savoir*, 134; Foucault, *Introduction*, 101. Foucault wrote *si confuse*, which Hurley mistranslated as "utterly confused."
8. Merrick, "Patterns and Concepts"; Merrick, *Sodomy*, introduction.

9. Extant sources do not explain the change from religious to classical terminology. Abbé Nicolas Théru denounced numerous sodomites in hostile language in the 1720s and 1730s, but the police themselves rarely used religious language in documents about same-sex relations. They conducted their operations more professionally and bureaucratically as the century progressed. A. Williams, *Police of Paris*; Milliot, *"L'Admirable police."* The word "pederasty," not to be confused, of course, with "pedophilia," first appears in police records dated 10 June 1746 (AB 11597, fol. 180) and 28 December 1747 (AB 11610, fol. 333) and in the fourth edition (1762) of the dictionary of the Académie Française.
10. Merrick, "New Sources and Questions"; Merrick, *Sodomy*, chap. 1.
11. Merrick, "Commissioner Foucault."
12. Convers Desormeaux, commissaire since 1761, worked with Desurbois, inspector since 1782, from June 1784 on, but Noël substituted for his colleague now and then, as in May and August 1785.

13. Y 11725 (January through June) and 11726 (July through December).

14. The other two cases involved denunciations (#28, #62). Only five patrols visited the Left Bank (#54, #83, #90, #97, #121).

15. According to documents in the Projet Familles Parisiennes database, Convers Desormeaux married Magdeleine Rolland, daughter of a royal surgeon's lieutenant, on 12 January 1764 (in the parish of Saint-André-des-Arts) and buried her on 17 April 1765 (in the parish of Saint-Etienne-du-Mont). He had several siblings, including a brother, a barrister in the Parlement, who died at age 42 on 16 November 1781, and a sister who married at age 42 on 3 March 1784.

16. The French phrases *ils se sont touchés*, *ils se sont maniés*, and *ils se sont faits des attouchements* could mean that men touched, fondled, and stroked themselves or each other. I have not specified who did what in English unless the text or context clarifies the meaning.

17. Desurbois named just two of his observers, Pierre Igou and one Antoine. See Y 11724, 18 September, 13 November 1784. For more on decoys generally and Antoine (Baude) specifically, see Merrick, *Sodomy*, chap. 5.

18. For examples in Foucault's papers, see FR, #81, #83, #143, #149, #150, and #154.

19. Two specifically denied hugging (#9, #151), which suggests that they regarded it as a meaningful gesture. For the only references to kissing, see #28 and #85.

20. We do not know what instructions the inspector gave his observers or why they occasionally refused to listen to men who accosted them, as in #184 and #189.

21. We can only wish the observers and the inspector had quoted more words, such as "the most indecent remarks about pederasty" (#77).

22. How did he know that a marquis paid a cobbler twenty-four sols every time he visited him (#38) or that a Canadian had had sex with a man in his room on the day of his arrest outside the Tuileries (#132)?

23. More than a few pederasts avoided or eluded observers, who could not always locate the inspector to secure arrests.

24. Desurbois had used the words "this type" before. See Y 11722, 29 March 1783; Y 11723, 25 April, 7 and 8 June 1784; Y 11724, 29 October 1784.

25. One man refused to take the oath (#142), and a few declined to answer any questions or make any statement (#95, #108/Bourgot and Gavard).

26. The papers from 1785 include just three formal interrogations: #28, #62, and #97/Cassina. For previous examples of the question in question, see Y 11723, 25 April, 25 May, 4 and 7 June 1784; Y 11724, 17 July, 31 October, 11 November 1784.

27. One man declared that he was, "on the contrary, given over to the debauchery of women." Y 11724, 29 October 1784.

28. See Turcot, *Promeneur à Paris*.

29. Prisoners often explained how long (days, weeks, months, years) they had known others and how they met in the first place.

30. #85/Regnier, #143/Aubrée, #214. One man noted that "lots of young folks" wore them. Y 11724, 17 November 1784.

31. Men who rejected advances revealed as much about solicitation as men who accepted advances, as in #5, #48, #73, #78, and #91.

32. #86/Verdier, #141/Robert, #195/Lapointe. See also Y 11724, 4 June, 29 September 1784; Y 11727, 20 October 1786.

33. For other references to amusement, see #29/Ponchel and #50/Miller as well as Y 11727, 14 February 1786; Y 11728, 9 September 1786.

34. See also #74/Abzac.

35. See also #120/Musbien, #124/Brelon, #174/Patelle, and #195/Bonnet.

36. For other uses of the same words, see #190, #193.

37. Another man "did not wish to believe that there were men who thought that way" (#62).

38. Prisoners mentioned three others with female nicknames: The Lovely Female Baker (#25), The Fat (or Pregnant) Woman (#75), and The Woman from Provence (#83). The papers from 1785 include one reference to rouge (#30) and two to cross-dressing (#33/Bertin, during carnival, and #215, just for fun) but no evidence of characteristic effeminacy. The papers from 1784 mention many more female nicknames, including The Lion Queen, The Mother of Jesus, and Venus with Lovely Buttocks. Desurbois noted only once that one man gave his arm to another "like a woman." Y 11724, 23 June 1784. Two men attended assemblies but did not mention that others dressed or talked like women there, as in 1748–49. Y 11724, 7 and 23 June 1784.

39. None of the men arrested in 1785 specified that he had immigrated to the capital for sex as well as work, but it seems possible, if not probable, that some of them did.

40. Four of six clergymen (#28/Le Clerc de Piervalle, #56/Deroche, #90/Gout de la Brande, #110/Taillardant, #127, #206/Guay) but none of six noblemen (#15/Vichy, #73/Mânes, #74/Abzac, #78/Belloy, #93/Voyepierre, #94/Beauharnais) confessed.

41. The yes-men included 22 percent in their teens, 34 percent in their twenties, 26 percent in their thirties, 12 percent in their forties, 5 percent in their fifties, and 2 percent in their sixties.

42. These words should be studied with the speaker's age in mind. For "boy," see #13, #29/Ponchel, #86/Droz, and #203/Bour. For "child," see #6, #70/Paillot, and especially #61, in which Dorgny, 33, called the 11-year-old Camus a "man," "young man," and "child."

43. In 1784, Desurbois caught four pairs in the act, ages 28 and 50, 25 and 49, 41 and 42, and 21 and 59. Y 11724, 12 July, 23 and 28 August, 6 September 1784.

44. Le Duc shared his bed with a man who had nowhere to spend the night and claimed that they "did nothing wrong together, even while sleeping together" (#81).

45. Y 11724, 11 December 1784. One man denied that he lived "together in relations of pederasty" with another. Y 11723, 23 April 1784.

46. One man debauched himself (#83/Portier), and three men gave themselves over (#62, #72/Lefevre, #75/Picard), in the active voice.

47. See #13/Lefevre, #68/Beaujar, #107/Petit, #130/Bertrand, #165/Schpiler, #167/Ribot, #176/Brondel and Blanchard, and #203/Mercier.

48. See also #140/Feron, #144/Tonnere, and #213/Brincman.

49. Marinot, for example, confessed that it was "the first time he amused himself in this way," but he said only that one man tried to stroke him and another made propositions to him (#81).

50. See #7/Lallement, #33/Liez, #89/Naudin, #122/Pavie, #130/de la Fosse, #132/Naudin, #139/Larpenteur, #183/Des Vignes, and #200/Cochois. For more references to comrades, see Y 11724, 11 June, 26 July 1784; Y 11724, 20 November, 4 December 1784; Y 11727, 3 and 25 April 1786.

51. For data, see Merrick, *Sodomy*, chap. 1, app. E. One unrepresentative man, 45, reported that he had been debauched by choirboys (#140).

52. Two other cases involved men aged 40, who debauched men aged 48 and 14. Y 11724, 7 September 1784; Y 11727, 12 April 1786.

53. For clergymen and noblemen, see #2, #12/Cujat, #16/Brillant, #77, and #106/Girard. For masters and servants, see #19, #34/Roumier, and #217/Guilbert.

54. Only one mentioned coercion (#213/Brincman), but see also Y 11724, 14 and 22 December 1784.

55. One man complained that others had tried to "turn him away from" women. Y 11724, 29 September 1784.

56. Convers Desormeaux asked a few men if they were married, as in Y 11723, 13 April 1784.

57. One asked about "a special female or male friend" (#92/Michelot).

58. Another man disliked married men. Y 11724, 11 December 1784.

59. #7/Lallement, #204/Montreuil. For married men in the preceding and following years, see Y 11723, 6 March, 25 May 1784; Y 11724, 6, 11, and 31 October, 20 and 21 November, 11 and 27 December 1784; Y 11727, 25 January, 8 and 20 February, 7 and 28 April 1786.

60. See also #13/Duval, #17/Picot and Bernard, #79/Cochois, and #177; Y 11723, 25 April, 7 and 13 June 1784; Y 11724, 11 and 24 October, 26 December 1784; Y 11729, 2 April 1787.

61. See also #16/Brillant, #161, #163, and #188; Y 11724, 4 December 1784; Y 11727, 16 February, 9 and 11 April 1786.

62. Although Claude Baurain declared that "this passion rules him to the extent he cannot rid himself of it" (#47).

63. For data, see Merrick, *Sodomy*, chap. 1, app. H. Just a few men mentioned oral sex: #62, #153/Foullon, and #199. See also Y 11724, 11 ("the horror that men given over to this vice call eating the world") and 27 December 1784; Y 11727, 9 April 1786.

64. Though two men declined to let another man "take his pleasure in the back as one takes one's pleasure with a woman" or "do to him what one does to a woman." Y 11723, 11 August 1784; Y 11729, 29 November 1787.

65. By using different nouns, such as "bugger" and "bardash," or the adjectives "active" and "passive."

66. In 1784 and 1786, nineteen and sixteen men, respectively, admitted that they had "consummated the crime." Six teenagers played the passive role, and just one played the active role, but men in their twenties, thirties, and forties played both roles. Several younger men penetrated older men.

67. One man did not even understand the phrase "put it in" (#40).

68. Laqueur, *Solitary Sex*. The police, of course, were most likely to arrest men who made spectacles or nuisances of themselves, such as Jean Baptiste Bonnier, apprentice shoemaker, who "spermatized" women's dresses inside Notre-Dame cathedral on 15 August (Assumption Day) 1734. AB 11245, fol. 76.

69. One man declared that "if he wanted to amuse himself, he would do it at his place." Y 11724, 9 August 1784. Only one "desired to be a prostitute" (#62). The police did not conflate male sex for pay with female prostitution, but police records provide abundant evidence for comparative gendered analysis.

70. See #30/Voisin, #44/Eugé, #63/Beauceron, #69/Jameau, #77/Barat, #84, #87/Pitot, #98/Chaudé, #129/Loulié, #135/Bourachaux, #191/Gouy, and #202/Grosmenil. See also Y 11723, 11 June, 24 October, 9 and 15 November 1784; Y 11727, 25 January, 21 February 1786.

71. The cases of two men who had sex with men for the first time suggest that others might have been vulnerable to seduction. Chaumette suspected that the stranger who accosted him was "inclined to this vice" but succumbed to propositions "that excited him" (#211). Candre "does not know how he let himself go to it and has never been inclined to it" (#201).

72. On 1 June 1724, Verain Guillay informed a decoy "that he did not like women, that he had done nothing but divert himself with men since his tender youth, that this pleasure was in his blood." AB 10255, fol. 285. On 7 June 1742, Louis Chambry declared that "this vice is in his blood and that it is not possible to correct it." AB 11456, fol. 239v.

73. Y 11729, 27 September 1787. Another man identified the man who had debauched him as a "pederast by profession." Y 11732, 28 November 1788.

74. Y 11727, 3 March 1786.

75. In #21, for example, did Bunel actually say "consummated" and then correct himself, or did the clerk expect him to say "consummated" and wrote the word, then crossed it out when Bunel said "masturbated" instead? The inspector also made some changes in his accounts.

76. For contents of pockets, see #46/Cellier, #132, and #220, as well as Y 11722, 15 October 1783; Y 11724, 7 December 1784. The police found not only letters but also an ode and story about pederasty in one man's room. Y 11727, 13 April 1786.

77. See #16, #21, #28, #32, #34, #42, #86, #142, #159, #165, and #192.

78. See also #141/Robert and #183/Teytaud.

79. Another alleged that at first he did not realize "that there is anything wrong in it." Y 11724, 15 November 1784.

80. Many of the relevant registers have not survived, so it is difficult to generalize about this subject.

81. Merrick, *Sodomy*, chap. 6.

82. But see Merrick, "Sodomy, Subculture, and Surveillance."

83. Y 11727, 28 April 1786.

84. Y 11727, 9 February 1786.

85. For good examples, see #58/Richeux and #107/Petit. For more references, from the preceding and following years, see Y 11723, 23 and 25 April, 4 June 1784; Y 11724, 10 and 24 July, 9 and 28 August, 19 and 29 September, 11, 22, and 30 October, 11, 15, and 29 November, 22 December 1784; Y 11727, 7, 8, 14, 15, 18, 26, and 27 January, 15 and 20 February, 5, 20, and 21 March, 7, 11, and 21 April, 12, 16, and 21 September 1786.

86. On masters and servants, see Merrick, *Sodomy*, chap. 3.

87. For such sources in English, see Merrick and Ragan, *Homosexuality*, parts 1 and 3; Merrick, *Sodomites*, part 2.

88. On 1791, see Sibalis, "Regulation of Male Homosexuality"; Ragan, "Same-Sex Sexual Relations."

JANUARY

1. Lawyer who represented clients and argued cases in court, as opposed to an attorney.

2. Parlement of Paris, the royal appeals court with jurisdiction over more than a third of the kingdom.

3. Honorary title attached to judicial offices such as commissaire and inspector.

4. Royal municipal court with jurisdiction over the capital and its environs.

5. Sieur, a more respectful title than Monsieur.

6. Gothic chapel in the Palais de Justice complex on Ile de la Cité.

7. The ramp down from quai des Orfèvres led to a watering spot on the Seine and archways that supported the buildings on the south side of rue Saint-Louis.

8. The oldest and largest hospital in Paris, on Ile de la Cité and the Left Bank, between the Petit Pont and the Pont au Double.

9. Member of the Congregation of the Mission, founded in 1625 by Saint Vincent de Paul, who lived in the former leper (or lazar) house in the priory at 107, rue du Faubourg Saint-Denis.

10. Located at 4, place Saint-Louis.

11. Gagné did not explain why he took communion for the first time at such a late age.

12. In the wing along the Seine on Ile de la Cité.

13. Y 13409, 20 February 1782, in Merrick, *Sodomites*, 124–25. In some cases the extant papers of the commissaires do not include documentation of previous arrests mentioned in reports.

14. Desurbois observed him in the Mousetrap with another man, who escaped, but Bourquin claimed he went there only to do his business. Y 11724, 21 November 1784.

15. On the Champs de Mars, founded in 1751, for the benefit of five hundred

young nobles whose parents could not afford to educate them properly.

16. In 1782, he identified himself as a bourgeois.

17. Honorific version of Monsieur, applied to men in the world of the law.

18. Royal court with jurisdiction over taxes and the royal domain.

19. Pierre Boudeville, 29, had two letters from Dessous in his pocket when he was arrested. He admitted that they had consummated the crime sometimes and masturbated other times. Y 11724, 15 December 1784.

20. French island colony in the Caribbean.

21. Member of the military regiments stationed in the capital.

22. At no. 49, constructed in 1780. French Guards slept two per bed in these and other new barracks.

23. See also #137/Ratz.

24. On quai du Marché Neuf on the south side of Ile de la Cité.

25. Commandery of the medieval religious and military of the Hospitallers of Saint John, 2–16, rue Du Sommerard. Artisans who lived and worked in the enclosure were not subject to guild rules.

26. Penitents of the Third Order of Saint Francis at 199, rue du Temple.

27. Odéon theater at 1, place de l'Odéon, completed in 1782.

28. Church between 55 and 73, rue Saint-Jacques. When Simon was arrested again, with his breeches down, in an alley at the New Market, he said he was 40 years old and not given over to pederasty. Y 11727, 8 April 1786.

29. Mentioned by René Deschamps, 39. Y11724, 7 December 1784.

30. For the arrest of Marie Gabriel, comte de Garspern, see Y 13408, 5 February 1781, in FR, #60.

31. Charles Olivier de Saint-Georges, marquis de Vérac (1743–1828).

32. Church at 30, rue Saint-Paul.

33. Victoire Escalis, widow (1779) of Jean Baptiste Ignace Elzéar de Sinéty, or Jeanne de la Porterie de la Garrigue (1750–1797), wife (1778) of André Esprit Louis de Sinéty.

34. Parisian residence of the dukes of Orléans, the most celebrated and notorious center of diversion and corruption in the city.

35. Lawyer who represented clients but did not argue cases in court, as opposed to a barrister.

36. Since 1757, on rue des Fossés de M. le Prince.

37. Limonadiers sold beer, cider, fortified drinks, sweet liqueurs, ice cream, coffee, and chocolate.

38. Y 13408, 21 May 1781, in FR, #89.

39. Seat of the Parlement of Paris and other royal courts, on Ile de la Cité, partly burned on 10 January 1776 and rebuilt 1783–86.

40. Head tax introduced in 1695.

41. Vestiges of the approximately semicircular fortification on the other side of the Saint-Antoine gate from the Bastille.

42. Carceral hospital in the southern suburbs of Paris.

43. Marshy area below the level of the boulevards near the intersection of rue Amelot, which followed the line of the old moat filled in 1777, and rue du Chemin Vert.

44. The crown leased the collection of taxes and operation of monopolies to an association of wealthy financiers known as Farmers General (or tax farmers).

45. On boulevard Saint-Michel, on the site of the gate in the city walls demolished in the seventeenth century.

46. Triumphal arch adjacent to the Bastille, erected in 1671 and demolished in 1778.

47. Everyone used the word *verge*, as opposed to any of its colloquial synonyms.

48. Presumably to provide cover for LaCroix when he had sex with others.

49. For the arrests of Jean François Buquet at ages 24, 26, and 27, see Y 13407, 6 October 1780, and Y 13409, 23 December 1782, in FR, #7 and #224; Y 11723, 7 June 1784. Asked, on the last occasion, why he continued to surrender himself to this vice, he replied, "It is in order to live when he has no work." Several men mentioned him. Y 11723, 8 June 1784; Y 11724, 11 September 1784; Y 11727, 26 April 1786. One, who met him in prison, declared that he stopped speaking to him because of his reputation. Y 11724, 7 November 1784.

50. The church and abbot's palace survive on boulevard Saint-Germain in the 6th arr.

51. Hospital for the elderly and indigent, as well as the insane, at 21, rue de Sèvres.

52. Title not just for abbots but for clergymen in general, especially those who had received no more than one (tonsure) or more of the minor orders.

53. He was arrested again for making propositions and exposing himself to a man who called him a bardash and had him arrested. At that time he worked for the architect Claude Nicolas Ledoux. Y 11728, 3 July 1786.

54. He had been arrested, warned, and released before and identified himself at the time as a native of Saint-Mâlo. Y 13409, 5 December 1782, in FR, #221.

55. Charles Hyacinthe Goulet, notary, 1766–1787.

56. Vichy (1740–1793) married (1764) Claude Marie Josèphe de Saint-Georges, and they had two sons.

57. Mentioned in FR, #83, #164, and #180.

58. Y 13409, 19 April 1782, in FR, #186.

59. Y 13408, 8 October 1781, in FR, #142. Some, but not all, references to procurement include the noun or verb. See, for example, #48, #129/Loulié, and #136.

60. In 1782, he gave his age in the same way.

61. Large tavern on rue Lamartine built and run by the Hassenfratz family.

62. Philippe Antoine Gabriel Victor Charles de La Tour du Pin (1723–1794) married (1748) Madeleine Bertin, and they had two children. One pederast listed the marquis as one of his protectors. Y 13407, 14 April 1780, in FR, #3.

63. Petr Aleksandrovich Buturlin (1731–1787), Russian ambassador to Spain, married (1759) Maria Romanova Vorontzova, and they had two children. See FR, #2, #8, #17, #34, and #46; Y 11724, 26 November 1784.

64. For the arrest of Cyprien Jérôme Picart de Saint-Hilaire, see Y 13409, 8 March 1782, in FR, #179.

FEBRUARY

1. Areintz was caught in the act, with his breeches down, in the Coal-Box with another man, who escaped arrest. He acknowledged that he had amused himself with men for two to three years and that he and the other man masturbated reciprocally. Y 11724, 15 September 1784.

2. In the middle of the bridge, next to the equestrian statue of Henry IV. Jaillot, *Rues*, 409.

3. 13, rue de la Montagne Sainte-Geneviève.

4. 73, avenue des Champs-Elysées.

5. 5, rue des Médicis.

6. University complex in the 5th arr.

7. Without a name, "Monsieur" means Louis XVI's brother, Louis Stanislas Xavier, comte de Provence (1755–1824), later Louis XVIII.

8. Saint-Germain fair, near Saint-Sulpice, from 1 February to Palm Sunday.

9. Four parallel to and five perpendicular to the central pathway in the parterre.

10. Martin Louis de Perrier, baron d'Usseau (b. 1745).

11. Former enclave of the Knights Templar, the medieval military order, in the 3rd arr.

12. Samuel Peixotto (1741–1805). See Merrick, *Sodomites*, 143–45.

13. From Epiphany to Ash Wednesday.

14. Member of the royal household cavalry. For more on Du Chenu, see appendix.

15. The police searched his room on 20 February and found nothing suspect.

16. On the site of the gate in the city walls demolished in the seventeenth century.

17. Bénigne Porret de Blosseville (1742–1828).

18. Between rue Saint-Nicaise and the courtyard of the Tuileries palace, on the east side of the garden.

19. Masked balls from 11:00 pm to 7:00 am on Sundays from Saint Martin's day (11 November) to Advent, on Sundays and Thursdays from Epiphany to Lent. The entrance fee was six livres per person. Hébert, *Almanach parisien*, 118.

20. Church at 2, impasse Saint-Eustache.

21. At this time the area planted with trees extended from place Louis XV to the roundabout between the Cours de la Reine and the gardens behind the homes along rue du Faubourg Saint-Honoré.

22. Les Halles, the central market, in the 1st arr.

23. This pathway, 65 toises long and 16 toises wide, was lined with chestnut trees. See Hurtaut and Magny, *Dictionnaire historique*, 3:729. One toise is equivalent to 6 feet.

24. On the Right Bank, between the Pont Notre-Dame and the Pont au Change.

25. La Monnaie, at 11, quai de Conti, constructed 1767–75.

26. On the north side of the garden.

27. The first Parisian newspaper published daily, as of 1 January 1777.

28. Tea flavored with syrup, not the cold dessert on modern menus.

29. Also mentioned in #71 as well as FR, #117; Y 11726, 27 April 1786.

30. He was arrested again later for extortion. Y 11728, 26 September 1786; Y 11729, 3 April 1787.

31. *Faire quanquan*, to make a lot of noise. For more references, see #215 and Y 11730, 27 September 1787.

32. He had three white handkerchiefs on his person, including one stuck in the belt of his breeches with an end hanging out. "If one of his handkerchiefs was in his breeches, he was very well allowed to put it there."

33. This marionette theater at 38, rue de Montpensier (68–75, Galerie de Montpensier) opened on 23 October 1784.

34. The duc de Chartres had the present buildings constructed between 1781 and 1784. He rented the lower floors to businesses and the upper floors as residences. The garden is surrounded by arcades on three sides.

35. This café at 121, Galerie de Valois, also mentioned in #33 and #69, opened in 1785. It delivered orders to customers by dumbwaiters in the middle of their tables.

36. At the northwest corner of the garden. The Orangery housed orange trees during the winter.

37. Philippe Guillaume des Deux-Ponts (1754–1807).

38. 57–60, Galerie de Montpensier.

39. The dauphin was the heir to the throne. That title belonged to the first son of Louis XVI and Marie-Antoinette, Louis Joseph, born 22 October 1781.

40. For promenades in 1785, see Jaillot, *Rues*, 308–11.

41. As a good example of bad spelling, the clerk wrote "comptant" instead of "content."

42. Antoine Eléonor Léon Leclerc de Juigné (1728–1811), archbishop as of 1781.

43. An unusual use of a colloquial collective noun for men who desired men. On such terms, see Courouve, *Vocabulaire*; Hennig, *Espadons*.

44. The circular basin between the quincunxes or the octagonal basin near the other end of the garden.

45. Donatien Alphonse François de Sade (1740–1814). His former valet Jacques André Langlois was arrested on 27 November 1780. FR, #32.

46. Or Opéra Comique, place Boieldieu, constructed 1781–83.

47. Claude Charles de Pleurre (1737–1810).

48. Circular space on the border between the 1st and 2nd arrs., with a pedestrian rather than equestrian statue of Louis XIV in the center.

49. Alexandre Fragnet, arrested during a pederasty patrol in the Champs-Elysées. Y 13409, 18 July 1782, in Merrick, *Sodomites*, 107.

50. The police found three work certificates, one of them forged, in his pockets.

51. When he was arrested again, he admitted that since his release from prison, he had surrendered himself to pederasty several times with several persons. Y 11727, 31 March 1786.

52. A man who avoided pederasts "and the places where they go" after his arrest in 1782 mentioned this tavern by name. Y 11723, 13 June 1784. See also FR, #72.

53. Joseph Magnus de Sparre (1704–1788) married (1730) Marie Antoinette de Chambige, and they had four children.

54. For another use of this noun, see Y 11727, 29 March 1786.

55. Perhaps Liez meant Roermond in the Austrian Netherlands.

56. 82, rue du Faubourg Poissonnière, constructed in 1772.

57. Barracks at 15, place de l'Estrapade.

MARCH

1. The former royal equestrian academy at 230, rue de Rivoli, on the north side of the garden.

2. Louis Joseph d'Ailly (1735–1794).

3. Jean Joseph Guénard acquired this costly venal office, which ennobled those who purchased it, in 1774.

4. When he was arrested again, outside the Tuileries, Brochet admitted that he had surrendered himself to pederasty for a year but insisted that he had "carried the debauchery only as far as masturbation." Y 11727, 5 March 1786.

5. In the monastery at 237–51, rue Saint-Honoré.

6. Jean Cosse, nicknamed Philippe, 26, domestic, unemployed at the time of his arrest. Y 11724, 24 October 1784. An Englishman gave him a watch for his obligingness. Y 11724, 31 October 1784. When he was arrested again, he identified himself as a hairdresser. Y 11727, 3 April 1786.

7. Variously identified as quai des Tuileries, quai du Louvre, and quai de l'Ecole.

8. As of this date clerks routinely used this wording: "places where pederasts and men given over to this vice gather."

9. Thirty leagues from Paris, by royal order on 12 August 1781, revoked on 7 July 1782. For his interrogation, see Y 13408, 26 July 1781, in FR, #117.

10. Over the moat between place Louis XV and the Tuileries.

11. Charles Philippe, comte d'Artois (1757–1836), Louis XVI's brother, later Charles X.

12. Laure Auguste de Fitz-James (1744–1814), wife (1762) of Philippe Gabriel Maurice Joseph de Hénin-Liétard de Chimay, lady-in-waiting as of 1770.

13. Marie Leczinska (1703–1768) married Louis XV in 1725.

14. The gray musketeers, as opposed to the black musketeers of the second company.

15. Jean Charles Pierre Lenoir (1732–1807), lieutenant general in 1774–75 and 1776–85.

16. See Y 13408, 16 August 1781, in FR, #122.

17. The French half (later Haiti) of the Caribbean island of Hispaniola. For other

references to the Americas, see #19, #68/du Doigt, #90/Despan, #102/Duperrier, #118, and #126/Laboubée.

18. For options and prices, see Hébert, *Almanach parisien*, 171.

19. For commentary on this case, see Merrick, *Sodomy*, 19–21.

20. Lent began on 9 February in 1785.

21. For another use of the same words, see #200/Sacquenet.

22. Gervaise de Latouche, *Histoire de Dom Bougre*. Father Casimir "reviewed all the famous buggers from Adam to the Jesuits and found among them Philosophers, popes, emperors, cardinals. He praised each one individually and, turning then to the injustice and blindness of those who attack a pleasure adopted and practiced by the greatest men, he went back to the story of Sodom. He maintained that this memorable event had been falsified, out of jealousy" (219).

23. For other uses of this language, see #172, #186/Bérault, and #193.

24. The Châtelet employed two categories of bailiffs, distinguished by the titles of "bailiffs with a rod" and "bailiffs on horse."

25. At the southeast corner of the garden.

APRIL

1. François Félix Dorothée des Balbes de Berton de Crillon (1748–1820).

2. Wife of Pierre Henri de Lupé (b. 1769).

3. Presumably Silvy.

4. Mentioned in Y 11727, 30 March 1786.

5. Mentioned in FR, #174 and #192.

6. For his previous arrests, see Y 13407, 6 October 1780; Y 13408, 25 December 1781; Y 11723, 7 April 1784, all in Merrick, *Sodomites*, 120–22, as well as #30.

7. Officials responsible for oversight of military provisions, armaments, and so forth.

8. Five percent income tax introduced in 1749.

9. Y 13408, 22 April 1781, in FR, #82. At that time he said he was born in Ornex, in the pays de Gex, and was more than 20 years old. When he was arrested again, outside the Tuileries, he said he was 26. Y 11727, 30 January 1786.

10. At 13–17, rue du Bac.

11. The clerk wrote that he loitered for a long time this evening "in places," without the usual "most suspect."

12. Jean Charles, vicomte de Carbonnières (1737–1794).

13. For rent for two sols. Hébert, *Almanach parisien*, 147.

14. Louis Maximilien de Lancry de Pronleroy (1713–1791).

15. In the hôtel d'Armenonville at the intersection with rue Verderet.

16. Spelled "jokquie" here and "jacquet," "jocquet," or "jockey" elsewhere; a young servant who drove a carriage or accompanied his master on horseback.

17. Treatment for fever, hemorrhage, incontinence, and more.

18. This oldest line of the sewer system drained into the Ménilmontant brook.

19. Perhaps *giroflée*, stock flower.

20. When Bigot was released from La Force, he promised to avoid suspect places, but he was arrested outside the Tuileries again. Y 11727, 18 January 1786.

21. For his arrest, see Y 13407, 9 October 1780, in FR, #11.

22. Ambigu Comique on boulevard du Temple, opened in 1769. The program for 20 April included *Mélite et Lindor*, *Les Déguisements*, *Les Deux frères*, and *Galatée*.

23. Not transformed (partly) into a museum until 1793.

24. Triumphal arch erected in 1672 at the intersection of rue Saint-Denis with boulevard de Saint-Denis and boulevard de Bonne Nouvelle.

25. There was a full moon the next night.

26. Founded in 1701 to supply the French army.

27. Nicolas Alexandre, vicomte de Virieu (1733–1811), held the title of gentleman-in-waiting to the comte de Provence, who occupied the palace.

28. For other cases involving pederasts who asked women to find men for them, see Y 11722, 6 October, 22 November 1783; Y 11723, 11 June 1784; Y 11727, 2 January 1786.

29. No one else mentioned this faculty.

30. The commissaire used the same verb (*habiter*) in both questions.

MAY

1. Along the north side of the garden, opposite the monastery of the Feuillants at 229–35, rue Saint-Honoré.

2. The extended family of Pierre Victor, baron de Besenval (1721–1791), commander of the Swiss Guards, includes many options.

3. Route between the Champs-Elysées and the Seine.

4. Between the Seine and the Cours de la Reine.

5. Entertainment complex in the Champs-Elysées, constructed in 1769–71, demolished in 1780.

6. The only reference to expulsion from the Tuileries.

7. Seminary of Saint-Nicolas-du-Chardonnet at no. 24.

8. Domestics of both sexes paid ten sols to register. Masters paid thirty sols when they hired domestics. "If they are not satisfied after ten or twelve days, the office secures others for them without further charge." Hurtaut and Magny, *Dictionnaire historique*, 1:701–2.

9. That is, he lived in an unfurnished rather than a furnished room.

10. Desurbois caught him and Charles Perrier, 50, domestic, in the Coal-Box with their breeches down, "seeking to surrender themselves to the crime of pederasty." Y 11724, 12 July 1784.

11. In 1784 he said he was 28.

12. Gabriel Claude Palteau de Veimerange (1739–1994).

13. Augustinian convent of the Daughters of the Assumption at no. 263.

14. They followed the lines of the city walls demolished in the seventeenth century and formed a semicircle between the Saint-Honoré and Saint-Antoine gates.

15. Perhaps they regarded the women they insulted as their rivals for the attention of men.

16. Jean Henri Bancal des Issarts, notary from 1783 to 1788.

17. In 1780 he said he was 20.

18. Y 13407, 13 December 1780, in FR, #36.

19. The only document that does not include separate statements.

20. In this establishment, also mentioned in #123, "one finds only cruisers and bardashes. Infamies and horrors it is not necessary to name take place in this café. The character of those who frequent it makes it easy enough to guess which. The police have it under surveillance, but their vigilant eyes are deceived. It would be wisest and safest to have this receptacle of tribades and sodomists closed." Mayeur de Saint-Paul, *Chroniqueur désoeuvré*, 47–48.

21. The building has arcades on three sides.

22. *The Hero* had seventy-four cannons and was involved in naval battles during the war for American independence.

23. For another case of sex at sea, see Y 11724, 2 December 1784.

24. Here and elsewhere the clerk shortened *raccrochement* to *racroc*.

25. Jacques Gabriel Louis Le Clerc de Juigné (1727–1807).

26. Seron later "had the weakness to accost the young man arrested with him on the Pont Neuf with the design of

amusing himself with him." Y 11727, 26 January 1786.

27. Jean François d'Abzac de Sarrazac (1747–1841) succeeded his brother Pierre Marie at the royal stables in 1781.

28. The Grandes Ecuries, as opposed to the Petites Ecuries, both on the place d'Armes, opposite the palace.

29. For more on Joret and Chauffour, see FR, #5, #12, #45, and #144.

30. Located near place Montaigne.

31. Jean Baptiste François Guilleminot Dugué (1727–1797), music director as of 1770.

32. Note that the phrase "consummated the crime," in this case, refers to anal intercourse with a woman.

33. Joseph François de Malide (1730–1812), bishop as of 1774.

34. The Tuileries had facilities for both sexes as of 1777.

35. Member of the military Order of Saint Lazarus of Jerusalem, founded during the Crusades to care for lepers.

JUNE

1. A women's hairstyle with rows of curls.

2. He was arrested again for violating his order of exile. Y 11728, 5 September 1786.

3. Located at 2–4, rue du Roi de Sicile.

4. He was arrested in the Mousetrap but insisted that "he has never been given over to pederasty and never surrendered himself to it." Y 11724, in Merrick, *Sodomites*, 129–30.

5. Jean Baptiste Nicolet (1728–1796) opened his Grands Danseurs theater at 58, boulevard du Temple in 1764. The program for 3 June included *Pierrot roi de Cocagne, Le Sabotier, La Cacophonie, Pierre Bagnolet et Claude Bagnolet son fils*, and *Les Forges*.

6. When he was arrested again, he claimed to be 23 but acknowledged that he had spent seventeen days in La Force, had been exiled, and had returned to Paris in December. Y 11727, 27 January 1786.

7. Jean François Levasseur, 26, maintained by a foreign lord, sought a man with more money to maintain him. Y 11724, 31 October 1784.

8. Opened on 2 July 1746, with the main entrance on rue Basse des Remparts.

9. He cut off the flaps, which he had in his pockets, in order to affix the rosettes.

10. No one else made such a claim.

11. He accosted men on boulevard du Pont au Choux but denied accosting anyone and having any "indecent intention." Y 11724, 8 November 1784.

12. He had been arrested before, on the boulevard du Pont au Choux, and released. Y 11724, 8 November 1784.

13. As of 1 March 1780.

14. The oldest planned square in Paris, called place Royale at this time, in the 4th arr.

15. The only usage of this word.

16. The ring of boulevards on the Left Bank, from the Invalides to the Salpetrière.

17. Located at 5, rue Descartes.

18. Louis Armand de Seiglière de Soyécourt (1722–1790) married three times (1748, 1763, 1773) and had one daughter, born in 1774. The clerk spelled the name Soycour, Saucour, and Soyecourt.

19. He married Marie Madeleine Cornu in 1748.

20. Not the same words that the inspector reported above.

21. The count (1756–1819) married (1783) Claudine Françoise Adrienne Gabrielle de Lézay Marnézia, and they had two children. His personal valet had been arrested and imprisoned the year before. Y 11724, 17 July 1784.

22. Léonor Anne Gabriel de Pracomtal (1773–1838).

23. In the southern suburbs of Paris.

24. Not Charles Louis Etienne de Fautereau (1741–1817), chevalier de Saint-Louis, who had no title. He married late for a nobleman and received a dispensation to wed (26 February 1772) his cousin Marie Anne Elisabeth de Fautereau.

25. The inspector caught him in the act, but the commissaire released him "upon his promises of correcting himself of this vice." Y 11724, 7 September 1784.

26. More than a few police reports, such as FR, #95, include references to men bathing and men watching men bathe in the Seine.

27. Daniele Andrea Dolfin (1748–1798), ambassador from 1780 to 1786.

28. He identified himself in the same way both times.

29. Presumably the old barrier at the end of rue des Vieilles Tuileries rather than the new gate, on rue Pasteur, in the wall constructed by the tax farmers in the 1780s.

30. Carceral hospital for girls (500 beds) and boys (120 beds) at 1, rue Lacépède.

JULY

1. Wives routinely sought permission, from the lieutenant general of police, to take refuge in convents when they initiated lawsuits for separation of persons (as opposed to property) from abusive husbands.

2. When he was arrested again, outside the Tuileries, he said he was 20 years old. Y 11727, 25 April 1786.

3. David Pierre Perrinet, receiver general for Flanders, on rue Charlot.

4. See FR, #72.

5. François Scipion de Grimoard de Beauvoir du Roure, born in 1760, officer in the French Guards, married (28 November 1779) Françoise Antoinette Louise de Noailles and died, without progeny, on 17 April 1782.

6. Louis Philippe Joseph d'Orléans, later Philippe-Egalité (1747–1793).

7. Fountain of the Four Seasons by Edme Bouchardon, constructed 1739–45, at 57–59, rue de Grenelle.

8. André Charles de Bonnaire de Forges (1740–1793), intendant des domaines et des droits domainiaux, on rue Vivienne.

9. The Hospital Order of Saint John of God.

10. For sick and poor soldiers and clergy, founded in 1780, located at 15, avenue du Général Leclerc.

11. In front of the city hall and along the Seine.

12. No one else used this language.

13. Listed in the 1785 *Almanach royal*, 145–59.

14. Louis XV laid the cornerstone of the church, now the Panthéon, in the 5th arr., on 6 September 1764.

AUGUST

1. Located at 42–44, boulevard Saint-Michel.

2. In principle, all property owners who inhabited the city for a year and a day and paid taxes there were entitled to the appellation and privileges of "bourgeois de Paris." In practice, however, this designation was generally applied to non-nobles who lived off their investments.

3. Frédéric Christophe Cassolet, 27, inlay vendor, had been arrested twice before. Merrick, *Sodomites*, 104; Y 11723, 23 April 1784. He cruised "with the greatest impudence" on the boulevards and in the Champs-Elysées, liked domestics and French Guards, debauched "young folks," and held orgies at his place.

4. He secured the job through the referral office for domestics.

5. Church at 2, place Sainte-Opportune.

6. François Henry d'Harcourt (1726–1802), duke as of 1783.

7. Catherine Scholastica Aubusson (1733–1815), married in 1752.

8. Annet Jacques Joseph de Rostaing de Champferrier (1731–1798).

9. Another man punched a pederast who propositioned him. Y 11727, 16 February 1786.

10. Arthur Richard de Dillon (1721–1806), archbishop as of 1763.

SEPTEMBER

1. Saint-Gervais et Protais, church on place Saint-Gervais.

2. Benedictine convent of the Perpetual Adoration of the Holy Sacrament at 66, rue de Turenne.

3. Hospital order housed at 241, rue Saint-Denis.

4. Philippe Jean Pelletan (1747–1829), professor in the medical faculty of the University of Paris.

5. He had been arrested and released before. Y 13409, 5 December 1782, in FR, #221.

6. When he was arrested (and released) before, he identified himself as a clerk. Y 11723, 29 March 1784.

7. Opposite rue Guénegaud. Jaillot, *Rues*, 20.

8. Listed in Jaillot, *Rues*, 573.

9. See #1/Juillien.

10. The record of this arrest, as opposed to the one documented in #140, has not survived.

11. Dominican convent razed for the construction of place de la Bourse.

12. For another case of parental intervention, see #108. Parents typically submitted complaints about wayward children to the lieutenant general of police. For examples, see Foucault and Farge, *Désordre des familles* and *Disorderly Families*.

13. Member of the Sovereign Military and Hospitaller Order of Saint John of Jerusalem, Rhodes, and Malta, founded in 1048. Brothers Alexandre Louis René Toussaint (1772–1857) and André Hector (1778–1806) Galard de Brassac de Béarn acquired this title as children, but, given their ages, neither one of them could be this Knight or the chevalier mentioned in #176, #180, or #213, who could be their father, chevalier de Saint-Louis.

14. Charles Jacques Louis de La Martellière, comte d'Orfeuille.

15. Desurbois reported that he loitered on the boulevard, accosted men, and went down to the Coal-Box with one of them, but he insisted that he merely answered questions about the time and other matters. Y 11724, 7 September 1784.

16. Prison for children incarcerated at the request of their families, at no. 107.

17. See Y 13408, 28 September 1782, in FR, #215.

OCTOBER

1. Convent of the English Daughters of the Conception at no. 46–50.

2. Presumably a tavern named after the village, in the 20th arr.

3. Hospital with three hundred (15 × 20, thus the name) beds for the blind at no. 28.

4. This seminary for poor students at 34, rue Sainte-Geneviève offered thirty-three endowed scholarships.

5. Y 13409, 14 September 1782, in FR, #214.

6. He was caught with another man in the Mousetrap, with their breeches down, but claimed he went there only to do his business. Y 11724, 23 August 1784.

7. In 1784, he said he was 49 years old.

8. Pierre Charles Laurent de Villedeuil (1747–1828), intendant as of 1785. Intendants of "justice, police, and finances"

represented the crown in provinces throughout the kingdom.

9. He had been arrested and released before. Y 13409, 20 December 1781, in FR, #223.

10. Y 13409, 20 December 1782, in FR, # 223.3.

11. Court with jurisdiction over issues involving finances and the royal domain.

12. Jacques Mathieu Augeard, marquis de Buzancy (1733–1805), secretary as of 1777. His "secret memoirs" do not include the word "pederasty."

13. Y 13408, 5 July 1781, in FR, #103.

14. No one else used the word *état* in this way.

15. In 1781, he said he was 48 years old.

16. Russian province, later Estonia and Latvia.

17. At 1, rue Montgolfier, constructed in 1765.

18. The buildings on both sides of the Pont au Change had five stories.

19. Royal abbey at no. 277 bis.

20. The extant registers from La Force in Archives de la Préfecture de Police, AB 321-29, cover the years 1788 to 1797, so it is not possible to study incarcerations in 1785.

21. Church at 254, rue Saint-Martin.

22. Etienne François d'Aligre (1727–1798), First President in 1768–71 and in 1774–88, had an official residence in the Palais de Justice complex, at the end of a passageway with a gate on rue Saint-Louis.

23. Perhaps Alexandre Guillaume de Galard de Brassac de Béarn (1741–1809) did not inherit the title of count until the death of his father in 1788. He had seven children with his wife (15 February 1768), Anne Marie Gabrielle Potier de Novion (1747–1793), between 1768 and 1779, including the sons mentioned in #154 (note 13), but nothing, as yet, links him to that street.

24. On 14 July, he told the commissaire he was born in Nancy and 21 years old.

NOVEMBER

1. No one else used this word.

2. For another use of this language, see Y 11727, 30 January 1786.

3. At the time of his arrest, Robert Lebas, called Grandmaison, 33, admitted that he slept with Louis Vallet, nearly 16, unemployed domestic, who denied it. Y 11724, 24 October 1784.

4. The list in the 1785 *Almanach royal* includes a Villemauzy on rue de Richelieu.

5. Des Vignes and Teytaud both promised not only to avoid suspect places but also "not to surrender himself to the debauchery of pederasty anymore." Convers Desormeaux warned at least one man "not to make himself suspected of pederasty again." Y 11723, 19 April 1784.

6. François Martial Augustin des Monstiers de Mérinville (1727–1802).

7. Fewer than eight miles from Teytaud's hometown.

8. It is not clear why Peigné included his associate's last name in his signature.

9. Pierre Clément Dassonvillez, commissaire from 1785 to 1791. He lived opposite rue de Montmorency.

10. The clerk wrote *venu a Paris pour voir des Paris* instead of *parents* (relatives).

11. No one else used this word.

12. Official of the Chambre des Comptes.

13. Entrances on rue de la Tonnellerie and rue Saint-Honoré. Jaillot, *Rues*, 22.

14. As a member of the Royal Academy of Painting and Sculpture, Maurice Quentin de la Tour (1704–1788) had rooms in the Louvre.

15. Gate at Place Blanche in the wall constructed by the tax farmers.

16. The only reference to sodomy, as opposed to pederasty, in 1785.

17. Monastery at 64, boulevard Saint-Michel.

18. Along the middle section of quai du Louvre.

DECEMBER

1. Frères des Ecoles (not Eglises) Chrétiennes at no. 2–10.
2. The royal monopoly on the sale of tobacco was established in 1674 and subsequently incorporated into the General Farms.
3. He had been arrested and imprisoned before. Y 13409, 2 January 1782, in FR, #159.
4. No one else used this language.
5. Charles Antoine Etienne de Choiseul-Beaupré (1739–1820).
6. Mercier presumably made this remark in response to Antoine.
7. Bathilde d'Orléans (1750–1782), wife (1770) of Louis de Bourbon (1756–1830).
8. To cross from the Left to the Right Bank.
9. On Sundays and holidays during the summer. Hébert, *Almanach parisien*, 118.
10. Ivan Sergeievich Bariatinsky (1740–1811), ambassador from 1773 to 1785.
11. Dmitri Alexseievich Gallitzin (1728–1803), Russian ambassador to Holland.
12. In one of the royal military orders.
13. Jacques François Pascal, executed on 10 October 1783 for the attempted rape and murder of an adolescent. See Merrick, "'Brutal Passion.'"
14. Nicolas Guy Brenet (1728–1792).
15. Madeleine Suzanne Adelaïde de Voyer de Paulmy d'Argenson (1752–1813), wife (1771) of Anne Charles Sigismond de Montmorency Luxembourg.
16. Square in the 1st arr., with an equestrian statue of Louis XIV in the center.
17. Church at 296, rue Saint-Honoré.
18. The church of the novitiates survives at 1, place Saint-Thomas-d'Aquin. Trelon was still unemployed when he was arrested again, outside the Tuileries. Y 11727, 3 March 1786.
19. Claude-Louis Châtelet (1753–1795).
20. The English options include Countess of Seven Points, literally as well as figuratively (e.g., Countess of Seven Quips).
21. Marie Gabrielle Charlotte Anne de Kergadiou (1736–1828).

WORKS CITED

A comprehensive bibliography on homosexuality in early modern France is available at Policing Male Homosexuality: 18th-Century Paris, https://coloradocollege.website/phs/historical-background/bibliography/.

Aldrich, Robert, ed. *Gay Life and Culture: A World History*. London: Thames & Hudson, 2006.

Almanach royal, année MDCCLXXXV, présenté à Sa Majesté pour la première fois en 1699. Paris, 1785.

Betteridge, Tom, ed. *Sodomy in Early Modern Europe*. Manchester: Manchester University Press, 2002.

Courouve, Claude. *Vocabulaire de l'homosexualité masculine*. Paris: Payot, 1985.

Crompton, Louis. *Homosexuality and Civilization*. Cambridge: Harvard University Press, 2003.

Dover, Kenneth. *Greek Homosexuality*. London: Duckworth, 1978.

Foucault, Michel. *An Introduction*. Vol. 1 of *The History of Sexuality*. Translated by Robert Hurley. New York: Pantheon Books, 1978.

———. *La Volonté de savoir*. Vol. 1 of *Histoire de la sexualité*. Paris: Gallimard, 1976.

Foucault, Michel, and Arlette Farge, eds. *Le Désordre des familles: Lettres de cachet des Archives de la Bastille au XVIIIᵉ siècle*. Paris: Gallimard, 1982.

———. *Disorderly Families: Infamous Letters from the Bastille Archives*. Translated by Thomas Scott-Railton. Minneapolis: University of Minnesota Press, 2017.

Gerard, Kent, and Gert Hekma, eds. *The Pursuit of Sodomy: Male Homosexuality in Renaissance and Enlightenment Europe*. New York: Harrington Park Press, 1989.

Gervaise de Latouche, Jean Charles. *Histoire de Dom Bougre, Portier des Chartreux, écrite parlui-même*. Rome [Paris]: chez Philotanus, [1740–41].

Hébert. *Almanach parisien en faveur des étrangers et des personnes curieuses*. Edited by Daniel Roche. Saint Etienne: Publications de l'Université de Saint-Etienne, 2001.

Hennig, Jean Luc. *Espadons, mignons & autres monstres: Vocabulaire de l'homosexualité masculine sous l'ancien régime*. Paris: Cherche Midi, 2014.

Higgs, David, ed. *Queer Sites: Gay Urban Histories Since 1600*. London: Routledge, 1999.

Hillairet, Jacques. *Dictionnaire historique des rue de Paris*. 2 vols. Paris: Editions de minuit, 1963.

Hurtaut, Pierre Thomas Nicolas, and Magny. *Dictionnaire historique de la ville de Paris et de ses environs*. 4 vols. Paris, 1779.

Jaillot, Jean Baptiste Michel Renou de Chauvigné, dit. *Les Rues et les environs de Paris*. Paris: Langlois, 1785.

Laqueur, Thomas. *Solitary Sex: A Cultural History of Masturbation*. New York: Zone Books, 2003.

Mayeur de Saint-Paul, François Marie. *Le Chroniqueur désoeuvré, ou L'espion du boulevard du Temple*. London [Paris], 1782.

Merrick, Jeffrey. "'Brutal Passion' and 'Depraved Taste': The Case of Jacques François Pascal." In *Homosexuality in French History and Culture*, edited by Jeffrey Merrick and Michael Sibalis, 85–104. New York: Harrington Park Press, 2001.

———. "Commissioner Foucault, Inspector Noël, and the 'Pederasts' of Paris, 1780–83." *Journal of Social History* 32, no. 2 (1998): 287–307.

———. "New Sources and Questions for Research on Sexual Relations Between Men in Eighteenth-Century France." *Gender & History* 30, no. 1 (2018): 9–29.

———. "Patterns and Concepts in the Sodomitical Subculture of Eighteenth-Century Paris." *Journal of Social History* 50, no. 2 (2016): 273–306.

———, ed. *Sodomites, Pederasts, and Tribades in Eighteenth-Century France: A Documentary History*. University Park: Penn State University Press, 2019.

———. *Sodomy in Eighteenth-Century France*. Newcastle: Cambridge Scholars Publishing, 2020.

———. "Sodomy, Subculture, and Surveillance in Paris, 1739–1747." *Early Modern French Studies* 45, no. 2 (2023): 199–223.

Merrick, Jeffrey, and Bryant T. Ragan, eds. *Homosexuality in Early Modern France: A Documentary Collection*. New York: Oxford University Press, 2001.

———. *Policing Homosexuality in Pre-Revolutionary Paris*. Policing Male Homosexuality: 18th-Century Paris; Foucault's Reports, 1780–83. https://coloradocollege.website/phs/foucaults-reports-1780-83-full-text/.

Milliot, Vincent. *"L'Admirable police": Tenir Paris au siècle des Lumières*. Paris: Champ Vallon, 2016.

O'Donnell, Katherine, and Michael O'Rourke, eds. *Queer Masculinities, 1550–1800: Siting Same-Sex Desire in the Early Modern World*. Houndmills: Palgrave Macmillan, 2006.

Ragan, Bryant T. "Same-Sex Sexual Relations and the French Revolution: The Decriminalization of Sodomy in 1791." In *From Sodomy Laws to Same-Sex Marriage: International Perspectives Since 1789*, edited by Sean Brady and Mark Seymour, 15–30. London: Bloomsbury, 2019.

Rocke, Michael. *Forbidden Friendships: Homosexuality and Male Culture in Renaissance Florence*. Oxford: Oxford University Press, 1996.

Sibalis, Michael David. "The Regulation of Male Homosexuality in Revolutionary and Napoleonic France." In *Homosexuality in Modern France*, edited by Jeffrey Merrick and Bryant T. Ragan, 80–101. New York: Oxford University Press, 1996.

Trumbach, Randolph. "London's Sodomites: Homosexual Behavior and Western Culture in the 18th Century." *Journal of Social History* 11, no. 1 (1977): 1–33.

Turcot, Laurent. *Le Promeneur à Paris au XVIIIe siècle*. Paris: Gallimard, 2007.

Williams, Alan. *The Police of Paris, 1718–1789*. Baton Rouge: Louisiana State University Press, 1979.

Williams, Craig A. *Roman Homosexuality: Ideologies of Masculinity in Classical Antiquity*. Oxford: Oxford University Press, 1999.

ANNOTATED INDEX OF MEN

Entries include, if known, the man's last name, first name (nickname), age, and occupation, as well as the outcome of the arrest and the document number.

ADDITIONAL ABBREVIATIONS

LG referred to lieutenant general of police
M   married
UN unemployed

Abzac, François, chevalier d', 35, W&R, #74
Adam. *See* Bour
Agneaux, Pierre, 25, gardener's assistant, P, #114
Albert, #168
Albert, Michel, 16, shoemaker's assistant, P, #144
Albin, Nicolas, 55, soldier, R, #87
Alexandre, Jean, 23, bookseller, P, #125
Allain, gemstone setter, #11
Ancelin, cook, #131
Antoine, #65
Antoine, coachman, #57
Antoine, domestic, #199
Antony, Joseph, 22, dragoon, P, #24
Areintz, Jean Philippe, 36, domestic, P, #18
Auberger, Jean, 17, apprentice binder, P, #90
Aubert, cook, #65
Aubert, priest, #2
Aubrée, Alexis, 30, student, W&R, #143
Audier, François, 24, domestic and cook, UN, P, #133

Badar, Antoine Joseph, 31, wigmaker's assistant, UN, P, #74
Badarou, Pierre, 15, apprentice saddler, P, #36; P, #97
Baffle, Antoine, 48, water carrier, W&R, #5
Baillaux, Pierre, 14, apprentice engraver, P, #97
Baillet, Jean François, 21, journeyman sword-furbisher, P, #117
Bailleux, Edme, 21, domestic, UN, W&R, #37
Bailly, Dominique Nicolas, 22, wigmaker's assistant, W&R, #37
Bailly, Jean, 39, personal valet, W&R, #19, #85, #203
Barat, Jean Baptiste, 22, tonsured cleric, P, #77
Barry, François (Samson), 42, bourgeois, W&R, #123
Barthélemy, Antoine, 21, grocer's assistant, UN, P, #70
Basse, Charles, 22, shoemaker's assistant, P, #92

Bâtonnier, Jean François, 20, domestic, W&R, #26
Baudi, #218
Baudière, Antoine Genin de, 22, bourgeois, W&R, #27
Baurain (or Beaurain), Claude, 50, cook, P, #30, #47
Béarn, chevalier de, #176, #180, #213
Beauceron, François Haranger du, 19, day laborer, P, #63
Beaugrand, Louis Claude, 28, writer, P, #208
Beauharnais, Claude, comte de, 28, M, military officer, W&R, #94
Beaujar, Pierre, 25, domestic, UN, P, #68
Bellanger, wood turner, #32
Bellat, Louis François Gabriel, 19, tailor's assistant, UN, W&R, #48
Belloy, Charles Joseph de, 34, former musketeer, W&R, #78
Benevald, Christian, 26, shoemaker's assistant, W&R, #97
Bennezé, Louis, 31, gauze worker, P, #184
Berard, Jacques Antoine, 24, former student, P, #122
Bérault, Jean Jacques Edme, 48, clockmaker, W&R, #186
Bernard, Germain, 20, upholsterer's apprentice, W&R, #133
Bernard, Jacques François (The Little Female Wigmaker), 40, hairdresser, W&R, #17
Bernard, Jean Louis, 22, tailor's assistant, P, #138
Berneron, Philippe, 21, tailor's assistant, UN, W&R, #112
Bertheaume, Nicolas François, 26, day student, W&R, #70
Berthellier, Charles Balthazar, 25, hosier's assistant, UN, P, #144
Bertin, Nicolas, 21, domestic, P, #33
Bertrand, #210
Bertrand, soldier, #107
Bertrand, Joseph, 33, domestic, UN, P, #130
Bertre, Jacques, 42, flannel vendor, P, #109
Besenval, chevalier de, military officer, #63

Besson, Antoine, 24, domestic, W&R, #167
Bidault, Jean Baptiste Etienne (Sheep's Head), 33, journeyman binder, UN, P, #80
Big Female Gilder. See Le Tourneur
Bigonnet, clerk, #170
Bigot, Louis Pierre, 25, sailor and journeyman mason, P, #58
Blanchard (chevalier de Monchevreuil), deserter, #46
Blanchard, Jean Baptiste Sébastien, 40, domestic, P, #18
Blanchard, Michel, 14, bootblack and errand boy, P, #176
Blondeau, Jean Louis, 21, pastrymaker's assistant, UN, W&R, #4
Boisseau, Etienne, laundryman, P, #189
Bongran, Jean François, 35, shoemaker's assistant, P, #138
Bonnet, Hubert, 22, stonecutter, UN, P, #195
Bornan, Guillaume, 31, smuggler, P, #158
Boucher, Eustache Robert Vital, 25, limonadier's assistant, W&R, #18
Boudard, François, 19, domestic, UN, P, #119
Bougere, Etienne (Dulis), 25, wigmaker's assistant, W&R, #141
Bour, Anzalen (Adam, Lallemand), 42, coachman, W&R, #203
Bourachaux, Jean, 16, domestic, UN, P, #135
Bourdelet, François, 30, journeyman engraver, P, #8
Bourgeois, Paul, 24, wigmaker's assistant, P, #217
Bourgot, André (Poignon), 21, day laborer, P, #108; #176; P, #177
Bourguignon, shoemaker's assistant, #170
Bourquin, Jean, 46, wigmaker, P, #3
Boutait, Georges Eléonor, 44, doorman, P, #153
Boyère, Pierre Patrice, 30, haberdasher and ironmonger, W&R, #5
Brelon, Louis, 31, day laborer, W&R, #124
Brillant, Pierre Jacques, 55, worked with wine vendor, P, #16

ANNOTATED INDEX OF MEN | 237

Brincman, Jean Michel Marie, 15½, tailor, P, #213
Brochet, Alexandre Charles, 33, upholsterer's assistant, UN, W&R, #35; P, #207
Brochier, Jean François, 24, student, S&R, #42
Brondel, Jean Baptiste, 15–16, errand boy, P, #176
Broquin, Jean Louis, 26, UN, W&R, #154
Brunet, Joseph, 30, journeyman mason, P, #162
Bucher, François, 31, surgeon, S&R, #204
Bunel, Jean Pierre, 40, shopkeeper's assistant, P, #21
Buquet, Jean François (Rag), #11, #15
Butin, Michel Jacques, 52, M, doorman, W&R, #7
Buturlin, Petr Aleksandrovich, count, M, #17

Callé, #21
Camort, French Guard, #10
Camus, Nicolas, nearly 12 or 13, day laborer, P, #61; P, #180
Candre, Louis, 43, wine vendor's assistant, UN, P, #201
Capriny, Mathurin Augustin, around 35, bill-broker, P, #62
Carié, André, 17, errand boy, P, #176
Carilliers, #89
Carin, Jean, tailor, UN, P, #37
Caron, domestic, #34
Carton, #17, #75
Cassegrain, Louis, 42, clerk, W&R, #41
Cassina, Camille, 30, secretary of the Venetian ambassador, LG, R, #97
Cassolet, doll vendor, #126
Caune, Salomon, 42, sword-furbisher, W&R, #123
Cellier, Nicolas Charles, 52, boardinghouse manager, P, #46
Cendre, André, 36, haberdasher's assistant, P, #50
Chabrier, Quentin, 23, shoemaker's assistant, W&R, #121

Chair, Alexandre, 42, tonsured cleric, P, #126
Champy, Nicolas Philippe, 19, soldier, P, #37
Charpentier, Charles, 28, grocer, R, #14; W&R, #21
Charpentier, Louis Isidore, 18, journeyman casemaker and soldier, P, #169
Charvais, secondhand dealer, #144
Chatenet, Olivier (Laurent), 53, journeyman smelter, P, #161
Chaudé, Pierre, 18, tailor, UN, P, #98
Chauffour, #75
Chaumette, Jean Charles Michel, 24, domestic, P, #211
Chauveau, #144
Chauveau, Jacques Daniel, 15, journeyman cabinetmaker, P, #142
Chedete, François Etienne, 40, doorman, UN, W&R, #5
Cheullot, canon, #77
Chevanne, Jean Baptiste, 25, wine vendor's assistant, P, #32
Chilliatre, Jean Baptiste (de Courval), 31, journeyman mason and soldier, W&R, #178
Cholette, Jean, 28, journeyman glazier, W&R, #87
Clautaux, Jean, 17, wigmaker's assistant, P, #212
Clément, #220
Clermont. *See* Pallardel
Cochois, Germain Claude, 36, UN, P, #200
Cochois, Jean Etienne, 20, florist, P, #79
Colle, Denis, 49, baker, P, #12
Collin, Louis Mathieu, 25, M, engraver, P, #179
Compagnat, Laurent (The Woman from Lyon), 29, limonadier's assistant, P, #69
Compiègne, #69
Comtois, domestic, #200
Corberon, Joseph Anne, 27, UN, P, #93
Cosse, #36, #210
Cotentin, Laurent, 28, domestic, W&R, #198

238 | ANNOTATED INDEX OF MEN

Countess of Seven Points. *See* Pallardel
Courval. *See* Chilliatre
Cujat, Mathieu, 34, manual laborer, P, #12

Daillant, Sébastien, 36, journeyman building painter and soldier, P, #67
Dallançon, Henry Louis, 33, limonadier's assistant, UN, P, #113
Dangois, Charles, 42, tailor's assistant, P, #141
Daniel, Jean Louis, 32, domestic, UN, W&R, #160
Danjou, Pierre, 29, cook, UN, P, #220
Daquin, Laurent, P, #95
Darras, Louis, domestic, #14
Daverdin, Antoine, 13, smelter, P, #115
David, Joseph, 30, hairdresser, W&R, #148
David, Louis Sébastien, 37, M, shoemaker, W&R, #104
Defrance, Thierry, 23, domestic, W&R, #38
Delagrange de Juniac, Louis François Justin, 16, student, P, #40
Delbaut, wine vendor's assistant, #99
Delcourt, cavalryman, #122
Denis, orderly, #2
Denot, Jean Marie, 29, porter, W&R, #82
Deroche, Jean Edme, 34, priest, S&R, #56
Deschamps, François Marie Antoine, 17, former grocer's assistant, UN, W&R, #56
Descourty, Charles François, nearly 18, tile-layer, W&R, #192
Desenneville, Jean Philippe Marie Denis, 41, commissioner of war, S&R, #145
Desgrignons, François Jobin, 40, clerk, W&R, #12
Des Hayes, painting vendor, #209
Desjardins, #139
Desjardins, gilder, #32
Desmarteaux, François, 16½, domestic, UN, W&R, #111
Despan, Jean Guillaume, 50, former shopkeeper, P, #90
Des Roches. *See* Nollan
Des Roziers. *See* Rozier
Dessous, Jean Etienne, 33, clerk, P, #3
Deure, French Guard, #33

Devaux, Louis, 13½, jockey, P, #194
Diet, Joseph, 31, journeyman currier, P, #128
Dieu, printer, #65
Doigt, François du, 28, domestic, W&R, #68
Donison, Christophe, 38, domestic, UN, P, #14
Dorat, Pierre François, 19, journeyman cooper, P, #106
Doré, Louis, 22, tailor's assistant, W&R, #39
Dorgny, Louis, 33, kitchen assistant, P, #61
Doricourt, Charles Pajot, 24, threadmaker, P, #59
Dory, #123
Dragon. *See* Foucault
Drouin, #218
Droz, Pierre Humbert, 43, clockmaker, P, #86
Du Chenu, garde du corps, #19
DuChesne, Louis Pasquier, 27, M, wine merchant, W&R, #59
Du Fossé, Charles Antoine, 38, fruit vendor, P, #127
Dugny, Nicolas Hyacinthe Juillien de, 23, journeyman printer, P, #146
Duhamel, Louis, 40, domestic, P, #210
Du Jardin, Charles, 21, cook, UN, W&R, #31
Dulis. *See* Bougere
Dumas, Jean, 18, errand boy, P, #176
Duperrier, Michel Alexandre, 39, domestic, W&R, #102
Duplessis, Jean Baptiste, around 20, fabric vendor's assistant, P, #134
Dupré, Pierre, 63, sold matches and tinder, P, #89
Durand, dyer, #29
Dutranoy (or Du Tranoy), Louis Joseph, 27, boardinghouse manager, P, #21; #217
Duval, Charles Antoine, more than 60, domestic, P, #196
Duval, Malo, 34, domestic, W&R, #13
Du Villard, Jean Baptiste, 16, apprentice wigmaker, P, #45

Emery. *See* Renezé
Etienne, domestic, #34
Eugé, Louis Marie, 16, shoemaker's assistant, UN, P, #44
Eve, Jacques Joseph, 27, music master, W&R, #88

Fargis, #220
Fat (or Pregnant) Woman, #75
Fautereau, marquis de, #96
Fayet, Louis, 20, domestic, UN, P, #116
Federitz, Emmanuel, 25, tailor's assistant, UN, P, #30
Feron, Thomas, 57, master building painter, W&R, #140
Finot, Hubert Jacques Gabriel, 21, clerk, S&R, #219
Foloppe, Jacques, 38, doorman, P, #109
Forch, André, 37, retired merchant, W&R, #168
Forget, Louis de, 19, UN, P, #138
Foriat, André Joseph, farrier, W&R, #108
Foucault, Thomas (The Dragon), 31, secondhand dealer, P, #100
Foujat, Etienne, 17, wigmaker's assistant, UN, P, #84
Foullon, Noël Pierre, 58, master beltmaker, P, #153
Frade, Jean Baptiste, 40, journeyman joiner, P, #147
Fragmere, #210
François, #116
François, wine vendor's assistant, #131
Franque, journeyman goldsmith, #144
Fraquerre, Alexandre, 36, domestic, P, #32
Frédéric, domestic, #114
Fussy, Charles, 18, doorman, P, #36

Gagné, Jean Louis, 29, orderly, UN, P, #2
Garet, Nicolas, 30, kitchen assistant, W&R, #21
Garnier or Gressier, #21, #36
Garon, Philippe Claude Noël (Parisian), 18, shoemaker's assistant, UN, P, #74
Garspern, Marie Gabriel, comte de, #6
Gaucher, François, 21, domestic, W&R, #11
Gautier, Joseph, 38, postilion, UN, P, #79

Gavard, Jean Baptite, 19, wigmaker's assistant, UN, P, #108
Gelé, Nicolas Hilaire, 36, mattress carder, P, #164
Georges, Jean Joseph (Saint-Fermin), 23, career in theatre, P, #21
Gérard, student, #219
Gérard, François, 24, student, W&R, #143
Geroflée, soldier, #58
Gillet, sculptor, #29
Girard, François, 32, personal valet, P, #106
Girard, Pierre, 14½, apprentice printer, UN, P, #192
Gombert, François, 21, kitchen assistant, UN, R, #21
Goran, Pierre, 27, butler's assistant, P, #45
Gossin, Pierre, 30, M, cook, W&R, #54
Gougère, wigmaker's assistant, #65
Gouldhorn, Jean, 37, valet, W&R, #94
Gout de la Brande, Pierre François, 44, priest, LG, R, #90
Gouy, François Joseph, 31, cook, UN, P, #191
Grandmaison, #180
Gréant, Joseph, 36, domestic, W&R, #60
Gressier, #21
Grosdemonge, Pierre Joseph, 34, cook, UN, P, #83
Grosmenil, Jean Léon (Martin), 23, employee of the tobacco office, P, #202
Groux, Louis, 32, former soldier and pastrymaker's assistant, P, #139
Guay, Laurent, 26, priest, W&R, #206
Guénin, Louis Jean Baptiste, 22, tailor's assistant, W&R, #111
Guilbert, François, 20, domestic, UN, P, #217
Guillaumet, Jean Guillaume, 52, street vendor, P, #91
Guinedou, Gabriel, journeyman mason, P, #28
Guyot, Simon, 37, clockmaker, W&R, #21

Hadet, Louis, 48, boardinghouse manager, P, #173
Hébert or Vébert, French Guard, #33

Henriet, Jean, 22, domestic, UN, W&R, #196
Herque, #59
Hervieux, Marc Antoine, 36, domestic, UN, P, #160
Hildebrand, Jean Jacques, 34, stocking worker, W&R, #149
Hoart, Pierre Nicolas, 66, retired jewelry vendor, P, #210
Hoffmann, Charles Joseph, 24, tailor's assistant, P, #170
Holy Female Savior. *See* Picot
Houdin, Louis, 32, cook, P, #131
Housel, Victor Daniel, 25, soldier, P, #202
Huby, Hugues Louis, 20, water carrier, P, #175
Hurel, Jean, 35, domestic, W&R, #216
Hurier, François Michel, 18, journeyman brushmaker, P, #190
Hurier, Jean Louis Moutin, 17, P, #124
Husson, Etienne, 19, coachman, W&R, #101
Hutin, #48
Hyacinthe, journeyman inlay worker, #36

Jacquet, Nicolas, 40, domestic, W&R, #123
Jalabert, François, 35, tailor, P, #16
Jameau, Henry François Nicolas, 25, journeyman playing card maker and soldier, P, #69
Jean, groom, #11
Jolly, Claude, 46, journeyman clockmaker, W&R, #149
Joret, #75
Jouan, René, 27, M, tailor, W&R, #66
Jourdain, lackey, #130
Jowe, Antoine Valérien de, 24, subdeacon and canon, W&R, #78

Laboubée, Jean, 39, wolf hunter, W&R, #126
La Chenaye, Louis Michel Alexandre Severet de, 26, employee of the Farms, P, #22
Lacoste, hairdresser, #17
Lacroix, jeweler, #144

LaCroix, Lambert, 42, day laborer, P, #10
Lafayette, Etienne Legivre de, 22, former clerk, UN, P, #154
Lafitte, domestic, #208
La Fosse, Antoine Marie de, 29, UN, P, #130
Lajeunesse. *See* Roussy
Lajeunesse, domestic, #33, #60
Lallemand. *See* Bour
Lallement, Thomas, 36, M, domestic, P, #7
Langlois, Louis, 20, domestic, P, #182
Lanois, #170
La Pérouse, Roch, 25, kitchen assistant, P, #60
Lapierre, domestic, #60, #128
La Place, Pierre, 29, baker's assistant, P, #149
Lapointe, Louis Claude, 21, limonadier's assistant, UN, W&R, #195
La Rivière, Jean Charles, 29, domestic, UN, P, #133
La Roche. *See* Roche
Larpenteur, Jean Nicolas, 32, grocer, S&R, #139
La Tour du Pin, Philippe Antoine Gabriel Victor Charles, marquis de, M, #17
Laubertin, Gabriel, 25, shoemaker's assistant, P, #135
Laurent. *See* Chatenet
Laurent, Guillaume Raimond, 25, haberdasher, P, #11
Laurent, Joseph Michel Jérôme, 25, M, domestic, W&R, #194
LeBeau, Louis, 17, limonadier's assistant, UN, P, #24
Lebel, André, 40, day laborer, W&R, #181
Le Cerf, Eustache, 33, glazier, P, #142
LeClerc, Jean Toussaint, 27, shoemaker's assistant, P, #47
Le Clerc de Piervalle, Maximilien, 30, priest, P, #28
LeComte, Joseph, 21, kitchen assistant, UN, P, #53
LeComte, Noël Henry, 26, wine vendor's assistant, P, #139

ANNOTATED INDEX OF MEN | 241

Le Comte, Olivier François, 34, domestic, UN, P, #31
Le Coq, Alexandre, 18½, saddler, W&R, #71
Ledoux, domestic, #60
Le Duc, Jean Baptiste, 30, domestic, UN, P, #81
Lefevre, master candlemaker, #46
Lefevre, Jean Baptiste, 43, innkeeper, P, #13
Lefevre, Louis Henry, 33, gardener's assistant, UN, P, #72
Lefuelle, Pierre Bruno, 20, fabric vendor's assistant, W&R, #180
Légal, Pierre, 20, wigmaker's assistant, UN, P, #65
Le Gendre, Alexisanne, 18, student and clerk, W&R, #91
Le Grault, Pierre François, 28, cook, P, #163
Lehardelay, Gaetan, 16, building painter, P, #180
Lejeune, bourgeois, #150
Lelancé. *See* Mercier
Le Leu, Elie, 23, wigmaker's assistant, UN, P, #4
Le Lief, Simon, 23, gauze worker, P, #101
Le Lièvre, Jacques François, 41, former wine vendor, P, #105
Le Maître, Alexandre, 22, clerk, W&R, #55
Lenoir, Mathieu, 22, domestic, P, #165
Le Plat, Isidore, 28, domestic, P, #211
LeRouge, Pierre Augustin Antoine, 26, gemstone setter, P, #43
Leroy, former domestic, UN, #45
Le Sueur, René Jean Baptiste, 51, journeyman joiner, P, #149
Le Tellier, Jacques, 62–63, retired wine vendor, W&R, #101
Le Tellier, Louis, around 30, domestic, W&R, #1
Le Tourneur, René (The Big Female Gilder), 25, painter and gilder, UN, P, #23
Levasseur, domestic, #32, #34
Levasseur, stationer, #83
Levasseur, toymaker, #10

Le Vise de Montigny, Charles Christophe, 18, apprentice jeweler, W&R, #111
Libéral, Jean, 18, shoemaker's assistant, P, #170
Librex, Henry, 25, domestic, W&R, #20
Liez, Joseph Sebastien, 30, master pastry-maker, P, #33
Ligneux, Louis Guillaume, 18, domestic, P, #208
Ligny, Charles de, 38, former haberdasher and innkeeper, UN, P, #115
Little Female Wigmaker. *See* Bernard
Loiseau, Emilan, 43, kitchen assistant, UN, P, #121; #204
Lorion, Etienne, 26, M, domestic, UN, W&R, #131
Loulié, André Marie, 23, domestic, W&R, #129
Lovely Female Baker, domestic, #25

Maille, Joseph, 33, domestic, P, #98
Mainot, Jean Jacques, 36, tree vendor, P, #173
Mallard, Charles Antoine, 43, domestic, UN, P, #69
Mânes, Jean Louis, marquis de, W&R, #73
Manny, Jean Baptiste, 45, domestic, P, #140
Manoury, Jean Baptiste, 27, tailor's assistant, W&R, #107
Marchal, Claude, 47, clerk, W&R, #10
Marchand, Jean, 32, domestic, P, #34
Marchandier, Jean Baptiste, 22, hairdresser, W&R, #183
Marinot, Jean Augustin, 20, earthenware worker, P, #81
Marion, sacristan, #170
Marion, Louis, 15, wigmaker's assistant, W&R, #47
Mariot, Martin, around 30, lackey, W&R, #51
Martin. *See* Grosmenil
Marville, de, #218
Matherne, Charles, 26, domestic, W&R, #27; P, #34
Maugrat, François, 28, quarrier, P, #87

Maujean, François, 24, shoemaker's assistant, P, #156
Maurice, Jean, 43, domestic, P, #76
Maurisset, Jacques Marie, 24, shoemaker's assistant, W&R, #24
Melard, Jean Baptiste Gabriel, 20, wigmaker's assistant, P, #210
Mercier, secondhand dealer in Bourges, #77
Mercier, François (Lelancé), 18½, domestic, UN, P, #203
Mercier, Nicolas, 28, cook, UN, P, #107
Mérigot, Pierre, 55, former military officer, W&R, #3
Michel, Jean Charles, 21, journeyman jeweler, UN, P, #166
Michelot, Claude, 22, limonadier's assistant, UN, W&R, #92
Mielot, Antoine Simon, 17½, pinmaker, W&R, #71
Mignot, François Nicolas, 21, glaziery worker and soldier, P, #158
Miller, Paul, 27, shoemaker's assistant, P, #50
Missy, Jean, 32, shoemaker's assistant, P, #113
Mitraff, Maxi, 20, secretary, W&R, #209
Modas, chevalier de Saint-Louis, #17
Molumard, Charles, 23, wigmaker's assistant, UN, W&R, #100
Monin, #96
Monnelle, Claude, 30, domestic, W&R, #38
Monneret, Claude Philibert, 44, valet, W&R, #155
Monnier, Pierre, 21, gauze worker, W&R, #178
Montreuil, Pierre, 48, M, innkeeper, P, #204
Morel, Benoît, 22, stocking worker, P, #114
Morin, fruit vendor, #163
Mougin, Guillaume, 18, journeyman jeweler, P, #189
Mulochot, Louis, 26, domestic, W&R, #120
Musbien, Nicolas, 50, archivist, P, #120
Mussard, Jacques Antoine, 20, clockmaker, W&R, #119

Nardeau, shoemaker's assistant, #138
Naudin, Jean, 27 or 28, tailor's assistant, W&R, #89; P, #132
Nicolle, Raphael, 56, porter, P, #54
Nollan (Des Roches), #46
Nollet, Michel François, 26, UN, W&R, #154
Nouvelet, Jean Claude, 21, journeyman upholsterer, W&R, #133

Orlan, valet, #66

Paillot, Louis, 22, postilion, UN, P, #70
Pallardel, Pierre (Clermont, Countess of Seven Points), 40, domestic, P, #215
Palliée, Pierre Nicolas, 17, apprentice upholsterer, W&R, #205
Pancelot, Charles, 46, day laborer, P, #158
Papelard, Pierre Etienne, 46, clerk, W&R, #109
Parisian. *See* Garon
Patard, Louis Michel, 19, French Guard, W&R, #5
Patelle, Pierre (The Stone), 65, domestic, UN, P, #174
Paular, Nicolas, 61, bourgeois, W&R, #151
Pavie, René, 32, cook, UN, P, #122
Pecquet, Pierre François, 18, grocer's assistant, R, #170
Peigné, Louis Antoine, 32, grocer and apothecary, W&R, #185
Peixotto, Samuel, banker, #19
Pélican, Charles, 26, domestic, P, #87
Pellé, Jean, 27, domestic, W&R, #152
Perrault, Simon, 28, domestic, UN, W&R, #65
Perretton, Gapella Auguste, 14, student, P, #212
Perrot, Antoine, 17, domestic, P, #203
Petit, Antoine, 30, journeyman turner, P, #129
Petit, Jean Baptiste Louis, 32, furniture vendor's assistant, W&R, #194
Petit, Joseph, 20, fruit seller, P, #25
Petit, Samuel Antoine Dittely, 31, former soldier, UN, P, #107

Petit, Sylvain, 25, domestic, W&R, #187
Philippe, Louis, 22, former clerk, UN, W&R, #60
Picard, #139
Picard, Jacques Louis, 28, tailor's assistant, UN, P, #75
Picart, François, 43, domestic, P, #59
Picot, Pierre François (The Holy Female Savior), around 50, domestic, W&R, #17
Piette, Antoine, 35, dragoon, P, #21
Piffault, Henry, 35, saddler's assistant, W&R, #116
Pilard, Pierre, 22, W&R, #70
Pingan, Barthélemy, 41, cook, W&R, #93
Pitot, Vincent François (Pointed Jerome), more than 50, banker, P, #87
Poignon. *See* Bourgot
Pointed Jerome. *See* Pitot
Ponchel, Charles, 18, worked with seed vendor, W&R, #29
Pontez, Julien de, 41, domestic, UN, W&R, #35
Portier, Charles, 22, journeyman building painter, P, #83
Potier, Guillaume, 30, breeches maker's assistant, UN, P, #64
Poupée, Pierre, mason, #211
Pousset, François, 33, former grocer's assistant, UN, P, #136
Pouteau, Louis, 20, feather vendor, W&R, #209
Prelaut, clockmaker, #67
Prévost, Philippe Jacques Jean, 43, bootblack, P, #57
Pringal. *See* Romegout
Proff, Antoine, 23, tailor, P, #142
Prudhomme, gauze worker, #189
Prudhomme, Pierre Henry, 26, box maker, P, #199
Pruneau, Jean Nicolas, 29, broker for silk vendors, S&R, #37

Quentin, Charles, 26, domestic, W&R, #186
Quentin, Jean François, 55, retired merchant, P, #142

Racine, Jean Baptiste, 48, domestic, W&R, #92
Rag. *See* Buquet
Raimbaut, Louis Dominique, 19, journeyman dyer, W&R, #82
Ramard, Gabriel, 26, cook, W&R, #31
Ratier, Jean François, 13, UN, W&R, #213
Ratz, Henry, 24, journeyman harpsichord maker, W&R, #137
Regnier, journeyman currier, #129
Regnier, Pierre, 19, wigmaker's assistant, UN, P, #85
Renaud, Jean, 27, domestic, P, #19
Renault, Jean, 24, former corporal, W&R, #144
Renezé, Jean Marie (Emery), 23, master wigmaker, W&R, #100
Ribot, Louis, 22, journeyman mason and soldier, P, #167
Ricard, #100
Ricard, Pierre Marin, 22, M, shoemaker's assistant, W&R, #24
Richeux, Jean Baptiste, 22, wigmaker's assistant, P, #58
Richomme, Claude, 16½, student worker, W&R, #8
Rieux, César Auguste Frédéric du, 48, former musketeer, W&R, #143
Robert, Nicolas, 17, tailor's assistant, UN, W&R, #141
Roberval, Pierre, 17, wallpaper worker, W&R, #102
Robin, Jean César, 59, bourgeois, P, #49
Roche, Nicolas (La Roche, Saint-Louis), 18, domestic, UN, W&R, #103
Rome, Augustin, 36, journeyman locksmith, P, #123
Romegout, Antoine (Pringal), 17, journeyman sculptor, P, #159
Rosse, baker's assistant, #135
Roumier, Etienne, 45, cook, P, #34
Roure, comte du, #106
Rousseau, domestic, #121
Rousseau, Philippe, 33, domestic, P, #172
Roussel, Jean Paul, 30, tailor's assistant, P, #157
Roussy (Lajeunesse), #60

Roux, Louis Etienne, 29, bourgeois, W&R, #52
Rouyer, Dominique Claude, 37, M, grocer, P, #46
Rouyère, Joseph, 24, coachman, P, #120
Rozier, Pierre (Des Roziers), 39, P, #39
Rullier, François, 63, caretaker, W&R, #193

Sabat, François, 20, kitchen assistant, UN, P, #73
Sacqueney, Philibert, 29, secondhand dealer, P, #200
Saint-Clément, Louis Denis, marquis de, 45, LG, S&R, #38
Saint-Fermin. *See* Georges
Saint-Hilaire, Cyprien Jérôme Picart de, #17, #59
Saint-Louis. *See* Roche
Saint-Louis, domestic, #76
Saint-Pierre, domestic, #33
Salmon, Jean Charles, 28, domestic, P, #6
Samson. *See* Barry
Santigny, apprentice upholsterer, #170
Sanzwoell, François Ferdinand, 16½, journeyman joiner and soldier, W&R, #8
Sauvage, Théophile, 18, student, W&R, #18
Schpiler, Denis, 21, floor polisher, P, #166
Seitivaux, Jean, 37, domestic, P, #118
Senemaud, Jean Baptiste, 18, journeyman jeweler, UN, P, #171
Séraphin, domestic, #68
Seron, Jean, 35, private library employee, W&R, #74
Servault, Etienne, 21, laundryman, P, #9
Sheep's Head. *See* Bidault
Sibille, Didier, 17, cobbler, W&R, #29
Silvie, chevalier de, #45
Simon, Louis, 45, domestic, P, #6
Simon, Nicolas Joseph, 17, cabinetmaker, P, #159
Soyécourt, marquis de, #91
Sparre, comte de, #34
Stone. *See* Patelle
Suchot, Claude Antoine, 46, parasol worker, W&R, #139

Suraune, Denis de, 32, apprentice goldsmith, P, #99

Taillardant, Jean Noël César, 36, monk, R, #110
Tellier, Jacques, 62–63, former wine vendor, W&R, #101
Ternisien, Jacques, 41, majordomo, P, #165
Terroux, Jacques, 21, watch-worker, P, #132
Tessier, Pierre, 33, baker's assistant, P, #125
Teytaud, Jean Baptiste, 21, student, S&R, #183
Thevenet, Jean Baptiste, nearly 18, domestic, P, #189
Thibout, Jacques, 25, grocer's assistant, S&R, #42
Thirion, Jean Baptiste, 44, dairyman, P, #168
Thomas, #48
Thomas, Jacques François, 20, upholsterer's assistant, UN, P, #96
Tonnere, Michel, 45, mathematical instruments worker, P, #144
Toussaint, #96
Toussaint, wine vendor, #67
Trelon, Antoine Rémy, 27, tutor, UN, W&R, #214
Trouillet, Alexis, 46, master shoemaker, P, #150
Tuquel, François, vineyardist in Dammartin, #211
Turbot, Pierre Louis, 16½, bootblack, P, #57
Turet, Antoine Pierre, 16, apprentice wigmaker, W&R, #175

Vandeuvre, Etienne, 50, dishwasher, P, #44
Vangette, Pierre Charles, 50, mattress carder, P, #104
Vangron, joiner, #16
Vauflard, François, 18, shoemaker's assistant, P, #218
Venet, Edme, 42, upholsterer's assistant from Lyon, P, #188

Verdier, Jean, 16, domestic, W&R, #86
Vichy, Abel Claude Marie, marquis de, 45, M, R, #15
Vignes, Jacques des, 61, notary in Pontoise, S&R, #183
Villecavoisin, François de, 21, day laborer, P, #197
Villelouays, Emmanuel, chevalier de la, 28, cavalry officer, W&R, #221
Vincent, Jacques Louis, 44, locksmith, P, #150
Voisin, Charles, 18, domestic, UN, P, #30
Vondière, wine vendor, #149
Voutancia, Antoine, 22, domestic, UN, P, #206
Voyepierre, Pierre de la, 43, M, governor, W&R, #93

Wafflard, Claude Paul, 31, journeyman inlay worker, W&R, #137
Woman from Lyon. *See* Compagnat
Woman from Provence, #83

GENERAL INDEX

This index does not include people, places, phrases, and topics that appear in almost every single document—most notably inspector Desurbois, commissaire Convers Desormeaux, the Tuileries gardens, the verbs "to pick up" and "to amuse oneself," and money—or matters covered in the Annotated Index of Men: marital status, occupations, unemployment, release, and imprisonment.

age, 8–9, 10
   "boy," 24, 30, 48, 102, 116, 121, 179, 197
   "child," 23, 30, 79, 80, 89, 170
   "old," 43, 48, 151, 163, 173
   "young," 24, 26, 27, 33, 36, 39, 42, 46, 54, 56, 66, 70, 73, 74, 76, 79, 80, 90, 91, 93, 96, 100, 101, 103, 107, 110, 112, 113, 114, 128, 130, 134, 144, 151, 152, 153, 154, 155, 164, 166, 172, 177, 178, 180, 182, 187, 188, 199, 200, 202, 204, 205, 206, 210
   "youth," 54, 105, 134, 142, 143, 148, 154, 205, 207
anal intercourse, 1, 11–12
   "active" and "passive" roles in, 27, 75, 76, 98, 111, 155, 164, 166, 171, 199
   "active" role in, 26, 43, 54, 66, 68, 76, 94, 103, 157
   "to consummate the crime," 11, 20, 24, 26, 27, 36, 38, 40, 46, 52, 53, 54, 66, 67, 68, 70, 73, 75, 76, 81, 86, 94, 98, 103, 110, 121, 129, 140, 143, 154, 155, 156, 157, 164, 166, 171, 190, 193, 197, 203, 213, 214
   "to fuck," 79, 80, 198
   "passive" role in, 20, 24, 27, 43, 52, 54, 67, 68, 75, 76, 77, 86, 110, 114, 121, 129, 140, 154, 155, 156, 171, 190, 193, 213, 214

   "to put it in," 62, 65, 68, 72, 73, 75, 80, 81, 82, 94, 120, 139, 147, 148, 150, 155, 160, 161, 187, 194, 206
arrest
   attempted bribery after, 30, 31, 111, 204, 205
   escape from, 23, 27, 28, 29, 30, 36, 37, 46, 49, 58, 59, 62, 67, 68, 69, 71, 74, 75, 92, 96, 99, 103, 104, 107, 109, 116, 130, 134, 149, 152, 153, 154, 155, 165, 166, 167, 168, 169, 173, 174, 180, 182, 184, 191, 195, 196, 197, 201, 202, 204, 205, 206, 210
   previous, 20, 26, 34, 35, 37, 52, 55, 58, 60, 61, 68, 85, 89, 112, 122, 128, 134, 142, 154, 156, 157, 162, 163, 165, 168, 170, 171, 173, 178, 180, 197
   resistance to, 43, 67, 101, 102, 103, 104, 106, 109, 130, 169, 183, 202, 210

balls, 39, 40, 52, 54, 201
bathing, 112, 113, 125
Bicêtre hospital, 27, 33, 34, 40, 41, 52, 53, 68, 74, 93, 96, 112, 197, 208
billiard parlors, 84, 167, 193
Bois de Boulogne, 133, 136

cafés, 35, 36, 42, 43, 44, 45, 46, 54, 60, 72, 77, 88, 89, 90, 114, 115, 134, 143, 178, 179, 207

248 | GENERAL INDEX

Champs-Elysées, 40, 52, 61, 62, 68, 69, 70, 73, 74, 75, 76, 84, 92, 110, 116, 118, 121, 124, 128, 129, 137, 138, 142, 143, 145, 147, 197, 203, 206, 214
Coal-Box, 27, 71, 85, 86, 88, 96, 102, 103, 109, 112, 115, 116, 117, 130, 132, 134, 149, 151, 152, 155, 157, 158, 159, 161, 162, 163, 164, 165, 166, 167, 168, 170, 179, 184, 185, 194
cohabitation, 9, 32, 121, 163, 170, 210
collèges, 35, 46, 62. 84, 106, 133, 140, 164, 177
Comédie Française, 57, 71, 72, 79, 90, 99, 100, 102, 105, 106, 107, 112, 132, 133, 176, 177, 178, 180, 185, 187, 189, 196, 199, 206, 208
    stoneyard at, 23, 25, 35, 79, 80, 101, 102, 106, 112, 133, 153, 166, 167, 176, 180, 185, 186, 187, 188, 189, 191, 192, 193, 196, 198, 204, 205, 206, 207, 208, 211
"costume" of pederasts, 4, 36, 44, 59, 61, 77, 84, 88, 121
    cravat, 42, 49, 50, 56, 58, 59, 77, 88, 91, 121, 124, 215
    earrings, 58, 77, 112
    perfume, 56, 103
    rosettes, 37, 44, 49, 50, 56, 59, 77, 78, 88, 91, 101, 121, 135, 153, 170, 208
    round hat, 24, 59
cross-dressing, 54, 208
"to cruise," 28, 34, 38, 53, 55, 58, 59, 60, 62, 68, 70, 76, 84, 85, 91, 96, 101, 103, 105, 109, 111, 112, 113, 114, 115, 116, 118, 120, 122, 128, 130, 132, 133, 134, 138, 140, 146, 149, 154, 157, 158, 159, 162, 163, 166, 168, 171, 172, 176, 180, 182, 188, 192, 197, 206, 208, 210, 213
    "to seek good luck," 102, 129

defecation, 21, 23, 26, 29, 30, 31, 32, 42, 67, 72, 73, 96, 129, 133, 144, 155, 157, 160, 162, 166, 167, 169, 170, 174, 175, 187, 189
drinking, 22, 24, 26, 35, 39, 58, 59, 60, 63, 76, 85, 89, 90, 98, 99, 105, 110, 117, 120, 121, 126, 138, 151, 153, 155, 156, 157, 158, 159, 160, 161, 164, 165, 167, 173, 174, 175, 178, 179, 182, 186, 187, 188, 193, 194, 203, 207, 214, 215

effeminacy, 2, 12, 121
"erection," 26, 30, 55, 69, 72, 73, 78, 79, 92, 102, 108, 184, 212
exile from Paris, 20, 27, 58, 68, 89, 93, 97, 111, 170, 197
extortion, 40, 46, 76, 82, 176, 178, 214

flagellation, 80, 82, 176
force, use of, 97, 177, 206, 207, 213
foreign countries
    Americas, 36, 61, 87, 106, 117, 130, 137, 142, 137
    Austria, 53, 154
    Belgium, 39, 78, 209
    England, 111, 130, 141, 177
    Germany, 37, 45, 56, 111, 113, 120, 146, 155, 157, 172, 197, 210
    Latvia, 170
    Luxembourg, 137
    Netherlands, 37
    Italy, 57, 79, 109, 112, 150, 163, 193
    Russia, 203
    Spain, 193
    Switzerland, 102, 131, 135, 141, 179
"friend," 23, 42, 45, 46, 47, 48, 50, 53, 57, 60, 89, 109, 111, 116, 121, 126, 137, 139, 142, 147, 161, 173, 214
    "comrade," 33, 48, 58, 78, 90, 145, 148, 172, 176, 177, 178, 186, 188, 207

gambling, 69, 78, 79, 124, 147
genitals
    "parts," 45, 96, 103, 139, 167
    "penis," 27, 79, 80, 139, 147, 148, 186, 194, 195, 201, 202, 210

Half-Moon, 27, 40, 86, 115, 149
hugging, 26, 66, 101, 131, 142, 159, 167, 174, 175, 214

kissing, 45, 46, 47, 81, 101

letters, 67, 83, 142, 177, 211
"libertinage," 81, 121, 197, 201
lieutenant general of police, 14, 61, 106, 113
Luxembourg garden, 38, 90, 96, 99, 100, 126, 127, 164, 176, 192, 211

manual contact
    caressing, 180, 197
    fondling, 29, 33, 65, 66, 67, 79, 80, 101, 102, 103, 107, 114, 118, 125, 128, 149, 151, 152, 154, 155, 172, 175, 176, 177, 180, 187, 189, 198, 204, 207
    placing hand on breeches, 45, 49, 68, 70, 73, 121, 134, 138, 165, 212
    stroking, 44, 90, 98, 122, 140, 148, 160, 162, 163, 164, 168, 174, 181, 182, 192, 195, 200, 204, 208; another man, 26, 57, 124, 127, 128, 154, 167, 174, 186, 191, 202; by another man, 57, 59, 85, 88, 98, 108, 124, 127, 128, 130, 131, 132, 135, 138, 147, 148, 155, 156, 166, 170, 175, 1190, 191, 195, 199, 204, 210, 211; "each other," 145, 192; "independently," 62, 130, 155, 156, 189, 196, 199, 201, 203, 211; "mutually," 38, 43, 81, 114, 122, 129, 130, 141, 166, 195; oneself, 116, 128, 170, 179; "reciprocally," 184, 204; through breeches, 73, 85, 29, 130, 131, 134, 135, 138, 139, 143, 145, 156, 170, 181, 186, 187, 191, 200, 203, 204; "together," 69, 131; "with" another man, 81, 105, 106, 107, 137, 142, 144, 147, 151, 152, 153, 161, 162, 166, 171, 175, 180, 181, 184, 186, 188, 190, 193, 194, 195, 196, 197, 198, 203, 209, 210, 211; with penis exposed, 186, 194, 195, 201, 202
    taking by the arm, 49, 75, 76, 95, 107, 119, 122, 123, 131, 134, 139, 143, 146, 148, 152, 154, 159, 164, 165, 185, 190
    touching, 80, 120; another man, 31, 79, 138, 148, 149, 151, 184, 196, 200; by another man, 31, 102, 137, 138, 139, 142, 148, 149, 169, 176, 182, 186, 191, 198, 200, 206; "each other," 86; "independent," 28, 39, 58; "mutually," 158; oneself, 39, 58, 117, 134, 210; through breeches, 148, 188; with penis exposed, 139, 147, 148, 210
    walking arm in arm, 35, 53, 70, 99, 100, 116, 131, 133, 155, 178
masturbation, 200, 203, 205
    by another man, 27, 30, 33. 46, 53, 69, 74, 75, 83, 100, 108, 136. 151, 152, 176, 177, 178, 184, 194
    "independently," 19, 24, 25, 28, 38, 39, 49, 50, 52, 55, 62, 65, 66, 71, 76, 78, 83, 86, 92, 93, 96, 98, 103, 107, 108, 110, 115, 124, 130, 140, 143, 144, 154, 155, 159, 162, 165, 174, 182, 183, 184, 185, 192, 193, 194, 195, 196, 206, 207, 209, 210, 211
    "to jerk off," 30, 43, 47, 167
    "mutually," 163
    of another man, 23, 46, 53, 69, 75, 83, 87, 100, 123, 176
    of oneself, 23, 27, 66, 74, 169, 180, 204, 207
    "to pollute," 108, 151
    "reciprocally," 55, 184, 204
    "with" another man, 24, 29, 55, 66, 67, 73, 101, 103, 137, 141, 142, 144, 149, 151, 152, 155, 157, 160, 161, 162, 165, 166, 167, 174, 180, 184, 187, 194, 195, 196, 197, 198, 203, 204, 205, 206, 210
"misfortune," 20, 50, 54, 61, 124, 165, 171, 199
monasteries, 23, 124, 198
Mousetrap, 19, 20, 21, 23, 24, 26, 28, 30, 32, 33, 41, 58, 61, 67, 72, 74, 75, 129, 144, 147, 157, 159, 160, 162, 168, 169, 170, 171, 173, 174, 186, 187, 192

"to oblige," 21, 103, 213
    "obligingness," 76, 84, 119, 122, 134, 154, 203
oral sex, 46, 80, 82, 160, 194

GENERAL INDEX

Orfèvres, quai des, 18, 19, 20, 21, 22, 23, 24, 25, 26, 27, 28, 29, 30, 31, 32, 33. 34. 35, 37, 38, 40, 41, 72, 73, 74, 75, 85, 136, 147, 148, 153, 154, 155, 156, 157, 159, 160, 162, 169, 171, 173, 174, 179, 181, 182, 185, 186, 187, 194
    under, 19, 20, 21, 24, 29, 30, 67, 133, 160, 168, 169, 174, 175
"orgies," 33, 213

Palais Royal, 24, 37, 39, 42, 43, 44, 45, 51, 52, 53, 54, 55, 57, 60, 62, 88, 91, 92, 95, 96, 100, 108, 110, 111, 112, 113, 115, 120, 121, 122, 123, 125, 126, 133, 139, 142, 148, 172, 173, 175, 182, 187, 190, 197, 198, 202, 208, 209, 213, 214, 215
"parties," 76, 81, 82, 88, 111, 157, 166, 202
"passion," 46, 68, 81, 203
place Louis XV, 39, 40, 49, 76, 84, 90, 91, 114, 118, 135, 138, 142, 157, 171, 188, 194, 201, 214
police practices, 2–3, 15
    observers, 4, 21, 23, 30, 32, 40, 43, 55, 57, 59, 68, 71, 72, 73, 74, 82, 87, 105, 107, 109, 116, 118, 119, 158, 163, 167, 183, 186, 201, 204, 205,
    pederasty patrols, 3, 37, 58, 61, 67, 71, 6, 84, 88, 91, 96, 99, 102, 105, 109, 112, 114, 116, 118, 122, 130, 132, 134, 138, 142, 145, 147, 151, 153, 157, 161, 162, 167, 1170, 71, 182, 188, 194, 201, 209, 214
prisons
    Châtelet, 41, 158
    La Force, 97, 165, 174, 187, 201, 202
procurement, 33, 34, 50, 69, 80, 81, 82, 113, 139, 145, 168, 169, 213
"prostitution," male, 12–13, 88, 154, 172, 197, 209

Saint-Germain fair, 36, 53, 54, 60, 90, 132, 161, 213
seminaries, 35, 46, 73, 84
sex between men
    curiosity about, 6, 19, 48, 73, 131, 179, 185, 202

"debauchery of men," 20, 56, 60, 65, 69, 86, 87, 91, 92, 93, 99, 105, 106, 108, 109, 111, 120, 123, 125, 126, 127, 128, 129, 131, 132, 134, 135, 136, 139, 146, 147, 149, 150, 151, 156, 157, 162, 172, 183, 184, 185, 186, 187, 191, 193, 195, 196, 197, 200, 209
"first time," 19, 38, 67, 80, 98, 114, 117, 132, 139, 142, 152, 168, 171, 174, 182, 188, 195, 196, 200, 202, 204, 206
hostility to, 21, 22, 29, 130, 143, 146, 170
in native region, 24, 88, 105, 145, 148, 156
"it has happened to him," 24, 28, 39, 112
out of indigence, 21, 50, 65, 83, 84, 87, 94, 101, 104, 114, 117, 139, 145, 170, 180, 184, 188, 197, 214
"pleasure," 98, 114, 134. 185, 214, 215
"sodomy," 191
"vice of liking men," 18, 22, 37, 40, 41, 68, 72, 74, 79, 83, 90, 99, 117, 121, 123, 131, 138, 141, 158, 162, 163, 199
sexual identity, 12–13
    "confirmed pederast," 58, 118
    "confirmed taste," 9, 96, 106, 161
    "for men," 131
    "given over to," 20, 21, 28, 31, 33, 34, 36, 38, 46, 49, 52, 54, 53, 55, 56, 60, 61, 62, 65, 68, 69, 70, 73, 74, 79, 81, 88, 90, 93, 96, 100, 105, 106, 111, 112, 115, 116, 118, 119, 120, 132, 136, 139, 143, 146, 148, 151, 154, 156, 158, 160, 165, 177, 181, 183, 186, 187, 203, 205, 208, 211, 213, 214
    "habit," 113
    "in his blood," 93
    "inclination," 46, 142
    "inclined," 134, 205
    "men of the cuff," 48
    "penchant," 30, 186
    "stripe," 179
    "taste," 4, 46, 71, 76, 153, 154, 182, 196, 204
    "temperament," 113

"to think that way," 80
"type," 5, 62, 71, 103, 140, 213
sleeping
    "together," 74, 98, 100, 114, 122, 134, 140, 144
    "with" another man, 19, 27, 33, 45, 65, 74, 76, 78, 93, 84, 90, 96, 97, 98, 108, 109, 112, 114, 115, 120, 121, 127, 129, 136, 137, 143, 145, 146, 148, 150, 166, 171, 173, 208
Sofa, 58, 61, 67, 88, 132, 156, 165, 168, 174, 210
"suspect places,"
    awareness of, 19, 21, 49, 64, 73, 84, 88, 105, 114, 131, 149, 180, 185, 193
    unawareness of, 25, 31, 32, 41, 73, 91

taverns, 20, 26, 27, 33, 51, 52, 56, 66, 75, 84, 119, 128, 137, 138, 161, 172, 174, 175, 179, 182, 202, 207, 213, 214
Terrace of the Feuillants, 82, 101, 107
theaters, 43, 44, 77, 173
    See also Comédie Française

theft, 33, 40, 41, 62, 93, 110, 158, 177, 178, 187, 208, 215
"trade," 80, 81, 109, 110, 170

urination, 18, 27, 29, 30, 32, 38, 43, 44, 65, 74, 79, 83, 85, 89, 92, 94, 101, 102, 104, 127, 128, 130, 136, 147, 149, 154, 167, 175, 180, 184, 185, 195, 209, 212

Versailles, 19, 211, 26, 36, 43, 59, 66, 71, 86, 92, 129, 140, 170, 213, 215

"weakness," 29, 33, 35, 69, 80, 108, 125, 152, 167, 191, 199, 206
women, 11, 45, 75, 81, 89, 97, 106, 111, 113–14, 124, 142, 196, 200, 201
    aversion to, 139, 156, 179
    avoidance of, 81, 96, 174, 190, 192
    no experience with, 62, 174, 185
    prostitutes, 22, 35, 54, 60, 74, 80, 81, 82, 94, 104, 132, 167, 168, 176, 207

www.ingramcontent.com/pod-product-compliance
Lightning Source LLC
Chambersburg PA
CBHW032336300426
44109CB00041B/1010